The Jasper Project: Lessons in Curriculum, Instruction, Assessment, and Professional Development

The Cognition and Technology Group at Vanderbilt

LEA LAWRENCE ERLBAUM ASSOCIATES, PUBLISHERS
1997 Mahwah, New Jersey London

Lawrence Erlbaum Associates, Inc., Publishers
10 Industrial Avenue
Mahwah, New Jersey 07430

Cover design by Kathryn Houghtaling

Library of Congress Cataloging-in-Publication-Data

The Jasper Project : lessons in curriculum, instruction, assessment, and professional development / the Cognition and Technology Group at Vanderbilt.
p. cm.
Includes bibliographic references and index.
ISBN 0-8058-2592-4 (cloth : alk. paper). —ISBN 0-8058-2593-2 (pbk. : alk. paper)
1. Mathematics—Study and teaching—Computer-assisted instruction. I. Cognition and Technology Group Technology at Vanderbilt.
QA20.C65J37 1997
510'.71'2—dc21 96-51912
CIP

Books published by Lawrence Erlbaum Associates are printed on acid-free paper, and their bindings are chosen for strength and durability.

Printed in the United States of America
10 9 8 7 6 5 4 3

Contents

Contents of the Companion CD-ROM

Preface

During the past 7 years, members of our Cognition and Technology Group at Vanderbilt (CTGV) have had the opportunity to work with hundreds of teachers and thousands of students throughout North America in the context of our *Adventures of Jasper Woodbury* problem-solving series. *Jasper* consists of 12 videodisc-based adventures (plus video-based analogs, extensions, and teaching tips) that are designed to improve the mathematical thinking of students from Grades 5 and up, and to help them make connections to other disciplines such as science, history, and social studies.

The experience of developing the *Jasper* series, testing it in classrooms, and redesigning it based on feedback has taught us more than we ever imagined when we first began the project. On some days, we describe our experiences with *Jasper* as a series of successive approximations toward success because each opportunity to test the *Jasper* series has resulted in new improvements. On other days, we view our experiences with *Jasper* as an ever-expanding lesson in humility. The more we have ventured beyond the ivory tower and into schools and classrooms, the more we have realized how uninformed we were about the realities of classrooms. The opportunities to learn from teachers, students, parents, administrators, and other community members have been extraordinary.

We wrote this book for two major reasons. The first was to help us organize the thoughts and experiences of over 90 members of our Learning Technology Center who have worked on the *Jasper* project. We have interacted with one another on a daily basis, but this is different from attempting to systematically organize our thoughts. Writing this book has helped us collaboratively reflect on our experiences and relate them to the broader literature in cognition and instruction.

The second reason for writing this book is to give others a chance to learn from our experiences. We have been very fortunate to receive research and development support from a number of foundations and federal agencies (see the acknowledgments). Hopefully, the information in this book serves as a partial payback for these investments. We anchor our discussions around our experiences with *Jasper*, but the issues we explore are relevant to any attempt to improve educational practice. Included in our discussions are issues of curriculum, instruction, assessment, and teacher learning (professional development). Each of these topics interacts with one another; hence, none of them can be ignored.

This book is designed for several different audiences. One audience is teachers who are using *Jasper* and want to learn more about it. *Jasper* teachers who have read preprints of this book have noted that it gave them a much broader perspective on why *Jasper* was developed and how it could be used.

A second audience includes teachers who are not using *Jasper* but are interested in issues of educational improvement. The opportunity to explore issues of curriculum, instruction, assessment and professional development within a single context (i.e., *Jasper*) helps people understand how all these topics interrelate.

A third audience for this book is undergraduate and graduate students who are studying topics such as cognition, education, and technology. We have used preprints of this book in several college courses and found that it was extremely well received by the students. The book tells a coherent story that helps students explore issues of curriculum, instruction, assessment, and professional development. The book also helps students understand the relevance of research programs for improving educational practice. Some of the research that we discussed is laboratory-based, some is classroom-based. Throughout our discussion, we emphasize the need for maintaining a balance of laboratory and classroom research.

When using this book for courses, we recommend that it be supplemented with additional books and articles. For example, we have used preprints of this book in conjunction with Bruer's *Schools for Thought* (1993), plus a number of relevant research articles. Needless to say, the choice of supplemental materials depends on the exact purposes of one's course.

The Jasper Project consists of a book and a CD-ROM. The CD-ROM contains video that illustrates important points discussed in the book. It includes the *Jasper* adventure *Rescue at Boone's Meadow (RBM)* plus video of "*Jasper* in the Classroom" that shows a teacher using RBM with sixth-grade students. The CD-ROM also contains examples of analog and extension problems, and examples from our SMART Challenge Series that is discussed in chapter 5.

The book is organized into seven chapters. In chapter 1, we provide an overview of the *Jasper* series and invite the reader to solve one of the adventures plus the extension materials that accompany it. In chapter 2, we discuss the theoretical and empirical work that gave rise to *Jasper*. In subsequent chapters, we discuss *Jasper* from the perspective of issues of curriculum (chapter 3), initial research on instruction and assessment (chapter 4), formative assessment (chapter 5), and teacher learning and community building (chapter 6). In chapter 7, we summarize the journey that the *Jasper* project has taken, and we highlight the major lessons learned.

We have found that this book need not be read in linear order. Some readers have preferred to read the introductory chapter and then proceed to the final chapter to see the lessons learned. After that, they have read the remaining chapters in order to fill in the gaps.

We hope that this book is useful to you the reader. We welcome any feedback and invite you to visit our Web site. The URL is http://peabody.vanderbilt.edu/projects/funded/jasper/.

ACKNOWLEDGMENTS

The *Jasper* project would never have been possible without the help of hundreds of talented and dedicated individuals. First, we thank the teachers and students who have worked with us to test and refine the *Jasper* series. The opportunity to work with them has been the highlight of our work.

Second, we thank members of our national advisory board who have helped us craft every *Jasper* adventure. Their input has ranged from ideas about mathematics, science, history, and appropriate uses of the English language to guidelines for creating role models that will motivate all students to learn. We have tried very hard to incorporate every suggestion made by every member of our advisory board. In some cases, this has not been possible due to limitations on script lengths, budgets, and other factors. Therefore, please do not hold our advisory board members accountable for any mistakes we may have made—we alone are responsible. Members of our National Advisory Board are listed later in this section.

The *Jasper* project would not have been possible without grant support from several important agencies. The James S. McDonnell Foundation provided research support that got us started and allowed us to study the effects of *Jasper* on student learning and understanding (No. 87-39 and No. 91-6). The National Science Foundation funded the development of 10 of the 12 *Jasper* adventures, plus the analog and extension problems to accompany these adventures (No. NSF-MDR-9050191 and No. NSR-MDR-9252990). A separate grant from the National Science Foundation has allowed us to study the effects of formative assessment in the context of our SMART Challenge series (No. NSF-MDR-9252908). Eisenhower grants have allowed us to work with teachers to implement a number of the *Jasper* adventures and assess their effects on student learning (Act P.L. 100-297, Title II). We are extremely grateful for all of this support. Nevertheless, the ideas expressed in this book reflect our opinions, not the opinions of the granting agencies.

We are especially grateful to Joe B. Wyatt, Chancellor of Vanderbilt University, and Bill Hawley, who served as Dean of Peabody College when we began the *Jasper* project. Dean Hawley took the risk of helping us fund the first two *Jasper* adventures so that we could establish a proof of concept. Chancellor Wyatt invited CEOs from nine different states to work with us to introduce the first four *Jasper* adventures into classrooms and study their effects. He also served on our advisory board and made extremely important contributions throughout the entire project. The *Jasper* project would never have been a success without these fundamental contributions from Vanderbilt University.

We also want to thank the writers, directors and production companies who worked with us to produce the *Jasper* adventures, plus companies who sponsored tests of *Jasper* and contributed their talents to the design of specific adventures. Specific groups and individuals are mentioned in the credits to the *Jasper* adventures. We thank each and every one of them for all their support and help.

In many parts of this book we borrow heavily from chapters that have been previously published, and we thank the publishers for permission to use them in this publication. The majority of these chapters have been published by Lawrence Erlbaum Associates. In chapter 4, we borrow from an article published in *Educational Technology Research and Development* (1992) by the Association for Educational Communications & Technology. It is reprinted by permission.

Members of our National Advisory Board are listed next. We follow this list with the names of people from the CTGV who have contributed to the *Jasper* project. We then list the writers, directors, producers, and production companies who helped create each adventure.

—The CTGV
February 2, 1997

THE NATIONAL ADVISORY BOARD

John Ahner
Mark Appelbaum
Jill Ashworth
Sallie Baliunas
Linda Barron
Otto Bassler
Gautam Biswas
David G. Bodnar
A. B. Bonds
Raffaella Borasi
Jomills Braddock
George Bright
Henry Casso
Alma Clayton-Pedersen
Deborah Davies
Edwin Duroy
Carol Edwards
John Halcón
Fred Humphries
Kim Humphries
Leigh Kahan
Kenneth Koedinger
Richard Lehrer
Frank Lester
Al Mance
Henrietta Mann
Molly Miller
Jim Minstrell
Luis Moll
Roy Pea
Nancy Ransom
María de la Luz Reyes
Geoff Roach
Sharon Robinson
Peter Salinger
Jackie Shrago
Jeff Swink
Charles Tortorella
Sara Tune
Emily Vanzee
Adelaide Vienneau
John Wikswo
Horace Williams
David Wilson
Chancellor Joe B. Wyatt

THE COGNITION AND TECHNOLOGY GROUP AT VANDERBILT

Jason Adair
Mary Alcantara
Paulo Alcantara
Jan Altman
Jill Ashworth
Brigid Barron
Linda Barron
Helen Bateman
Kadira Belynne
Bunny Bransford
Jason Bransford
John Bransford
Melinda Bray
Sean Brophy
Kay Burgess
Kristin Carlson
Andrew Cohen
Diane Cohn
Beverly Conner
William Corbin
Nathalie Coté
Thad Crews
Karen Cunningham
Trefor Davies
Hoan Davis
Dave Edyburn
Daniel Farmer
Benjamin Ferron
Marcy Gabella
Michael Gaines
Steve Garrison
Laura Goin
Elizabeth Goldman
Josh Goldman
Seth Goldman
Susan Goldman
Rachelle Hackett
Hope Hall
Ted Hasselbring
Charles Hausman
Helen Heath
Daniel Hickey
Cindy Hmelo
Jim Johnston
Ronald Kantor
Charles Kinzer
Ralph Knapp
Jeff Laughlin
Xiaodong Lin
Johan Madson
Taylor Martin
Cynthia Mayfield-Stewart
Delessa McNair
Linda Miller
Carolyn Millican
Elliott Mitchell
Allison Moore
Joyce Moore
John Morris
Doug Morse
Mitchell Nathan
Dana Neubauer
Tom Noser
Steve Owens
James Pellegrino
Anthony Petrosino
Jay Pfaffman
Faapio Po'e
Kirsten Rewey
John Rieser
Vicki Risko
Darryl Roberts
Daniel Rock
Henry Savage
Karl Schmidt
Daniel Schwartz
Teresa Secules
Diana Sharp
Robert Sherwood
Diana Slatopolsky
Karen Smart
Susan Spicer
Carolyn Stalcup
Jason Stephens
Seth Strauss
Jeff Swink
Laura Till
Jay Tomlin
James Van Haneghan
Keisha Varma
Sashank Varma
Nancy Vye
Drew Wallen
Susan Warren
Jackie Welch
Tamara Wilkerson
Susan Williams
Andy Wilson
Michael Young
Linda Zech

CREDITS

Journey to Cedar Creek

Writer, Producer, and Director	Thomas Sturdevant

Rescue at Boone's Meadow

Writer, Producer, and Director	Thomas Sturdevant

The Big Splash

Executive Producer	Kitty Moon
Director	Larry Boothby
Producer	Chuck Strader
Writer	Thomas Sturdevant
Produced by	Scene Three, Inc.

A Capital Idea

Executive Producer	Kitty Moon
Director	Mark Ball
Producer	Buck Ford
Writer	Thomas Sturdevant
Produced by	Scene Three, Inc.

The Right Angle

Executive Producer	Kitty Moon
Director	Larry Boothby
Producer	Greg Alldredge
Writer	Tony Vidmer
Produced by	Scene Three, Inc.

The Great Circle Race

Executive Producer	Kitty Moon
Director	Larry Boothby
Producer	Greg Alldredge
Writer	Dan Butler
Produced by	Scene Three, Inc.

Get Out the Vote

Director	Donna Culver
Producers	Donna Culver, Wendy Smith
Writers	Dan Butler, Donna Culver, Wendy Smith
Produced by	Culver Productions

Blueprint for Success

Director	Donna Culver
Producers	Donna Culver, Wendy Smith
Writers	Donna Culver, Loree Gold
Produced by	Culver Productions

Bridging the Gap

Producer and Director	Donna Culver
Associate Producer	Wendy Smith
Produced by	Culver Productions

Working Smart

Executive Producer	Bill Nelson
Writer, Producer, and Director	Charles S. Cobean
Produced by	Little Planet Publishing

The General is Missing

Executive Producer	Bill Nelson
Writer, Producer, and Director	Charles S. Cobean
Produced by	Little Planet Publishing

Kim's Komet

Executive Producer	Bill Nelson
Writer, Producer, and Director	Charles S. Cobean
Produced by	Little Planet Publishing

1

Overview of the *Jasper* Series

OVERVIEW OF THE *JASPER* ADVENTURES

The *Jasper* series consists of 12 videodisc-based adventures (plus video-based analogs, extensions, and teaching tips) that focus on mathematical problem finding and problem solving. The 12 adventures are illustrated in Fig. 1.1. Each adventure is designed from the perspective of the standards recommended by the National Council of Teachers of Mathematics (NCTM). In particular, each adventure provides multiple opportunities for problem solving, reasoning, communication, and making connections to other areas such as science, social studies, literature, and history (NCTM, 1989, 1991).

Jasper adventures are designed for students in grades 5 and up. Each videodisc contains a short (approximately 17-minute) video adventure that ends in a complex challenge. The adventures are designed like good detective novels, where all the data necessary to solve the adventure (plus additional data that are not relevant to the solution) are embedded in the story. *Jasper* adventures also contain embedded teaching scenes that provide models of particular approaches to solving problems. These episodes can be revisited on a just-in-time basis as students need them to solve the *Jasper* challenges.

Descriptions of the *Jasper* Adventures

Summaries of the 12 *Jasper* adventures appear in Appendix A. The adventures can be used in any order, although they do differ in complexity. In general, the adventures in the left-most column of Fig. 1.1 are the simplest and those in the right-most column are the most advanced.

Some teachers like to focus on a particular area (e.g., trip planning, geometry) and have students proceed from the simplest to most complex adventures in that area. Other teachers prefer to use one adventure from each topic area (trip planning, statistics, geometry, algebra). They usually have students begin with the simplest adventures in each area and graduate to the more difficult ones in succeeding years. Other teachers mix and match the adventures in ways that help them integrate *Jasper* instruction into other content areas. For example, *Get Out the Vote* is especially good for linking to social studies and history; *Bridging the Gap* is excellent for focusing on endangered species and changing populations, and so forth.

FIG. 1.1. The 12 *Jasper* adventures.

Solving a *Jasper* Adventure

Our experiences indicate that, in order to understand *Jasper*, it is imperative to attempt to solve at least one of the adventures. It is not sufficient to simply watch *Jasper*; the important experience is in the solving of it. (A motto that accompanies *Jasper* is, "It's not just a movie; it's a challenge.") The challenge is most fun and meaningful when solved collaboratively.

We include the *Jasper* adventure *Rescue at Boone's Meadow* on the CD-ROM that accompanies this book. We strongly recommend that you watch it and attempt to solve it (ideally, with one or more friends) before proceeding further. If you do not have access to a CD- ROM player, use the external summary of the adventure provided in Appendix B. However, please note that, for many reasons that will be discussed throughout this book, the use of *Jasper* summaries is far less desirable than the use of the video adventure.

DESIGN OF THE *JASPER* SERIES

Each adventure in the *Jasper* series was developed according to a set of design principles that emerged as we studied students' problem solving. As a result, the *Jasper* series is different from many other materials produced for mathematics. The following sections describe eight features of *Jasper* that differentiate it from many traditional approaches to mathematics instruction.

Jasper Helps Students Learn Mathematics While Solving Problems in Authentic Contexts

Often, students study mathematics by first learning isolated skills. Then they apply the skills by solving narrowly defined problems that provide practice for the skills. When students use *Jasper*, they learn mathematics as they try to solve the challenge. They develop and learn mathematical concepts and skills as they need them through just-in-time instruction. Although some teachers who use *Jasper* for the first time feel the need to teach all of the relevant concepts and vocabulary to students before they watch the adventure, teachers who use *Jasper* usually report that students learn mathematics (concepts, skills, symbols, and vocabulary) as they attempt to solve the challenge.

The use of mathematics in authentic contexts supports students' reasoning, problem solving, and communication skills, all standards identified by the NCTM (1989). In accordance with the national standards, each adventure provides multiple opportunities for using these skills and making connections to other areas such as science, social studies, literature, and history (NCTM, 1989, 1991). In her review of the *Jasper* Series for *Technology and Learning*, Eiser (1993) stated: "Of the products we have looked at, the one that most fully incorporates the ideas expressed in the NCTM standards—including mathematical sophistication, stress on group work, and real-world relevance, is the *Jasper* Series."

A *Jasper* Adventure Provides a Context That Helps Students Integrate Concepts in Mathematics As Well As Mathematical Knowledge With Knowledge of Other Subjects

In traditional mathematics classrooms, students often study one concept or skill at a time. For example, they might study fractions, followed by decimals, followed by percentages, and so on. In a *Jasper* adventure, there are several concepts and skills that are embedded in the context of the story. Students can begin to develop an understanding of these skills and concepts concurrently by using their own knowledge to reason about the story. This often results in different strategies and mathematical concepts being used by different groups as they solve the challenge. For example, in solving *The Big Splash*, students must estimate the number of students in Chris' school who will buy a ticket to the dunking booth, using some sample data that Chris collected. Some students reason about the data using fractions although other students use percentages. As students share their solutions, they have the opportunity to connect their understanding of fractions with their understanding of percentages. Learning mathematics in the context of the video story provides many opportunities for students to make these types of mathematical connections.

Each *Jasper* adventure also includes links to other subjects and opportunities for students to learn things in addition to mathematics. For example, in *Rescue at Boone's Meadow*, the character Larry explains the aerodynamics of an ultralight aircraft and how the wings help the plane stay in the air. This scene can anchor a discussion about science in the same way that other scenes anchor discussions about mathematics. As one *Jasper* teacher said, "In life, things that we learn are not separated. *Jasper* helps learning be more like real life."

Jasper Takes Advantage of the Power of Video and Interactive Technologies

The *Jasper* adventures are in visual rather than textual formats and are on videodisc rather than videotape. Video allows a more veridical representation of events than text. It is dynamic, visual, and spatial, and students can more easily form rich mental models of the problem situations (e.g., Johnson-Laird, 1985; McNamara, Miller, & Bransford, 1991; Sharp et al., 1995). This characteristic is particularly important for nontraditional students and for students with little knowledge in the domain being studied (Bransford, Kinzer, Risko, Rowe, & Vye, 1989; Johnson, 1987). Teachers who have used *Jasper* have told us that their students who had difficulty in reading were able to contribute to *Jasper* solutions and gained new respect from their peers.

Videodisc technology also has random-access capabilities that allow teachers almost instant access to information for discussion (see Sherwood, Kinzer, Bransford, & Franks, 1987). This makes it easy for students to re-explore the video in order to find the relevant data and just-in-time embedded teaching.

At the simplest level, *Jasper* adventures require only a videodisc player with a handheld controller or barcode reader. A single player on a cart can be moved from classroom to classroom. Students can re-explore the story by using the rapid scan or frame numbers on a handheld remote videodisc controller (see Fig. 1.2), or using barcode technology (see Fig. 1.3).

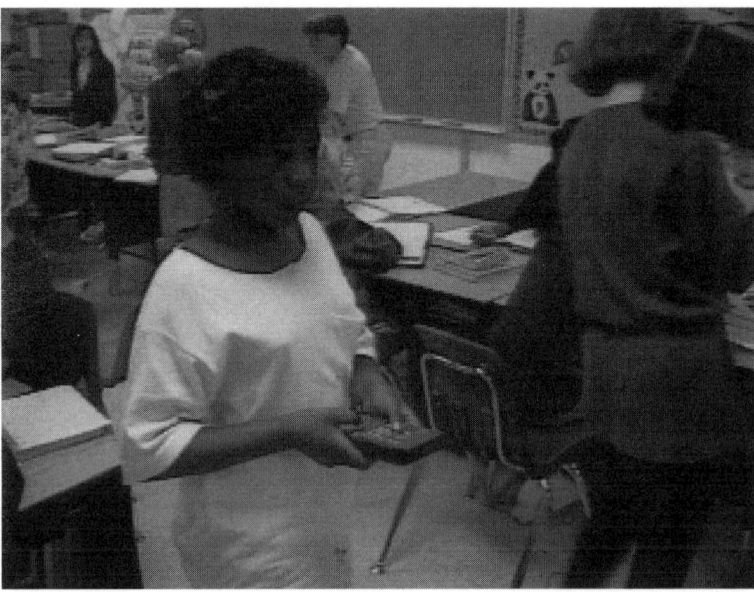

FIG. 1.2. Student using a hand-held videodisc controller.

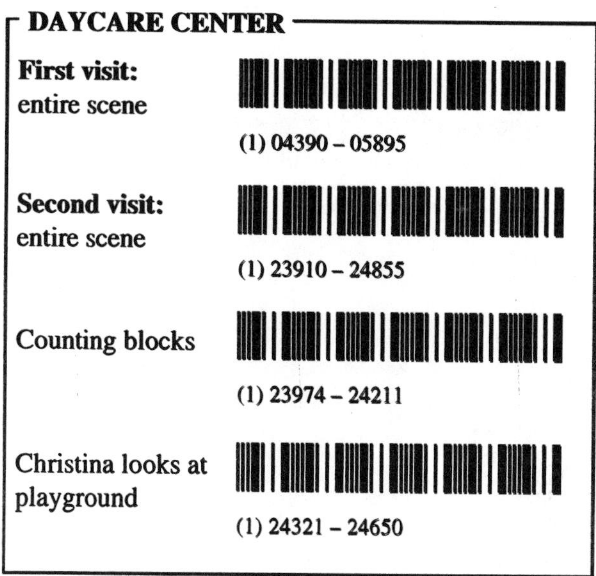

FIG. 1.3. Barcode technology.

At more sophisticated levels of implementation, *Jasper* includes optional computer software. For example, computer map controllers allow students to click on locations that are represented in the story and return to them almost instantly. A map controller for *Rescue at Boone's Meadow* is illustrated in Fig. 1.4.

We discourage the use of *Jasper* on videotape because it is cumbersome to rewind the video in order to find relevant data. As a result, teachers who use videotape tend to hand out fact sheets with all the data from the video presented on them. When students use fact sheets (such as the story summary in Appendix A), we find that their thinking tends to be driven by the facts on the sheet rather than by their own attempts to generate relevant subgoals and to then search for data needed to achieve these goals. Real-world problems rarely present themselves in the form of fact sheets that contain all the relevant data. Fact sheet-driven thinking is not the approach that *Jasper* is designed to promote. As the picture quality of CD-ROM technology reaches that of videodisc, it will likely offer an additional interactive platform for using *Jasper*.

Jasper Adventures Support Inquiry

As noted earlier, *Jasper* adventures are not designed primarily for entertainment. A motto that accompanies *Jasper* is, "It's not just a movie; it's a challenge."

Jasper challenges are designed to help students understand the kinds of problems that can be solved through mathematical inquiry. Experts in a domain often forget how much they know about applications of the concepts they are teaching. When these remain tacit, students fail to understand why, when, and where various

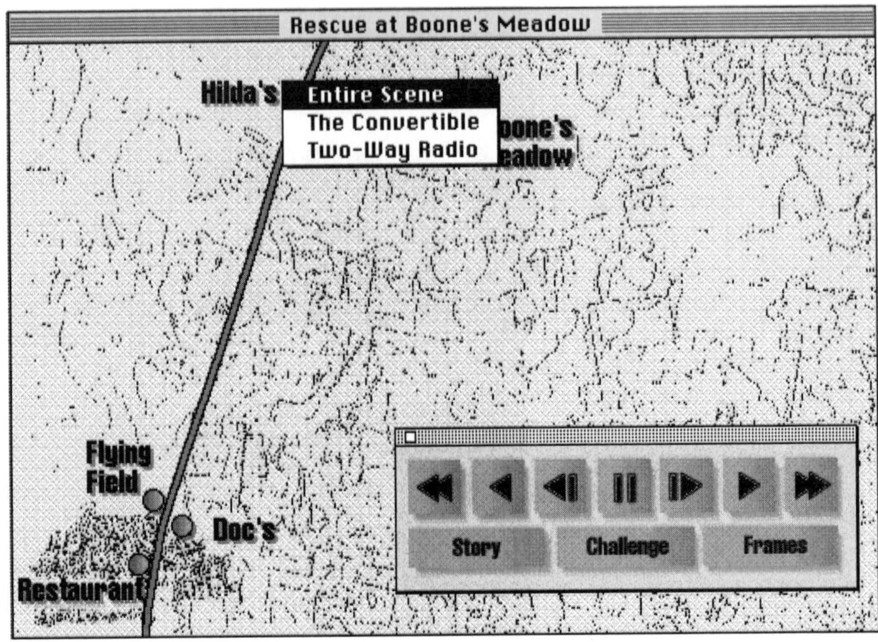

FIG. 1.4. Screen from computer map controller.

concepts and procedures are applicable. They may be able to answer direct questions about content they have been taught, but still lack the ability to spontaneously use it in any other context, despite its relevance. When this happens, the students' knowledge remains inert (Whitehead, 1929).

Jasper adventures also include embedded teaching that often takes the form of modeling by experts (Brown, Collins, & Duguid, 1989). Modeling helps students in two ways. First, by watching an expert perform in a particular environment, students develop a better understanding of the appropriate performance in that environment. Modeling can also provide coaching and scaffolding for students as they develop their own skills (e.g., Vygotsky, 1978, 1986). Without a certain level of preparation, however, students are often overwhelmed with information and do not know what to attend to and what to ignore (e.g., Bransford, Goldman, & Vye, 1991; Bransford, Sherwood, Hasselbring, Kinzer, & Williams, 1990). The models in the *Jasper* series are presented as part of the story line of the adventures, but students are not expected to learn effectively through their initial exposure to the models. Videodisc technology makes it easy for students to return to the models as needed while attempting to solve the *Jasper* challenge. This just-in-time exposure to information allows students to re-explore models after relevant questions that define a need to know have been generated.

Students Must Generate As Well As Solve Problems

Problem generation is an important aspect of problem solving and mathematical thinking, but our early work with middle school students in problem solving made us realize that most students are not very good at it (see Chapter 4). Traditional word problems usually have explicit goal structures and, hence, do not encourage students to generate goals on their own.

Jasper adventures end with challenges that specify a general goal for the students. Nevertheless, in order to solve the challenges, students must identify a number of subproblems and generate subgoals on their own. After students have watched the video story, teachers usually engage the class in a discussion where students suggest, and the teacher or a student records, the subproblems they must solve. Some teachers leave it to collaborative small groups of students or individuals to identify and solve their own subproblems. In either approach, students are active participants in identifying and solving problems. Our data indicate that fifth-grade students can become very good at complex problem formulation on tasks similar to *Jasper* after working with *Jasper* in cooperative learning groups for four to five class sessions (see Chapter 4).

A *Jasper* Adventure Provides Opportunities for Collaboration Over an Extended Period of Time

The complexity of the challenges makes them difficult to solve alone and, thus, provides an authentic purpose for collaboration. Data indicate that students enjoy group work and perform better when they work together (Barron, 1991; Rewey, Barron, Rieser, Bransford, & Goldman, 1992; Vye et al., in press).

As students work together over multiple class periods (from several days to several weeks) to solve a challenge, they have repeated opportunities to communicate about mathematics, share their ideas about problem solving, and receive feedback that helps them refine their thinking. As groups present their solutions to the class, they discuss the strengths and weaknesses of different solution strategies. This process helps students consider and analyze alternative solutions, interpret and understand other groups' reasoning, and communicate in the context of solving authentic problems.

Jasper Affords Students the Opportunity to Develop a Deep Understanding of Mathematical Concepts

Each videodisc adventure also includes video-based analog and extension problems. These problems help students engage in what-if thinking by revisiting the original adventures from new points of view. For example, after finding a way to rescue a wounded eagle in *Rescue at Boone's Meadow* (most students' solutions involve the use of an ultralight airplane that is featured in the adventure), students may see analog problems where they are asked to rethink how the presence of headwinds or tailwinds could affect their original solution (see Fig. 1.5). Slight

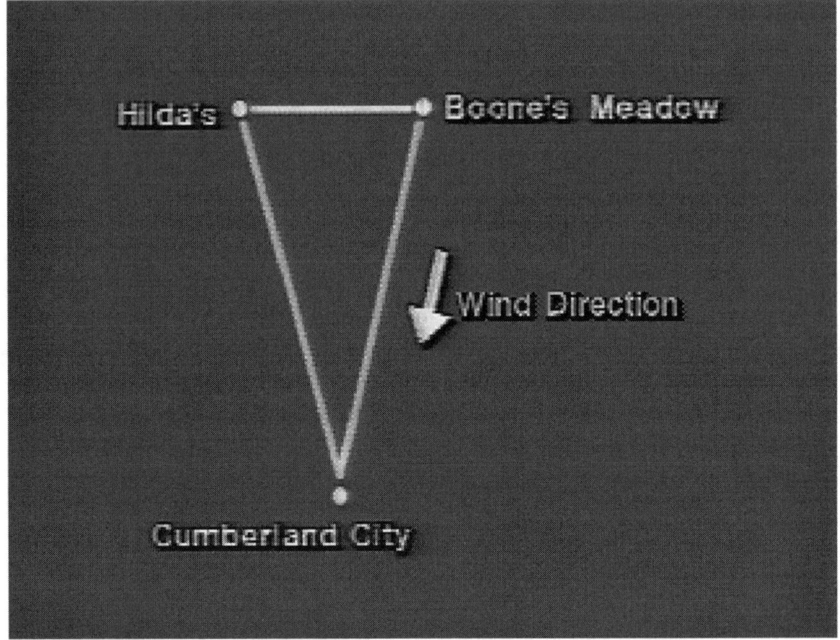

FIG. 1.5. Graphic of headwind problem from *Jasper* Analogs.

changes in wind conditions can have large effects on the feasibility of the solutions that students had generated earlier.

In addition to analog problems, there are video-based extension problems with each adventure. These are designed to help students see how the thinking involved in solving a *Jasper* adventure relates to other kinds of activities. For example, students who attempt to rescue the eagle in *Rescue at Boone's Meadow* are invited to compare the thinking they did about the ultralight with the thinking that Charles Lindbergh did when planning his trip from New York to Paris. The *Jasper* extension materials include video segments of Lindbergh's flight (see Fig. 1.6 or *Rescue at Boone's Meadow* Analogous Problem 6 on the CD-ROM).

The analog and extension problems were developed because our research team and our collaborating teachers began to worry that students' understanding and transfer were not as flexible as we wished. In Chapter 4, we discuss data that confirm these concerns, plus data that show the benefits of working on analog and extension problems.

Jasper Provides Positive Role Models

A goal of the *Jasper* series that we take extremely seriously is to provide positive role models for students from all backgrounds. We cannot provide a wide range of role models in any particular adventure. However, across the series we have been able to include a diverse set of heroes and heroines. Our national advisory board has played a major role in helping us achieve this goal.

The *Jasper* series is named after Jasper Woodbury, who attempts to solve the problem in the first *Jasper* adventure (*Journey to Cedar Creek*). However, Jasper is not the primary problem solver in the remaining adventures. Emily (an African-American female) is the heroine in *Rescue at Boone's Meadow*; Julie (an Hispanic female) is the primary problem solver in *A Capital Idea*; Chris (an African-American male) is the hero in *The Big Splash*; Paige (an American Indian) is a heroine in *The Right Angle*; Donna (a wheelchair-bound African-American female) is the heroine in *The Great Circle Race*.

It is gratifying that our attempts to portray positive role models have not gone unnoticed. In her review of the *Jasper* Series for *Technology and Learning*, Eiser (1995) stated, "Without making an issue out of race, religion, gender or appearance, the videos are remarkably free of stereotypes. It is only in looking back that you notice the woman gas jockey, the black principal, the Native American and Hispanic heroines." (p. 58).

In addition to its focus on people, *Jasper* attempts to provide models of community service and collaboration. Stories include a focus on the importance of voting, recycling, forming school-business partnerships that host career days for students and undertake community projects, and so forth. Throughout the adventures, students see a great deal of collaborative problem solving.

JASPER-RELATED PROJECTS

Our experiences with *Jasper* indicate that it becomes an even more valuable experience for students when they follow up their work on a *Jasper* adventure with

FIG. 1.6. Analogous problems can help students apply *Jasper* learning to real-world situations, such as planning Lindbergh's historic transatlantic flight. Reprinted with permission from the National Air and Space Museum, Smithsonian Institution (SI Neg. No. 87-8992).

more personalized, student-generated projects that are related to the adventure. For example, students who have solved a distance-rate-time adventure such as *Rescue at Boone's Meadow* have been given the opportunity to work either individually or in groups to design their own trip-planning adventures and present them as challenges to their classmates (e.g., Williams, Nathan, Moore, Goldman, & CTGV, 1994). Students who have solved *The Big Splash* (where they help one of the video characters collect data for a business plan to secure a loan for a booth at the school's fun fair) have generated their own ideas for school-related projects, collected data on the degree of school-wide interest in these projects, and written grant proposals that, if successful, will allow them to actually carry out their projects. Similarly, students who have solved *Blueprint for Success* (where they help the characters in the adventure design a playground for a donated piece of land) have been given the opportunity to design a playhouse that has a set of constraints on materials, size, safety requirements, and so forth. Successfully designed playhouses have actually been built by community members and donated to preschool programs throughout their city.

The addition of student-generated projects to the *Jasper* experience has a number of advantages. One is an increased sense of ownership by the students; they like generating their own ideas and especially like the opportunity to create something (e.g., a business plan, a child's playhouse) that is actually used in some way by members of the community. The opportunity to engage in such projects also represents an excellent transfer task that allows students to re-apply the skills they developed while solving the *Jasper* adventure. For example, students creating business plans for their own school's fun day need to re-apply what they learned about sampling techniques and sample size in *The Big Splash* in order to collect data about student interest in their proposed projects. Students designing playhouses must re-apply and refine the lessons learned about scale and requirements for architects' drawings that they learned while solving *Blueprint for Success*.

There are also important advantages to having students collaboratively solve a relevant *Jasper* adventure prior to engaging in student-generated projects. We have conducted several studies that convince us that the quality of student-generated projects is superior if students have first had the opportunity to solve a relevant *Jasper* adventure rather than simply begin with the projects themselves (Moore, Sherwood, Bateman, Bransford, & Goldman, 1996). The opportunity to solve the *Jasper* adventures gives all students a chance to approach their projects with a strong base of knowledge acquired from the modeling and problem-solving activities available through *Jasper*. Solving *Jasper* problems also helps students develop the ability to work together and collaborate.

SMART Challenges Anchored Around *Jasper*

An optional feature of *Jasper* involves the video-based SMART Challenge series. The goal of the Challenge series is to break the isolation of typical classrooms by linking classes of students and teachers together to form a community that is attempting to solve various *Jasper*-related challenges. SMART stands for Special Multimedia Arenas for Refining Thinking. These arenas use telecommunications, television technology, and Internet technology to provide students and teachers with feedback about the thoughts of other groups who are attempting to solve a particular *Jasper* adventure. Students can look at others' work and decide whether they want to revise their own. Samples of the SMART Challenge programs can be viewed on the accompanying CD-ROM.

As an illustration, students working on *Blueprint for Success* may see data from 60 other students about relationships between the length of the legs for their A-frame swing sets and the desired height of their swing sets (see Fig. 1.7). Students also see visual representations of various types of designs. Figure 1.8 shows a design for an A-frame swing set where the length of the legs equals the desired height of

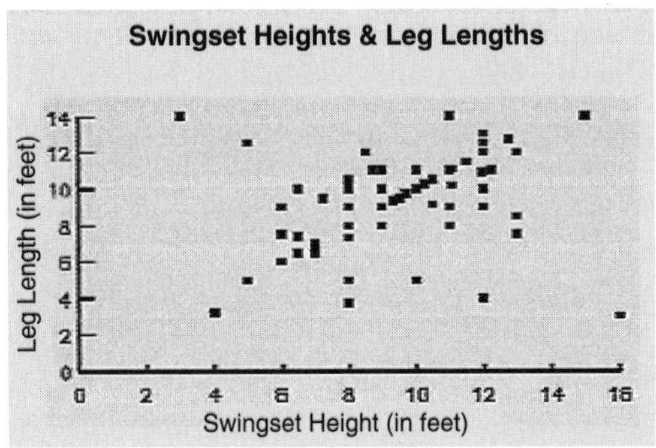

FIG. 1.7. Scatter plot of data relevant to swing design from SMART Challenge program.

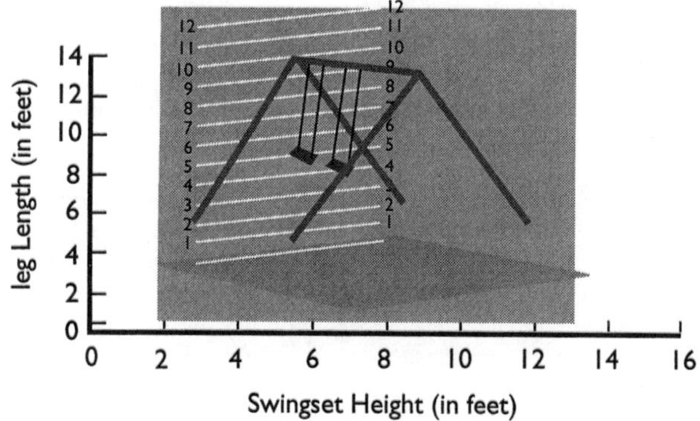

FIG. 1.8. Visual representation in a SMART Challenge program where desired height of the swing set is equal to the length of each leg.

the swing set. This design is one that is commonly suggested by many students. The visual model helps students see that this design does not work.

SMART Challenges also include the introduction of just-in-time tools that help students conceptualize the subproblems they are working on in the *Jasper* adventure. For example, Fig. 1.9 shows a static representation of a dynamic scene that, when played as full-motion video, lets students see the top view of a swing set, slide, and sandbox. The specification of top views is necessary for accurate architectural drawings. Without visual models, many students have a difficult time imagining appropriate top views.

Additional video tools provide dynamic information that helps students conceptualize concepts such as rate, sampling, and so forth. Other tools show examples of models that students and teachers can use in their classrooms. For example, one tool shows how to make a graph-paper ruler that lets students measure the length of the diagonals on graph paper. Another tool shows how to use string and graph paper to experiment with relationships between perimeter and area.

SMART Challenges have been extensively studied in the context of *Rescue at Boone's Meadow, The Big Splash,* and *Blueprint for Success* (Barron et al., 1995; CTGV, 1994). The addition of SMART Challenges to the *Jasper* series has been shown to have a value-added effect on achievement relative to *Jasper* alone. Data from SMART Challenges are presented in Chapter 5 (see Fig. 1.10).

It is worth noting that the SMART Challenge model extends beyond *Jasper*. The general features of the model are designed to be useful for any problem-based or project-based curricula. We began our SMART research with *Jasper* but are currently extending it to other areas such as science.

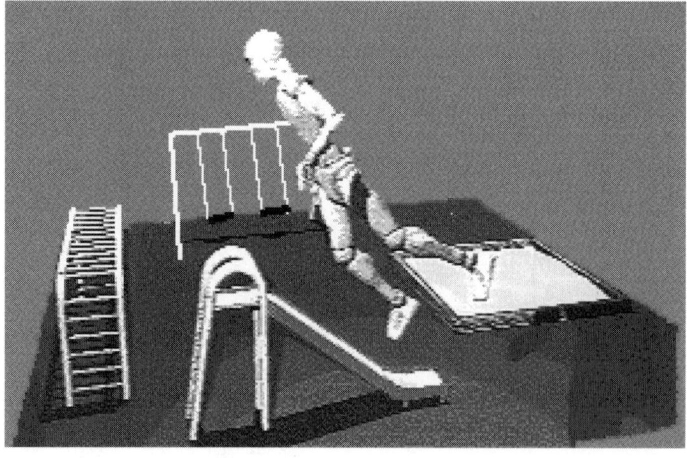

FIG. 1.9. Static representation of a dynamic SMART Challenge scene that lets students see a top view of playground equipment.

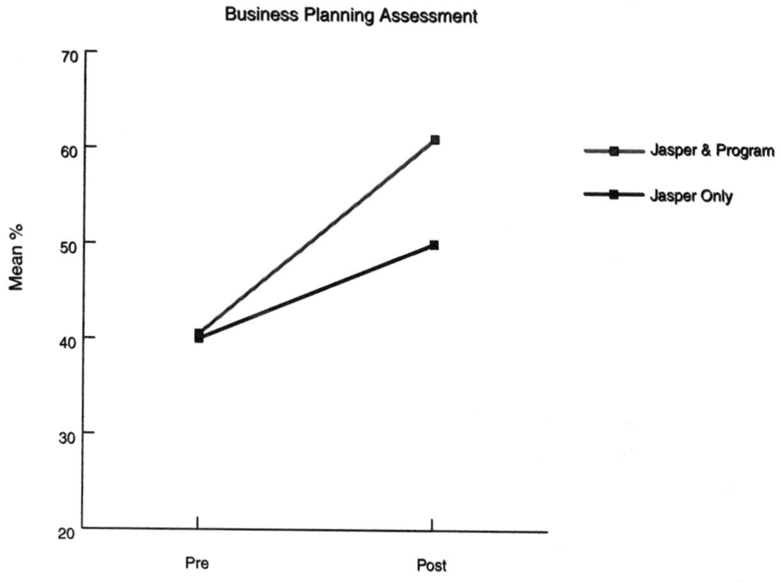

FIG. 1.10. Data from a study of the effects of SMART.

Software Support for *Jasper* and SMART

We noted earlier that, at its simplest level, *Jasper* requires only a videodisc player that can be controlled by a handheld controller or barcode reader. As we have worked with *Jasper* in classrooms, we have looked for situations where software support could make *Jasper* easier to use and increase its beneficial effects.

Jasper Adventure Player and *Adventure Maker* software programs provide additional opportunities to extend students' learning by providing computer tools that support problem solving and allowing students to create their own computer-based adventures that they can present to others to solve (Fig. 1.11). Developed with Biswas and Crews of Vanderbilt's Computer Science Department, the software lets students create new adventures, keeps track of students' answers to problems, and then provides a simulation of the consequences of the answers that they have proposed. *Jasper SMART Tools* software lets students create their own mathematical tools that help them work smart (Fig. 1.12).

We are continually working with teachers to find ways that software support can make their teaching easier. For example, in conjunction with teachers, we have designed and successfully piloted a simple piece of software for efficiently providing feedback about students' blueprints while working on *Blueprint for Success* (Fig. 1.13). The software also allows the teachers to efficiently specify where students might go to get help revising their blueprints. CD-ROM-based resources that allow students to access particular animations and dynamic visual scenes that can help them achieve their goals are being piloted.

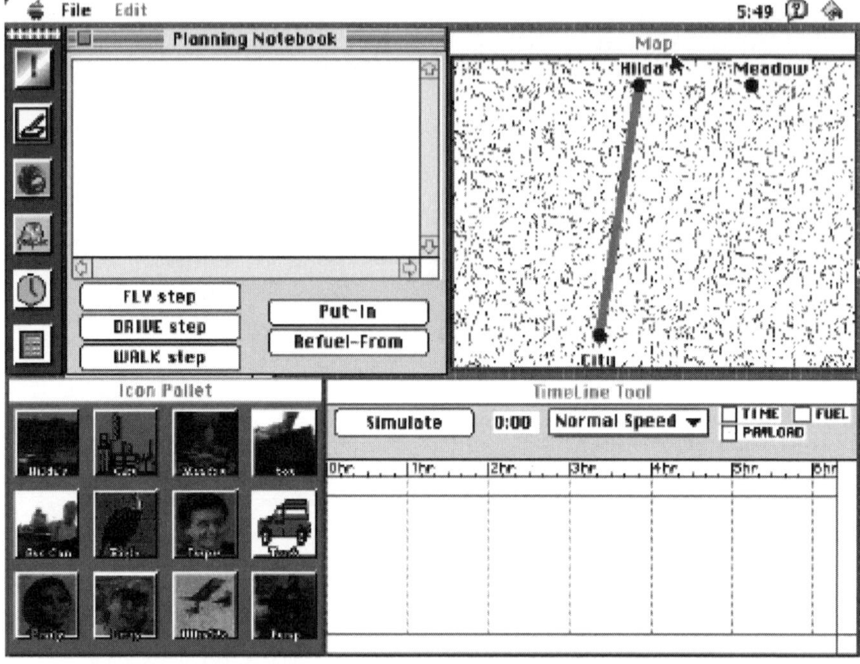

FIG. 1.11. A screen from the *Jasper* Adventure Player Software.

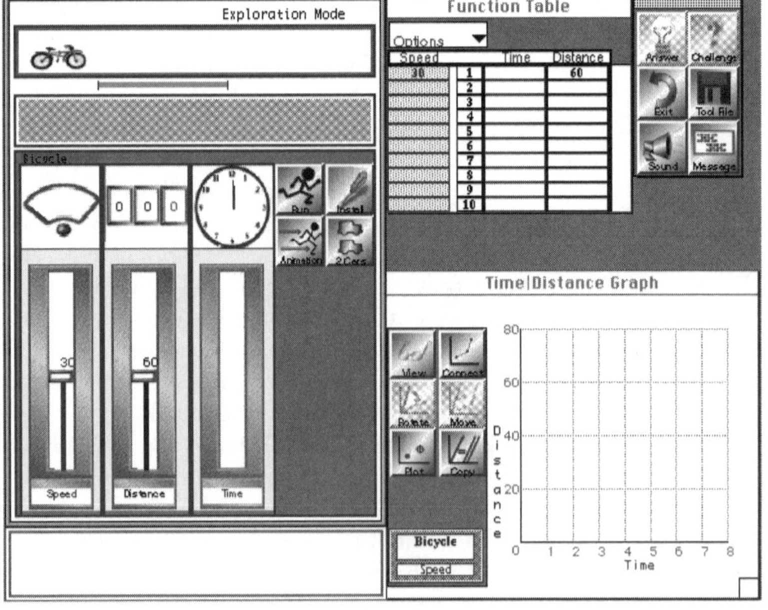

FIG. 1.12. A screen from the *Jasper* SMART Tools software.

Swing: How's My Scale?

Linda

Class List

List Cards

1 of 9

- Recheck the ☐ **front view** and/or ☐ **side view** of your swing. You need to show what your scale is.
- Recheck the ☐ **front view** and/or ☐ **side view** of your swing. I used your scale and came up with different measurements than you did.
- Good work! I used your scale and found that some of the measurements on your ☐ **front view** and/or ☐ **side view** of your swing are not quite right, so recheck them.
- Good work! I used your scale and found that almost all of your measurements are correct. But a few of the measurements on your ☐ **front view** and/or ☐ **side view** of your swings are not quite right, so recheck them.
- Good work! I used your scale and found that almost all of your measurements are correct. But recheck the side view of your swingset. I don't agree with your measurement of the length of your swing's legs.
- Great job!! You included a scale and the measurements on your drawings are correct.

Other Comments

FIG. 1.13. A HyperCard program for helping teachers give feedback about blueprints.

SUPPORT FOR PROFESSIONAL DEVELOPMENT AND COLLABORATION

We have learned a great deal from teachers about effective ways to support their implementation of *Jasper*. In our very first professional development sessions, the formative assessment we received from teachers and business leaders provided information that fundamentally changed how the Vanderbilt group conducted workshops (see Chapter 6). This information has been valuable to many other groups as well. We have continued to learn from teachers and, with their assistance, have developed materials to support the implementation of *Jasper*.

A Model of Collaboration and Dissemination

In the *Jasper* Implementation Project of 1990–1991 (see Chapters 4, 6), we used an innovative model of collaboration among teachers, researchers, and corporate supporters with the goal of maximizing the support for the classrooms using *Jasper* for the first time and establishing a team of experts that would, in turn, teach others in their community to teach with *Jasper*. The sponsoring corporation funded the purchase of equipment and professional development activities for a team of two teachers and one corporate collaborator for the first year. The corporate collaborator was on leave to work 20 hours a week with the teachers, providing technology and other support in the classroom. This model of collaboration and dissemination was successful in many ways. In at least five sites, the corporate support continued for several years as the original teachers trained other teachers and *Jasper* spread district-wide in Grades 5 and 6. Although this model did perpetuate the spread of *Jasper* in these sites, it was not a model that we could easily replicate in new sites. The initial and ongoing organizational costs made it impractical for our group to implement again on that scale (CTGV, in press).

The CTGV Model for Professional Development

Our work with teachers has helped us develop a model for building a learning community for teachers that is consistent with and builds on the *Jasper* instructional model. We start with an anchor (often it is a *Jasper* adventure) that provides a common experience and challenge to engage teachers in question generation and discussion. Teachers generate ideas and strategies for using *Jasper* with their students. The facilitator of the professional development becomes a member of the learning community, sharing other teachers' experiences and ideas for using *Jasper*. We have found that this type of collaboration can result in better teaching and learning than having experts explain the correct use of *Jasper*. We have used this model with over 600 teachers in more than 20 workshops.

Interactive Teacher Development Materials

We have also used the design principles for *Jasper* to develop an interactive video that teachers can use with or without a facilitator. This "*Jasper* in the Classroom" video shows a sixth grade classroom at various times during a 5-day period as they solve a *Jasper* adventure (see the enclosed CD-ROM). The video serves as an anchor for teachers as they analyze and discuss different classroom processes and generate ideas for using *Jasper* with their students.

Materials accompany the video to help teachers reflect and analyze the classroom video segments. There are also comments and suggestions by experienced *Jasper* teachers to help scaffold teachers' thinking about different ways to use *Jasper*.

The *Jasper* series includes several additional types of support for helping teachers successfully implement it in their classrooms. Extensive print materials accompany each adventure and provide information about mathematics content as well as pedagogy. Videos that accompany each adventure show general tips for teaching.

Many of the *Jasper* adventures also include a variety of visual teaching tools that teachers can use to enhance their own understanding of concepts used in solving the adventure. These teaching tools can later be shown to the students as well. For example, a teaching tool for *Blueprint for Success* shows a front, side, and top view of a swing set and slide to help students as they create their blueprints. A teaching tool for *Bridging the Gap* provides a visual model for proportional reasoning. Some of the teaching tools are on the videodisc that contains the *Jasper* adventure. Others are derived from the SMART Challenge programs (described earlier) and reside on a separate CD-ROM. We are also creating a World Wide Web site where *Jasper* teachers can learn from one another.

Jasper as a Tool for Community Building

A highly positive benefit of *Jasper* is one that we did not anticipate originally but was brought to our attention by teachers (CTGV, 1994). It involves opportunities for community building. Parents, administrators, business leaders, and others like to know what students are learning. They can be shown a *Jasper* adventure and then asked to solve it (usually in groups). Students can act as their guides to keep them from doing too much floundering. This format has worked extremely well in many different settings (e.g., CTGV, 1994). It can be used with any problem-based curriculum where the nature of the overall problem is relatively easy to convey.

The use of *Jasper*-like problems also facilitates activities such as cross-age mentoring and long-distance discussions among students and teachers. For example, college students at Vanderbilt have solved *The Big Splash* and then worked with inner-city sixth graders as the latter solved the adventure and prepared for presentations. Initial contacts among the groups have been face-to-face, but the rest of the mentoring was conducted via desktop videoconferencing. Discussions among mentors and mentees are much more fruitful when they can be anchored around a specific context, such as a *Jasper* adventure.

Anchors such as *Jasper* also facilitate long-distance communication among students and teachers. By sharing a common referent (e.g., see the discussion of Buhler in Bransford & Johnson, 1973), it is much easier for groups to communicate.

SUMMARY

Our goal in this chapter is to provide an overview of the 12 *Jasper* adventures plus analog and extension materials and support for professional development. We also argue that *Jasper* cannot be understood unless you try to solve at least one of the adventures.

A copy of the adventure *Rescue at Boone's Meadow* is available on the CD-ROM with this book and we strongly suggest that you try to solve it. A video of *RBM* being used in a classroom is also available on the CD-ROM.

Subsequent chapters explore the *Jasper* series in more detail. In the next chapter we discuss the theoretical and empirical work that gave rise to *Jasper*. Following this we explore *Jasper* from the perspective of issues of curriculum (Chapter 3), initial research on instruction and assessment (Chapter 4), explorations of formative assessment (Chapter 5), and teacher learning and community building (Chapter 6). In Chapter 7, we end with a discussion of lessons learned that are relevant not only to *Jasper*, but to all efforts to support school reform.

2

The Genesis of *Jasper*

The *Jasper* series arose from several research projects that were being conducted in 1984 when we began the Learning Technology Center (LTC) at Peabody College, Vanderbilt University. At that time, we never envisioned creating products such as *Jasper* because we defined ourselves as a research rather than a development center. However, it soon became apparent that typical materials such as textbooks and end-of-chapter word problems made it extremely difficult to create the types of learning environments that we wanted to study. In addition, we wanted to collaborate with teachers and, therefore, needed materials that they were eager to use in their classrooms. As a result, the development of high quality materials to support learning became an important part of our center's research plan.

RESEARCH ACTIVITIES THAT SET THE STAGE FOR JASPER

When the LTC began, we were engaged in three major research projects that provided foundations for *Jasper*.

The Inert Knowledge Project

The first project focused on an issue that Whitehead (1929) called the inert knowledge problem. *Inert knowledge* is knowledge that can be recalled when people are specifically prompted to remember it, but that is not spontaneously used to solve problems even though it is relevant.

Bereiter (1984) provided an excellent illustration of failures to utilize important information. He noted that a teacher of educational psychology gave her students a long, difficult article and told them they had 10 minutes to learn as much as they could about it. Almost without exception, the students began with the first sentence of the article and read as far as they could until the time was up. Later, when discussing the strategies, the students acknowledged that they knew better than simply to begin reading. They had all had classes that taught them to skim for main ideas, consult section headings, and so forth. But they did not spontaneously use this knowledge when it would have helped.

A number of laboratory and classroom studies suggested to us that the inert knowledge problem was ubiquitous (e.g., Bereiter, 1984; Bransford, Franks, Vye, & Sherwood, 1989; Gick & Holyoak, 1980; Perfetto, Bransford, & Franks, 1983). Evidence also suggested that the degree to which knowledge remained inert was strongly affected by the way that information was learned initially (e.g., Adams et al., 1988; Lockhart, Lamon, & Glick, 1988; Simon, 1980). The idea of overcoming inert knowledge became a major goal of the learning environments that we wanted to create.

The Logo Project

A second research project that strongly influenced our thinking was the Vanderbilt Logo project. We worked in fifth-grade classrooms to help students learn to program in Logo (e.g., Papert, 1980) and attempted to assess the effects of Logo on general thinking and problem solving. Several important lessons emerged from this research:

1. It was clear that the opportunity for students to create their own products in Logo was highly motivating. This sensitized us to the importance of helping students construct their own products, arguments, and ideas rather than simply learn to reconstruct facts that others had presented to them.
2. Although Logo programming was engaging to students, it became clear that engagement did not ensure the kinds of learning that we had envisioned. For example, we found that students often used trial-and-error to type in commands that let the Logo turtle wrap around the screen a number of times. Often, this produced an interesting-looking design that was then shown to others. The design would appear in other students' programs because there was a spirit of sharing in our Logo classrooms. Nevertheless, students merely copied lists of commands from one another and, hence, did not learn planning skills or goal-directed Logo programming skills (e.g., Bransford, Stein, Delclos, & Littlefield, 1986).
3. With guidance by the teacher, students could be helped to engage in more planning, and less random trial-and-error, without losing their enthusiasm for Logo programming (e.g., Bransford, Stein, Delclos, & Littlefield, 1986; Littlefield, Delclos, Bransford, Clayton, & Franks, 1989; Littlefield, Delclos, Lever, Clayton, & Bransford, 1989). This resulted in better learning on the part of students and, eventually, in better transfer to other types of thinking-related activities (e.g., Littlefield, Delclos, Lever et al., 1989).

These experiences helped us realize a methodological flaw in many studies of the effects of Logo programming that were being conducted at that time. Researchers were asking whether experience with Logo transferred to other types of tasks, and many found no evidence of transfer. But they also failed to ask whether students had learned to program in Logo in the first place, versus simply being engaged in a lot of random trial and error. Without an adequate degree of initial learning, one cannot expect transfer to occur (e.g., Littlefield et al., 1988; Littlefield, Delclos, Lever et al., 1989).

The experiences also emphasized the importance of teacher guidance in any attempt to introduce and evaluate the effects of technology. Furthermore, as teachers focused more explicitly on particular pedagogical goals (e.g., learning to plan, learning to understand principles of geometry), there was a greater probability of observing transfer from Logo (e.g., CTGV, 1996a; Lehrer, Lee, & Jeong, 1994; Mayer, 1988; Salomon, 1992). These findings fit with other observations that the ability to think is not simply a function of thinking skills but, also, of access to powerful conceptual tools (e.g., Bransford, Sherwood, Vye, & Rieser, 1986; Bransford, Vye, Kinzer, & Risko, 1990; Chi, Glaser, & Farr, 1991; Salomon, 1993; Salomon, Perkins, & Globerson, 1991).

4. Logo helped create a social context that sparked conversations outside, as well as inside, the classroom. For example, one of our children was taking Logo in school. When he came home, numerous conversations about Logo arose spontaneously. In one case, he and his father were waiting in line to see a movie and began discussing the procedures needed to create a polygon of any number of sides. They could not wait to get home and test their thinking. Overall, a great deal of Logo talk occurred outside of school.

The teacher in school was impressed by the son's programming skill; she had no idea of the amount of time outside of class that he spent talking about Logo and trying it out. This experience helped us appreciate the power of home–school connections for learning and the fact that many students can have learning opportunities at home that are invisible to their teachers. It also helped us realize the value of a shared context (in this case, Logo programming) for conversations and further inquiry.

The Dynamic Assessment Project

A third set of research activities that set the stage for *Jasper* emerged from the Vanderbilt Dynamic Assessment Project, a project that focused on alternative assessments of children (e.g., Bransford, Delclos, Vye, Burns, & Hasselbring, 1987; Vye, Burns, Delclos, & Bransford, 1987). The purpose of this project was to assess individuals' responsiveness to opportunities to learn (e.g., Brown, Bransford, Ferrara, & Campione, 1983; Campione & Brown, 1987; Feuerstein, Rand, & Hoffman, 1979; Lidz, 1987) and to assess their zone of sensitivity to instruction (Vygotsky, 1978; Wood, Wood, & Middleton, 1978).

The methods of dynamic assessment were different from those used in standardized, static assessments such as intelligence tests and achievement tests where help or hints on the part of the tester invalidate results. An important component of dynamic assessment involves a systematic attempt to actively change various components of tasks and approaches to teaching in order to find the conditions that are most effective for each child. Therefore, the Dynamic Assessment Project brought us face-to-face with issues of curriculum, instruction, and assessment. As part of the Dynamic Assessment Project, we began to work with fifth-grade students who were having trouble in reading and mathematics. Our experiences with the development of learning environments designed to help these students are discussed in a later section.

TOWARD A NEW VISION OF EFFECTIVE LEARNING ENVIRONMENTS

Taken together, the work on overcoming inert knowledge, Logo, and dynamic assessment suggested the possibility of creating new environments for learning that could help people gain access to important areas of knowledge and skill that may have been difficult for them to reach without these new environments. New methods of skill acquisition such as the Graduated Length Method (GLM) of teaching skiing provided a particularly exciting vision of what might be possible. In one of our articles (Bransford, Sherwood, & Hasselbring, 1988), we discussed a paper by Burton, Brown, and Fischer (1984) that illustrates the importance of creating alternate pathways to important competencies. Their example involved learning to ski, but it seemed relevant to a wide variety of areas, such as the development of important competencies in literacy, science, and mathematics. We wrote:

> The development of the "Graduated Length Method" (GLM) of teaching skiing a number of years ago was a breakthrough that made successful and enjoyable skiing available to thousands of people who had not previously been considered candidates for participation in the sport. In the GLM method, several elements of the task are carefully and systematically manipulated by a skillful coach so that the learner skis in a series of increasingly complex situations, each requiring an extension of the skills learned in the previous, less complex environment. So, a novice skier is given very short skis, no poles, and is put on a gentle slope. The short skis make turning easier and allow practice in developing rhythm, an essential component of successful control. The lack of poles helps the student to focus on balance and on the movement of the skis. The gentle terrain greatly reduces the frightening speed that novices often experience on steeper slopes and allows them to build confidence and to practice important movements that are critical for success on the more demanding slopes.
>
> In the course of training, the GLM coach analyzes the performance of the learner at each level of instruction and makes decisions about when and what to change, based on the successes and failures of the student. Gradually, longer skis are introduced; wider, narrower, or steeper slopes are presented; the snow conditions are also varied; poles are added. An important characteristic of the GLM method is that, even at the simplest level of instruction, the student is actually skiing rather than engaging in isolated exercises (e.g., balancing on a wooden beam) that have dubious relevance for the actual performance of complex skilled behavior and that are often not motivating to pursue.
>
> The GLM method also depends on effective teaching. For example, changes in the types of skis, types of slopes, and so forth are made at points when the coach decides they will help either to advance the student to the next level or to make the student

> aware of current errors that need to be debugged. The coach might have the student ski in soft, powdery snow so that a lack of rhythmic turning could be clearly visible in the tracks left by the skis or, if the student was not using the skis properly in negotiating turns, the coach might move the location to an icy area, where the proper use of edges of the skis is critical in staying upright. [These environments provided rich sources of feedback to the students.] Overall the GLM method is designed to make it easier for instructors to teach and students to learn.
>
> For present purposes, the important point involves the relationship between (a) people's abilities to develop an important competency (skiing) and (b) cultural practice regarding established methods of teaching. Prior to the GLM approach, many people had great difficulty learning to ski. It was tempting to conclude that some people simply had the ability and many others did not. Given the GLM method, however, thousands of persons who would otherwise have failed were able to succeed (Bransford, Sherwood, & Hasselbring, 1988, pp. 174–175).

HARNESSING THE POWER OF NEW TECHNOLOGIES

The vision of successful learning environments such as the GLM motivated us to ask whether new computer and video technologies could help us create new kinds of learning materials and activities. Our attention was attracted to the rapidly increasing availability of computer and video technologies that began to emerge in the mid-1980s. How might these tools be used to provide learning benefits analogous to the power of the GLM?

Beyond Electronic Workbooks

Research available at that time suggested strongly that students needed something more than technology-enhanced worksheets that helped them develop isolated sets of skills and memorize factual content (e.g., see CTGV, 1991). Students especially needed to learn to think for themselves and to solve problems (e.g., Feuerstein, 1979; Linn, 1986; Mann, 1979; Nickerson, 1988; Segal, Chipman, & Glaser, 1985). Work with Logo (e.g., Papert, 1980) suggested uses of technology that might enhance thinking rather than develop only isolated skills.

Beyond Isolated Sets of Thinking Skills

One approach we considered was to develop computer programs that taught general learning and problem-solving strategies such as how to solve verbal and figural analogy problems, how to solve different types of logic problems, and so forth. However, we became aware of the research literature that demonstrated the pervasive role of content knowledge in empowering people to think effectively (e.g., Bransford, Sherwood, et al., 1986; Chi et al., 1991; Simon, 1980). As noted earlier, the importance of introducing students to powerful conceptual ideas in the context of Logo (e.g., ideas about geometry) began to show up in that literature as well (CTGV, 1996a).

We decided to avoid attempts to teach general thinking and learning strategies and, instead, to embed strategy and skill instruction within the context of particular subject matters such as literature, science, and mathematics. A major challenge was to create environments that would help students acquire and organize knowledge in ways that would render that knowledge useful rather than inert when solving problems.

Attempts to Develop Simulations

Our first thoughts about creating meaningful learning environments involved the idea of developing computer-based simulations that students could explore while learning new information. These simulations would involve the need to use relevant content knowledge to solve problems that the students faced.

We built a prototype for the area of mathematics that asked students to solve word problems such as how much fence a person needed to completely fence a rectangular piece of land with a specified length and width (e.g., 100 feet by 80 feet). Students entered their answers and then saw a simulation of their approach. Many middle school students made the common mistake of adding only the length and width of the pen to determine the amount of fence they needed and hence answering 180 feet rather than 360 feet. In their simulation, they could see that their piece of land was only 1/2 fenced.

We hoped that simulations such as these could be designed to help students learn to read word problems more strategically, to acquire concepts such as perimeter, area, and volume, and to begin to understand the conditions under which each concept was most useful. (For example, perimeter is usually important in fencing a piece of property; area is important if you want to order grass seed for property; volume is important for making that property into a swimming pool.)

However, it soon became apparent that the type of installed machines in schools (mainly Apple IIs and IIes at that time) were not sufficiently powerful to support the kinds of simulations we envisioned. Because we wanted to study how technology was actually used in classrooms rather than only in laboratory settings (see CTGV, 1996a), a consideration of the installed base of machines was important to us.

Overcoming Constraints on Computing Power

In 1985, we were fortunate to meet Don Nix and his colleagues from the IBM Thomas J. Watson Research Center, who introduced us to interactive videodisc technology. The ability to randomly access video materials seemed to have profound implications for new uses of the video medium. Instead of being confined to linear, television-like programs, interactive videodisc technology made the re-exploration of video information much easier (e.g., Bransford, Sherwood, et al., 1988).

The use of the videodisc medium also meant that we could provide high-quality, dynamic visual images without having to deal with the severe limitations on processing capacity imposed by the computers then available in classrooms. We began to explore ways to use the video medium to create realistic problem-solving environments that students and teachers could share, explore, and analyze. This line of thinking developed into an approach to instruction that we have come to call *anchored instruction*. The approach is described next.

ANCHORED INSTRUCTION

Anchored instruction represents our attempt to overcome the inert-knowledge problem by creating meaningful problem-solving environments that permit sustained exploration by students and teachers. A major goal is to help people understand the kinds of problems and opportunities that experts in various areas encounter, and to see how experts use knowledge as tools to identify, represent, and solve problems. A related goal is to help students integrate their knowledge by exploring the same situation (anchor) from multiple points of view (e.g., as a scientist, mathematician, historian).

The Role of Previously Acquired Knowledge

Anchored instruction is motivated by a belief in the crucial role of the knowledge that people bring to learning situations. Not all instruction needs to begin with explicitly presented anchors. In many cases, people bring their own knowledge to the learning setting, and this functions as an anchor that makes information meaningful.

As an illustration, our initial article on anchored instruction refers to a story from Lefrancois's (1982) *Psychology for Teaching* (Bransford, Sherwood, et al., 1990). The story begins with an imaginary archeologist who uncovers some stone tablets in a cave. The tablets tell the story of Oog:

> *Oog writes that it occurred to him that a great many children of the People did not know very much. They did not know that they should walk on the top of the hills where their scent would be carried away into the skies, rather than at the bottom where the scent would find its way to the beasts that lie on the hillsides. They did not know that the huge Bela snake hides among the branches of the Kula berry bushes, not because the snake likes the berries, but because he likes the children. Of this they were ignorant, even as they were ignorant of the skills required to fashion the houses of the People so that the rain would not come in, and of a thousand other things that the People should know.* (p. 5)

The story continues with an account of how Oog became a teacher and taught the People, and of how the People flourished because of the information they learned.

Lefrancois' story about Oog is fiction. Nevertheless, it does an excellent job of illustrating the powerful role of education in people's lives. We can imagine that people in Oog's time would go out of their way to listen to the information he supplied because it was so important for them.

But note that Oog used a very traditional approach to instruction: telling. His use of a transmission model represents an approach to instruction that is often criticized today. We argued that Oog's method of teaching was appropriate, given the level of understanding that the learners brought to the situation. They could easily grasp the relevance of what he was saying because of their extensive life experiences. Thus, Oog's students presumably experienced the problems associated with dangerous animals, protecting their children, and building effective shelter. Under conditions such as these, there is a time for telling. The information is meaningful because it maps onto knowledge of problem situations that the learners have already acquired.

Compensating for a Lack of Experience and Knowledge

We emphasize the importance of anchored instruction because, in many educational settings, there is an absence of features that are present in the story about Oog. Students often have not had the opportunity to experience the types of problems that are rendered solvable by the knowledge we teach them. They treat the knowledge as an end rather than as a means to important ends. In geometry, many students memorize terms but fail to understand how knowledge of the mathematical properties of simple shapes provides one with the power to measure the world (Zech et al., 1994; Zech et al., in press). In science, students often do not appreciate how new concepts and theories can render perplexing problems solvable and make previously puzzling sets of data cohere (e.g., Hanson, 1970; Sherwood, Kinzer, Bransford, et al., 1987). In the humanities, students often fail to see how sets of classic writings provide important perspectives on current problems. The common denominator in all these cases is that new information is treated as facts to be learned rather than as knowledge to be used.

A major goal of anchored instruction is to help students experience the kinds of problems that experts in an area encounter and to understand how core concepts in a discipline help clarify these problems. We want to help them transform knowledge from mere facts into useful tools. We also want to provide a common context that can be explored by students, teachers, parents, and others so that they have a common ground for communication (see Bransford & Johnson, 1972, 1973).

Examples of early work on anchored instruction in the areas of literacy and science can be found in Risko et al., 1989; Sherwood, Kinzer, Bransford, et al., 1987; Sherwood, Kinzer, Hasselbring, & Bransford, 1987; Bransford, Vye, et al., 1990. In the next discussion, we explore the work in mathematics that led most directly to *Jasper*.

SPECIFIC EXPERIENCES THAT GAVE RISE TO *JASPER*

The *Jasper* series arose most directly from our use of anchored instruction in the context of the Vanderbilt Dynamic Assessment Project (see previous discussion).

As part of that project, we worked with middle school students who were having difficulties in school, especially in areas such as reading and mathematics. We decided to focus on helping students learn to solve word problems because they involved an emphasis on both reading comprehension and mathematics.

Early Work on Word Problems

Our work on word problems was conducted with fifth- and sixth-grade students who were having difficulties in school, especially in areas of reading and mathematics. As discussed in Bransford, Zech, et al. (1996), we presented students with written versions of simple word problems such as the following:

1. *Tony rides the bus to camp every summer. There are 8 other children who ride with him. The bus travels 9 miles an hour. It takes 4 hours to get there. How far away is the camp?*
2. *John is standing in front of a building. The building is 8 times as tall as John. John is 16 years old. John is 5 feet tall. How tall is the building?*

Nearly every student with whom we worked used an approach to solving word problems that was mechanical rather than based on an attempt to understand the problem. For example, a typical answer for the first word problem was 8 + 9 + 4 = 21. The following explanation about solution strategies was quite typical:

Interviewer: Why did you decide to add the numbers?
Student: Because it said like "How far away is the camp?" How is to add.

Interviews relevant to the second problem also involved a search for key words in the problems. For example, one student (who was quite typical) stated:

Student: I saw the building is 8 *times* as tall as John so I know to multiply.
Interviewer: What did you multiply?
Student: 16 and 7 and 8.

Our experiments suggested to us what mathematical thinking meant to these students. Mathematical thinking was the procedures used to solve numerical problems. The procedures involved a search for key words that specified the operations to perform on the numbers (i.e., add, subtract, multiply, or divide). The numbers to be operated on were rarely attached to meaningful elements of the problem context. For example, both of the problems include numerical information that was clearly irrelevant (i.e., the fact that 8 other boys rode with Tony; that John is 16 years old). Despite this fact, students consistently attempted to use the irrelevant information in every problem we gave them. Basically, students demonstrated extremely poor comprehension of the problems they were being asked to solve.

As we searched the literature on word problems, we discovered that our findings were similar to those reported by other researchers. Several investigators showed that, instead of bringing real-world standards to their work, students seem to treat word problems mechanically and often fail to think about constraints imposed by real-world experiences (Charles & Silver, 1988; Silver, 1986). For example, Silver asked students to determine the number of buses needed to take a specific number of people on a field trip. Many of them divided the total number of students by the number that each bus would hold and came up with answers like 2⅓. The students failed to consider the fact that one cannot have a functioning ⅓ bus.

Studies by Reusser (1988) also provided dramatic evidence of many students' problems with word problems. He gave schoolchildren the following type of problem in the context of other mathematics problems:

> There are 26 sheep and 10 goats on a ship. How old is the captain?

Approximately ¾ of the students in Reusser's study attempted to provide a numerical answer to the problem. Their overwhelming tendency was to ask themselves whether to add, subtract, multiply, or divide rather than ask whether the problem made sense.

Several authors questioned the generality of Reusser's findings and conducted their own version of his experiments:

> Our reaction to Reusser's data was that this must have been a special group of students who had been taught poorly. We gave the problem to one of our own children who was in fifth grade. Much to our surprise, and dismay, the answer given was 36. When we asked why, we were told 'Well, you need to add or subtract or multiply in problems like this, and this one seemed to work best if I add (Bransford & Stein, 1993, p. 196).

Support for Problem Comprehension

Our approach to working with students focused on efforts to improve their ability to understand the problems they were solving. We began to investigate the use of video-based scenarios that could help students generate mental models of situations (e.g., see McNamara et al., 1991). In several studies, we used the first 12 minutes of the film *Raiders of the Lost Ark* where Indiana Jones travels to South America to capture the golden idol (e.g., Barron, Bransford, Kulewicz, & Hasselbring, 1989; Bransford, Hasselbring, et al., 1988). We asked students to imagine that they wanted to return to the jungle to obtain some of the gold artifacts that Indiana left behind. If so, it could be important to know dimensions of obstacles, such as the width of the pit one would have to jump, the height of the cave, the width of the river and its relationship to the size of the seaplane, and so forth.

The goal of learning about potential obstacles and events guided the selection of mathematically based problems that were derived from scenes from the movie segment. We decided to use known standards (e.g., the height of Indiana Jones) to estimate sizes and distances that were important to know. For example, one problem asked students to estimate the width of the pit they would have to jump if they returned to the cave. This information could be estimated by finding a scene where Indiana used his bullwhip to swing over the pit. Through the use of freeze frame, we were able to show a scene of Indiana swinging with his outstretched body extending halfway across the pit. Measurement on the screen (either by hand or through the use of computer graphics) allowed students to see that the pit was approximately two Indianas wide. Students were also encouraged to create visual and symbolic representations of problems, and they received individualized feedback about the strengths and weaknesses of their approach to each problem. All instruction was one-on-one.

Effects of learning in the video context were compared with the effects of learning in a control condition in which students received one-on-one instruction in solving and representing written problems without the use of the video context. The results indicated strong benefits of the video context on students' abilities to solve analogous transfer problems that occurred both within and outside the context of Indiana Jones (see Bransford, Hasselbring, et al., 1988). Students in the video condition also showed marked improvements in their abilities to visually represent problems. Figure 2.1 shows pretest and posttest representations of an Indiana Jones problem that asked students to estimate the dimensions of various objects in the video.

Pretest

Indiana Jones is lying across the pontoon. The pontoon is 3 times as long as Indiana Jones. The plane has 2 pontoons. If Indiana Jones is 6 feet tall, how long is the pontoon?

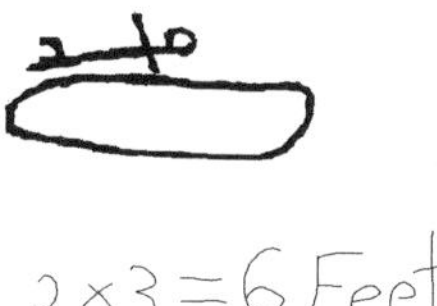

Posttest

Indiana Jones is lying across the pontoon. The pontoon is 4 times as long as Indiana Jones. The plane has 2 pontoons. If Indiana Jones is 6 feet tall, how long is the pontoon?

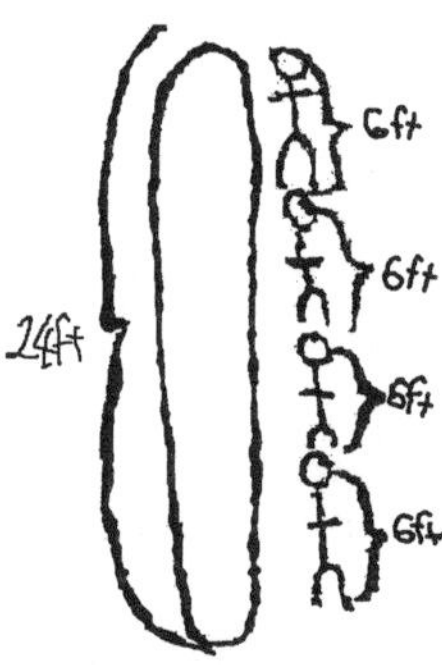

FIG. 2.1. Pre- and Postdata on children's attempts to solve *Raiders* problems.

Our findings with *Raiders of the Lost Ark* were encouraging to us, the students, and their teachers. Students enjoyed working on problems in the context of *Raiders*, and most of them exhibited a major shift in their abilities to explain the nature of the problems they were trying to solve, represent these problems visually, and explain their work. They also showed evidence of transfer to real-life settings. For example, students began to use known heights (e.g., of one another) to estimate the height of trees, flagpoles, and other objects in their environment.

Needs for New Problem Contexts

We began to worry about a limitation of our work with *Raiders*, namely, that the type of problems we were able to devise was too restricted. The primary problem type involved simple measurement problems given some standard. In particular, we helped students see that there was some object (e.g., the width of the cave, the length of the pontoon on the plane) that was important to measure and that was X number of Indiana Joneses long (e.g., If Indiana Jones were Y feet tall, how long was the object?). Students could learn to do well on this type of problem yet still lack a deep understanding of what they were doing. In particular, we were worried about what Dunker (1945) called the functional-fixedness problem. Given a change in problem type so that new solution strategies must be generated, people often remain functionally fixed and attempt to apply familiar solution strategies even though they are no longer relevant. Working with only a single problem type is almost a sure way to get people functionally fixed.

The manner in which the *Raiders* movie was edited precluded us from generating additional problem types in that context. For example, we would have liked to develop problems that involved dynamic rather than static approaches to measurement. An example involves efforts to estimate the width of the forest in *Raiders*, given that it took Indiana Jones X seconds to run through it, going at a speed of Y miles per hour. A similar problem could be written for the width of the large field that separated the forest from the river where the airplane was parked.

Unfortunately, the movie did not let us see continuous sequences of Indiana Jones running so that students could time them. Instead, we saw Indiana Jones going into the forest, then halfway through it, then going into the clearing and suddenly leaving the clearing, and getting to the river. The kinds of edits that appeared in the movie did not support the scenes we needed to help students begin to think about rate. (Movie directors and editors know that continuous scenes shot from a single perspective tend to be visually boring.)

The River Adventure

The limitations on creating additional problem types in the *Raiders* context prompted us to think about creating our own videos that included the kinds of scenes and data needed in an educational context. We eventually designed and produced our own prototype videodisc, *The River Adventure*. In this adventure, the viewer is told that he or she has won a 1-week trip on a houseboat and must do all the planning for food, gas, water, docking the boat, and so forth. Data concerning the boat (e.g., its length, width, height, cruising speed, fuel consumption, and capacity), the route, marinas along the route, and so forth, were all embedded in the video. The students watching the video had to determine when and why to use various sets of data to help them achieve particular goals. For example, one important consideration in planning for the houseboat trip is to reserve a dock at a marina that is the appropriate size for the boat. The houseboat's dimensions are not explicitly given in the video; instead, students see scenes of a 6-foot person on the boat and could use them to estimate its length, width, and height (analogous to using Indiana Jones as a standard in our earlier work).

The adventure also requires students to call the dock (via marine radio) and provide their estimated time of arrival. This means that students had to use scenes to estimate the speed of the boat (e.g., the number of minutes to travel between mile markers on the river) and then use the boat speed to determine how long it would take to travel the distance to the dock (the distance was discoverable by exploring the map included on the videodisc). The adventure includes additional data such as fill times for the water tank in order to estimate its capacity, estimates of amount of water needed for various tasks, and so forth. Overall, the adventure includes all the embedded data needed to plan for the trip.

As we discussed elsewhere (e.g., CTGV, 1994), we used the same type of instructional approach described for *Raiders* to help students learn to understand, represent, and solve problems in *The River Adventure* context. However, we worked with multiple problems so that functional fixedness was less of a threat. Results were highly encouraging: Students liked the challenge and were able to transfer to post-test problems. Examples of pre- and posttest data are illustrated in Fig. 2.2.

Beyond Well-Defined Word Problems

As we thought more about our assumptions of mathematical thinking, we began to question the fact that our approach to using *Raiders* and *River Adventure* still involved a traditional word-problem format. All we had added was video support. Thus, as students watched the video, we stopped it in order to present word problems to them. By doing so, we explicitly defined the problems to be solved rather than helped students learn to generate and pose their own problems. The latter seemed important for developing the kind of mathematical thinking necessary to solve complex problems in the real world (e.g., Bransford & Stein, 1993; Brown & Walter, 1990; Lave, 1988).

Historical accounts of great mathematical thinkers (e.g., Turnbull, 1993) provide ample evidence of the importance of identifying and posing problems rather than simply solving problems that others presented to them (see also Brown & Walter, 1990). For example, Eratosthenes made ingenious use of simple principles of geometry to accurately estimate the circumference of the earth. Similarly, Thales estimated the height of a pyramid by using simple geometric principles based on shadows. (The trick was to determine the length of the pyramid's shadow given that part of it was covered up by the pyramid). In both cases, the thinkers essentially

Pretest

Students view a still frame of a boy lying across the bow of the houseboat. The announcer notes that the boy is 6 feet tall. One can see perceptually that the boat is twice as wide as the boy. The interviewer asks: Can you think of a way to figure out how wide the boat is?
Student 1: "Multiply?" When the interviewer doesn't answer right away the students says, "Divide?" He eventually draws the following:

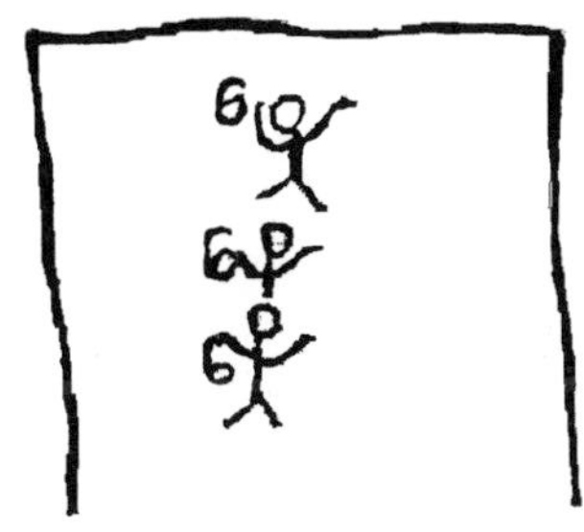

Posttest

Students view a still frame of a garbage can sitting on the bow of the houseboat. The announcer notes that the can is two feet tall. One can see perceptually that the top of the boat is about 6 cans high. The interviewer asks: Can you think of a way to figure out how tall the boat is? The student draws the following and then explains the math:

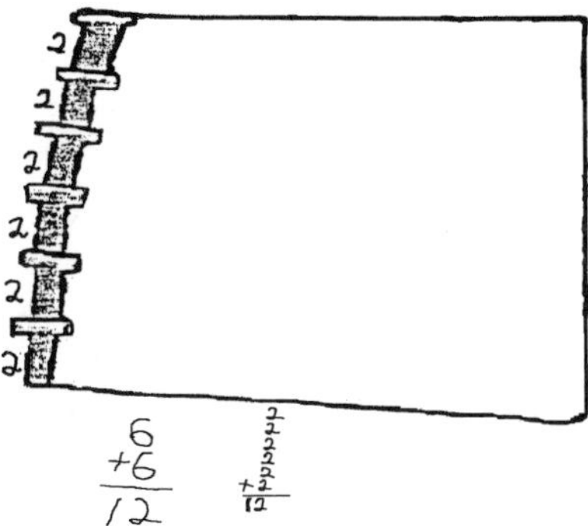

FIG. 2.2 Pre- and posttest data on children's attempts to solve *River Adventure* problems.

generated their own word problems rather than solved well-defined problems provided by someone else.

At a less complex level of mathematical sophistication, the need to generate problems and subproblems arises frequently in everyday life. As a simple example, imagine the task of going from one's house to a breakfast meeting at 8:30 in a new restaurant across town. First, one needs to identify the existence of a problem to be solved; namely, the need to determine the time one should leave in order to make the breakfast meeting on time. To solve this general problem one has to generate subproblems such as "How far away is the meeting?" "How fast will I be able to drive?" and so forth. The ability to identify the general problem and generate the subproblems to be solved is crucial for real-world problem solving. We consider it to be an important component of mathematical thinking. We also believe that typical uses of applications problems do not develop such generative problem-finding and problem-formulation skills (Bransford & Stein, 1984; Brown & Walter, 1990; Charles & Silver, 1988; Porter, 1989; Sternberg, 1986).

Research on Problem Generation

We used *The River Adventure* to study problem generation by collecting baseline data on people's abilities to engage in the types of mathematical thinking necessary to plan for the houseboat trip. Members of our research team worked with three groups of individuals: college undergraduates, academically successful fifth graders, and fifth graders who exhibited delays in their mathematics development and were receiving special services. After watching the video, students were given a structured interview consisting of several levels of questions. The initial questions were general and open-ended and were designed to assess students' abilities to articulate and elaborate important categories to consider in planning the trip (e.g., fuel, estimated time of arrival, food, water, etc.). Subsequent questions were designed to tap students' abilities to collect relevant data and formulate mathematical solutions for specific aspects of the plan (e.g., "How might you estimate the dimensions of the houseboat?").

The results of the planning questions suggested that most college students were relatively good at identifying and elaborating the important categories to consider to adequately plan for the trip (this was not surprising because the categories were mentioned at the beginning of the video). In contrast, fifth-grade students, both academically successful and mathematics-delayed, were much less likely to mention key categories. When a category was mentioned, the responses of the students tended to be quite general (e.g., "You need to bring enough water."). Students' responses almost never involved quantitative thinking such as systematic attempts to estimate how much water would be needed for a 1-week trip. In addition, nearly all the fifth graders had a difficult time identifying the relevant mathematical data that would be needed for solving the problems associated with their plans, such as determining the boat's dimensions or estimating arrival time. Not surprisingly, mathematically delayed students had even greater difficulty in these areas than their academically more successful peers (Furman et al., 1989; Montavon, Furman, Barron, Bransford, & Hasselbring, 1989).

We also found that the more structure we provided in our questioning, the better our participants responded. (These findings have also been replicated in the context of our *Jasper* series; see CTGV, 1994.) By the time we reached our third level of questioning, we were essentially presenting participants with simple, well-defined word problems (e.g., If this boat is twice as wide as this boy lying on the deck, and this boy is 6 feet tall, how wide is the boat?). The fact that everyone did much better at level 3 questioning than level 1 (with 1 being the most general level) shows that they had the potential to answer many of the questions but were unable to initially because they had difficulty formulating relevant subproblems. The fact that these results were found even for students who scored very high on tests of mathematics achievement suggested that the process of problem formulation was a part of mathematical thinking that was worth targeting in our instruction.

Collaboration With Classroom Teachers

As we began to develop instructional procedures for using *The River Adventure* to teach problem formulation as well as problem solving, we had the opportunity to work with a number of experienced mathematics educators and mathematics teachers in the context of a research project undertaken by members of our Technology Center: Elizabeth Goldman, Linda Barron, and Bob Sherwood. They received a National Science Foundation grant in mathematics-teacher preparation that brought them in contact with experienced middle school mathematics teachers in our area. The teachers proved to be extremely helpful to our work. For example, when we discussed problems in the curriculum that they wanted to improve, a major concern centered around word problems. The teachers were enthusiastic about the possibility of videodisc-based problem settings like our *River Adventure*. However, they were not at all enthusiastic about the production values of our prototype. They helped us see that, as researchers, we could get by with such a prototype because we created a special event that got children out of their scheduled classes. When something was introduced as regular instruction, however, the teachers wanted it to be interesting to the students. Our prototype was too boring. Because our primary goal was to develop partnerships with classroom teachers, their views of our prototype were taken very seriously. Our collaboration with them eventually led to the development of *The Adventures of Jasper Woodbury* problem-solving series.

THE DEVELOPMENT OF *JASPER*

The first *Jasper* adventure, *Journey to Cedar Creek*, is modeled after the original *River Adventure*. It features an old cruiser that has no running lights and a temporary gas tank; Jasper wants to buy it to fix it up. After he travels up river to buy it, students have to decide if the old cruiser can make it home before sunset and whether Jasper has enough fuel for the trip and enough cash to purchase fuel.

The second *Jasper* adventure, *Rescue at Boone's Meadow*, was designed to re-introduce the distance-rate-time considerations from the first *Jasper* adventure plus add a new twist: Namely, that there are many more possible solution paths. *RBM* features a wounded eagle and an ultralight airplane that can be used to rescue it. Students are asked to find the fastest way to rescue the eagle and state how long it would take. They also have to consider issues of fuel and its effects on the payload limits of the ultralight.

The first two *Jasper* adventures allowed us to replicate many of the effects found with *Raiders* and *The River Adventure*. For example, we found that even the highest achieving sixth graders (on standardized tests of math achievement) had a very difficult time formulating subproblems that they needed to solve in order to solve the adventures. When these subproblems were explicitly defined for them, they were much better able to solve the problems they faced (e.g., CTGV, 1993b).

We also found that instruction in the context of *Jasper* had powerful effects on students' abilities to formulate and solve subsequent complex problems. In contrast, students whose instruction consisted of the one- and two-step word problems that comprised the overall *Jasper* problem showed very poor abilities to transfer to new complex problems (e.g., CTGV, 1993a, 1993b, 1994; Van Haneghan et al., 1992). These findings are discussed in more detail in Chapter 4.

As our work progressed, we began to realize that our design strategy had been to begin with authentic adventures (either ones such as *Raiders* that were already available or ones we were able to film) and add the mathematics later. We developed a new strategy of beginning with mathematics concepts and deriving our adventures from them. The NCTM standards (1989) were invaluable for thinking about the types of mathematical concepts that seemed particularly important for middle school students. We eventually decided to focus on the areas of introductory statistics, geometry, and algebra (including pre-algebra). These ideas are discussed further in Bransford, Zech, Schwartz, Barron, Vye, and the CTGV (1996).

SUMMARY

The *Jasper* Series arose from several different projects being conducted within our Center: the Inert Knowledge Project, the Logo Project, and the Dynamic Assessment Project. These three projects eventually gave rise to the concept of anchored instruction, which was first applied to learning in the areas of literacy and science. We then moved to the area of mathematics.

Initial work in the area of mathematics helped us understand the impoverished view of mathematical thinking held by many middle school students. In an attempt to help them understand problem domains where mathematical thinking is useful, we worked with videodisc-based programs such as *Raiders of the Lost Ark*. Initial work in this context was very encouraging, but we soon found the need to expand the range of problem types that we presented to students. Therefore, we created our own prototype, *The River Adventure*.

Work with *The River Adventure* was also highly encouraging. However, teachers helped us see that our prototype was too boring for normal classroom use; we needed adventures that were more interesting and exciting. Our goal was to collaborate with teachers on research, so we listened carefully to their concerns. The opportunity to collaborate with them eventually led to *The Adventures of Jasper Woodbury*.

The first two *Jasper* adventures were modeled after *The River Adventure*. Subsequent *Jasper* adventures were designed by beginning with a specification of big ideas in mathematics and then developing the adventures. The NCTM (1989) guidelines were extremely helpful for developing the adventures. In addition to the trip-planning *Jaspers*, we eventually focused on the areas of introductory statistics, geometry, and algebra.

3

Jasper From the Perspective of Curriculum Design

In this chapter, we discuss the *Jasper* series from the perspective of philosophies of curriculum design. *Jasper* is designed to encourage sustained thinking about authentic problems. Its close cousins are case-based learning (e.g., Gragg, 1940; Hallinger, Leithwood, & Murphy, 1993); problem-based learning (e.g., Barrows, 1985; Duffy, Lowyck, & Jonassen, 1993); and project-based learning (e.g., Collins, Hawkins, & Carver, 1991; Dewey, 1933). These approaches to curriculum design are different from many others; for example, the design of general thinking skills curricula and the design of typical textbooks with applications problems at the end of each chapter. We discuss each of these next.

TEACHING GENERAL THINKING SKILLS

The design of curricula for teaching general thinking and problem-solving skills has a long history (e.g., see Mann, 1979). Examples include Feuerstein, Rand, Hoffman, and Miller's *Instrumental Enrichment* (1980); Whimbey and Lochhead's *Problem Solving and Comprehension* (1985); Sternberg's *Intelligence Applied* (1986) and a host of books on learning skills and problem solving (e.g., Adams, 1979; Bransford & Stein, 1993; Brown & Walter, 1990; Hayes, 1990). Thinking-skills programs can be very valuable for students (e.g., Segal, Chipman, & Glaser, 1985). Our point is simply that their design is different from the *Jasper* design.

Thinking-skills programs tend to emphasize general strategies that cut across content areas; for example, strategies for remembering such as the use of acronyms and acrostics; general strategies for solving problems such as breaking problems into parts, beginning with simple cases, working backwards; strategies for increasing creativity such as brainstorming, fractionation, attempting to abstractly define one's goals from at least two different perspectives, and so forth (e.g., Bransford & Stein, 1993).

The types of problems presented to students in thinking skills courses usually minimize the need to acquire new content knowledge. For example, in Whimbey and Lochhead (1985), students think aloud as they practice taking systematic approaches to problems such as:

If today is Monday, what day was 2 days before yesterday?

The concepts in this problem are familiar to most people; they involve only an understanding of the days of the week and how they are ordered. This is very different from having to tackle problems that require knowledge of concepts such as exponents, logarithms, or density.

The Importance of Content Knowledge

Sherwood, Kinzer, Bransford, et al. (1987) discussed a problem that illustrates the crucial role of content knowledge in everyday problem solving. Their problem was posed in the context of the movie *Raiders of the Lost Ark*. In the movie, Indiana Jones attempts to remove a golden idol from a cave. The idol is booby trapped; Indiana Jones attempts to compensate for its weight by replacing it with a small bag of sand. If we assume that the idol is solid gold and that its volume is approximately 2,000 cubic centimeters (approximately the size of one half-gallon of milk), how might we get a relatively precise estimate of its weight without using any gold objects or a scale?

Sherwood and colleagues noted that this problem requires considerable knowledge of the concept of density. For example, tables of densities indicate that the density of solid gold is 19.3 grams per cubic centimeter; it is an extremely dense metal (the density of lead is only 11.2 grams per cubic centimeter). On earth, a solid gold idol with a volume of 2,000 cubic centimeters would weigh approximately 60 pounds. Without knowledge of the concept of density, it is difficult to imagine that the Golden Idol problem could be solved.

A problem-solving column that appeared in the magazine *Dogfancy* (McLennon, 1991) provides an additional illustration of the role of specific knowledge in problem solving. In one issue of the magazine, a dog owner wrote that he installed a dog door for his two dogs. One used it all the time. The younger one (5 years old) used it to go out, but would never use it to come back in. What could the owner do to make the younger dog use the door?

The dog expert began her reply by asking whether the door offers the dog the same angle of entrance from each side. She then stated: "One of my dogs alerted me to this one. When I placed a large flat stone as a step outside the door, he was able to go through in both directions in the same body posture" (p. 68). Note that the pet owner's problem reminded the expert of a similar problem that she herself had encountered and solved. These remindings of similar problems often occur to experts and, hence, make their problem solving relatively routine (e.g., see Schank, 1990).

The expert realized that the angle of the entrance might not be the feature that was responsible for the dog owner's problem. Therefore, she also discussed other possible causes of the problem such as sunlight that might be reflected off the door from the outside and that might keep the dog from entering, or the flap of the door might have hit the younger dog in the face when it was following the older dog from the outside, hence making it wary of the entrance, and so forth.

Overall, the expert's discussion of the possible causes of the problem, plus her suggested solutions, seemed to come from a great deal of specific knowledge that she had accumulated over her career. Because she had considerable experience, it is a good bet that most problems that people ask her to solve are relatively routine to her. Many theorists argue that specific experiences are represented in memory as cases that are indexed and searched so that they can be applied analogically to new problems that occur (see Kolodner, 1991; Riesbeck & Schank, 1989; Schank, 1990). This is very different from the idea that expertise is derived from the top-down application of a general set of problem-solving skills.

Content and Skills in *Jasper*

The *Jasper* series attempts to teach thinking in contexts that are rich in content as well as in the need for general strategies. The assumption is that thinking is enhanced by access to powerful conceptual ideas and not simply through access to a general set of thinking skills (e.g., Bransford, Sherwood, et al., 1986; Bransford & Stein, 1993; Chi, Bassok, Lewis, & Glaser, 1989). *Jasper* borrows from the traditions of the thinking-skills movement because it helps students develop a sense of agency that allows them to identify and define problems and systematically explore possible solutions. However, *Jasper* also introduces students to powerful concepts. Examples include the idea of making predictions about a population by extrapolating from a sample that is representative of that population, creating scale models that allow one to make inferences about the real thing, using invariant mathematical properties of simple shapes such as triangles and squares to measure the earth, and creating mathematical models of situations and designing Smart Tools for solving a wide variety of problems (e.g, Bransford, Zech, Schwartz, Barron, Vye, and the CTGV, 1996). These ideas require a great deal of specific content knowledge; for example, specific knowledge about what makes a sample representative and how to extrapolate from it to the total population, and specific knowledge of the invariant mathematical properties of triangles such as isosceles right triangles and why they are so useful for measurement. Without knowledge of the specifics, students are unable to use these ideas to guide their thinking.

THE DESIGN OF TYPICAL TEXTBOOKS

An emphasis on the importance of content knowledge is hardly new to the educational community. Most instruction is content-based. However, this content is usually presented in a manner that is different from curricula like *Jasper*. In particular, textbooks tend to emphasize the presentation of facts and principles, followed by application problems that appear at the end of each chapter. A classic article by Simon (1980) on problem solving and education helps clarify problems with the approach adopted by typical textbooks. He began with an explanation of the inadequacy of knowledge of mere facts.

Why Facts Are Not Sufficient

Simon (1980) argued that the knowledge representation underlying competent performance in any domain is not based on simple facts or verbal propositions, but is instead based on productions. Productions involve "condition-action pairs that specify that if a certain state occurs..., then particular mental (and possibly physical) actions should take place" (Anderson, 1987, p. 193). Productions thus provide information about the critical features of problem situations that make particular actions relevant. Knowledge-based theorists such as Newell and Simon (1972) and Anderson (1983, 1987) provided important insights into the need to help people conditionalize their knowledge—to acquire knowledge in the form of condition–action pairs mediated by appropriate goal-oriented hierarchies, rather than as isolated facts.

Simon echoed Whitehead (1929) and Gragg (1940) in noting that many forms of instruction do not help students conditionalize their knowledge. For example, he argued that "textbooks are much more explicit in enunciating the laws of mathematics or of nature than in saying anything about when these laws may be useful in solving problems" (p. 92). It is left largely to the student to generate the condition–action pairs required for solving novel problems. Franks, Bransford, Brailey, and Purdon (1991) noted that one of their favorite examples of the lack of explicit emphasis on conditionalizing one's knowledge comes from a textbook on experimental design. On page 195 of the book was a section entitled "Which Test Do I Use?" It stated: "How to choose a statistical test was postponed until now so that various aspects of data analysis could be presented." The text then included a discussion of the uses of various statistics. The entire discussion totaled 13 sentences in length.

The importance of conditionalizing one's knowledge can also be illustrated by considering how an understanding of proverbs contributes to wisdom. Imagine that a person learns a list of proverbs such as:

1. "Too many cooks spoil the broth."
2. "Many hands make light work."
3. "Haste makes waste."
4. "He who hesitates is lost."
5. "Absence makes the heart grow fonder."
6. "Out of sight, out of mind."

The ability to recite proverbs from memory is quite different from knowing when and why each is most applicable. Indeed, when taken out of context, many proverbs seem to contradict one another (e.g., note 1 vs. 2, 3 vs. 4, 5 vs. 6). Wise individuals who benefit from their understanding of proverbs have conditionalized their knowledge. For example, they know the conditions under which "Too many cooks spoil the broth" versus "Many hands make light work." The "too many cooks" proverb usually applies to situations in which it is difficult to break a task into a set of independent components. Cooking a particular dish is a good example; different people's attempts to contribute can interfere with one another. In contrast, if you are working in someone's yard, one person can cut the grass, another can trim the hedges, another can weed and water the flowers. Under conditions where each task can be pursued independently of the other, "Many hands make light work."

At a general level, the idea of conditionalizing one's knowledge is related to the ability to understand why, when, where, and how particular types of knowledge are useful. This understanding allows us to use knowledge as a tool to solve important problems. Our ability to use physical tools requires a similar type of understanding. Consider the knowledge necessary to know when, where, how, and why to use a particular type of scissors. Examples of different types of scissors, and some of their contexts of usage, are provided in Fig. 3.1 (cf., Bransford & McCarrell, 1974). If you

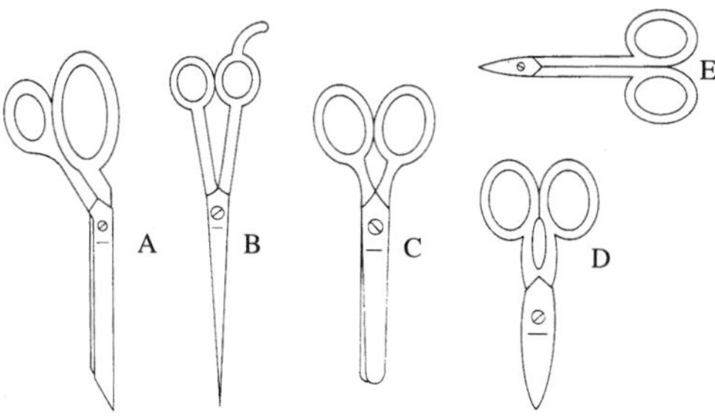

Structure	**Function**
A. Dressmaker shears	
heavy	because of type of use.
one hole larger than other	so that two or three fingers will fit in larger hole—allows greater steadiness as one cuts cloth on flat surface.
blades off-centered and aligned with finger hole edge	so that blade can rest on table surface as cloth is cut—again, greater steadiness.
B. Barber shears	
very sharp	to cut thin material; i.e., hair.
pointed	permits blades to snip close to scalp and to snip very small strands of hair.
hook on finger hole	a rest for one finger which allows scissors to be supported at various angles—hence greater maneuverability.
C. Pocket or children's scissors	
blunt ends	so scissors can be carried in pocket without cutting through cloth; so children can handle without poking themselves or others.
short blades	allows greater control by the gross motor movements of the child just learning to cut.
D. Nail scissors	
wide and thick at pivot point	to withstand pressure from cutting thick and rigid materials; i.e., nails.
slightly curved blades	to cut slightly curved nails.
E. Cuticle scissors	
very sharp blade	to cut semi-elastic materials; i.e., skin of cuticles.
small, curved blades	to allow maneuverability necessary to cut small curved area.
long extension from finger holes to joint	as compensation for short blades necessary for holding.

FIG. 3.1. Examples of different kinds of scissors and their functions.

could recognize different examples of scissors but had no idea about the contexts in which each was used most appropriately, your knowledge would not be conditionalized.

Applications Problems and Their Shortcomings

Simon argued that effective learners are assumed to acquire the conditionalized knowledge necessary for effective problem solving by working through examples and sample problems. In mathematics classes, for example, word problems found at the end of each chapter can help students move from knowing that something is true ($5 + 5 = 10$; $A^2 + B^2 = C^2$) to knowing when, why, and how particular concepts and procedures are applicable. Lesgold (1988) provided an insightful discussion of the role of applications problems in helping students learn to solve problems rather than simply retrieve previously told facts.

It seems clear that didactic instruction about facts, concepts, and skills is enhanced by the use of applications problems. Nevertheless, there are also shortcomings of traditional word problems and their uses. We discussed several limitations in CTGV (1992a).

First, traditional applications problems often fail to help students think about realistic situations. Instead of bringing real-world standards to their work, students seem to treat word problems mechanically and often fail to think about constraints imposed by real-world experiences. See Chapter 2 for elaboration of this point.

A second problem with applications problems is that most of them assume only a single correct answer. This leads to misconceptions about the nature of problem solving and it inadvertently teaches students for a single answer rather than seek multiple answers. In addition, because typical word problems are difficult for many students to understand (due to reading problems) and often seem arbitrary, it becomes especially difficult to present students with problems that reflect the levels of complexity characteristic of many real-world problems (CTGV, 1990). This limitation of the word-problem format becomes increasingly noteworthy in the context of recommendations from many researchers (Baron, 1987; Frederiksen & Collins, 1989; Resnick & Resnick, 1991) that instruction and assessment must focus on students' abilities to perform holistic, authentic tasks rather than on their ability to demonstrate that they have acquired the piecemeal skills and facts that make up complex performances. For example, the ability to solve sets of simple (i.e., one- and two-step) well-defined problems is not equivalent to students' ability to solve realistic, complex problems that are ultimately decomposable into the same set of simple problems (CTGV, 1993a; Van Haneghan et al., 1992).

A third limitation of traditional applications problems involves the habits of mind that they develop. Generally, applications problems can be solved by thinking back to the information in the chapter or chapters that one has been studying. This means that the goal of one's search is to retrieve previously presented information rather than rely on one's own intuitions. This may limit the development of people's abilities to think for themselves.

A fourth limitation of traditional applications problems is also important: They explicitly define the problems to be solved rather than help students learn to generate and pose their own problems. Mathematical thinkers tend to generate their own problems. Examples of the importance of the generative skills of finding and defining problems are discussed in Chapter 2.

Overall, traditional uses of textbooks frequently lead to a problem that was discussed in Chapter 2: the inert knowledge problem. Whitehead (1929) defined *inert knowledge* as knowledge that is accessed only in a restricted set of contexts even though it is applicable to a wide variety of domains. In Simon's (1980) terminology, information presented in typical text-based curricula is often stored as facts that are not conditionalized. Without information about why, when and how to use our knowledge (about its conditions of applicability), it does us little good.

Experiences With Inert Knowledge

Many people who have taught using traditional curricula have experienced the inert knowledge problem. One of our favorite examples involves a story relayed by Ann Michael (cf., Bransford, 1993). For several years, she served as a clinical supervisor for college students who were beginning a practicum where they learned to provide language therapy for children who were language-delayed. The students with whom Michael worked had all taken the required college course on theories of language and their implications for therapy. This was designed to prepare them to do language therapy. Nevertheless, when Michael worked with the students in the clinical therapy sessions, there was almost no carryover from this course. Michael concluded that the college course must have been very poorly taught.

Soon thereafter, Michael was asked to teach the college course on theories of language and their implications. She did what she considered to be a highly competent job and was pleased with the general performance of the students on her tests. A year later, she reencountered a number of her college students in the clinical practicum on language therapy. Much to her surprise and dismay, these students also showed almost no evidence of using anything they had learned in their language course. Many could remember facts when explicitly asked about them, but they did not spontaneously use the knowledge to help them solve problems in the clinic.

Michael noted that, this time, she was less willing simply to conclude that her college students performed poorly because they had a poor instructor. She knew how hard she had tried to prepare the students, and she knew that they did well on her tests. The experience motivated her to explore problems with traditional approaches to instruction and to design a series of studies to attempt to overcome these problems. Her studies (Michael, Klee, Bransford, & Warren, 1993) illustrate some of the advantages of problem-based curricula. We discuss these advantages later. For present purposes, it is sufficient to note that Michael's experiences fit well with Whitehead's (1929) observations that much of the information acquired in school tends to remain inert.

Many others have had experiences similar to Michael. For example, several members of our group have had the opportunity to talk with Howard Barrows of the

Southern Illinois University School of Medicine. He pioneered problem-based learning for medical students; we wanted to know what motivated him to advocate such a radical change in instruction. He described experiences with medical students, who took his clinical course in medicine, that were strikingly similar to the experiences described by Michael. In clinical settings, where students needed to access knowledge that was relevant to the problems presented by clients (rather than merely recall facts about biology or neurology), the students acted as if they had not had the background preparation. In Whitehead's terminology, what they had learned remained inert.

An article published in 1940 by Gragg provides additional information about problems with traditional approaches to curriculum design. He taught in the Harvard Business School and found that employers of Harvard business graduates complained that the students were not prepared for action. Their knowledge was not in a form that enabled them to identify and define important problems and make reasoned decisions. Gragg argued that wisdom can't be told, and advocated new approaches to instruction that introduced students to important concepts and strategies in the context of working through real cases of business problems. Case-based approaches to business instruction are still used in the Harvard Business School, and are commonly used in many other American professional schools today (see later in this chapter).

We noted in Chapter 2 that a number of investigators have begun to conduct controlled, experimental studies of the inert knowledge problem. For example, studies conducted by Asch (1969), Gick and Holyoak (1980), Hayes and Simon (1977), Perfetto et al. (1983), Reed, Ernst, and Banerji (1974), and Weisberg, DiCamillo, and Phillips (1978) provided evidence that relevant knowledge often remains inert even though it is potentially useful. Researchers have also shown that opportunities to learn in the context of actually solving problems makes knowledge less inert (e.g., Adams et al., 1988; Gick & Holyoak, 1983; Lockhart, Lamon, & Gick, 1988; Novick, 1988).

Concerns About Habits of Mind

In addition to concerns about inert knowledge are concerns that traditional approaches to instruction also tend to deprive students of opportunities to develop the habits of mind necessary for effective lifelong learning. For example, students often develop misconceptions about the kind of thinking necessary to solve real-life problems, and their own abilities to think.

Schoenfeld (1989) noted that many college students who enter his mathematics course at the University of California, Berkeley seem to have serious misconceptions about the nature of everyday problem solving. Many assume that if they cannot solve a problem in 5 minutes, it is basically unsolvable by them. They appear to have little idea that many everyday problems are solved only because of sustained effort that may take place over the course of days, weeks, and often months. Students need opportunities for sustained thinking about complex problems in order to experience the fact that positive changes in their thinking (the appearance of mini-insights into the problem) do, in fact, occur over time. A major goal of Schoenfeld's approach to teaching is to help students discover their own abilities to solve mathematics problems on their own.

Duffy (1992) noted that many teachers do not believe in their abilities to think and invent when it comes to instruction. Many cannot imagine that they can have better ideas about instruction than the experts who write the curriculum guides. As a result, they tend to rely on what Duffy called the absentee prescriptions of master curriculum developers, and often miss opportunities to adapt instruction to fit their students' particular needs and goals. Most likely, the teachers Duffy worked with had taken courses in which they were told about good instruction rather than being helped to invent, evaluate, and modify their own approaches to instruction. Exclusive reliance on fact-based approaches to instruction has the potential to undermine students' beliefs in their abilities to identify and define problems and invent solutions on their own.

CURRICULA ORGANIZED AROUND AUTHENTIC PROBLEMS

In recent years, a number of investigators have begun to revisit some age-old approaches to curriculum and instruction—approaches that provide opportunities for students to acquire relevant content knowledge while attempting to understand and solve authentic problems that arise within particular disciplines. By acquiring knowledge in the context of solving authentic problems, students are more likely to understand how, why, and when it is useful (e.g., Brown, Bransford, Ferrara, & Campione, 1983; Brown, Collins, & Duguid, 1989). As a consequence, it is less likely to remain inert.

Cases, Problems, and Projects

A number of professional schools, such as law schools, medical schools, business schools, and schools of educational administration, are using case-based and problem-based instruction. Williams (1992) provided an excellent review and analysis of case-based and problem-based learning in law schools and medical schools. Bridges and Hallinger (1995) discussed case-based and problem-based learning in schools of professional practice such as educational administration.

There are a number of differences between case-based and problem-based approaches to curriculum and instruction that we do not have time to consider (see Bridges & Hallinger, 1995; Williams, 1992). Nevertheless, we will describe a few examples. Law schools often used case-based instruction (Williams, 1992). Their cases typically consist of an actual problem and the proposed solution to it; for example, the solution proposed by a court of appeals, the supreme court, and so forth. Students discuss the case and relate the proposed solutions to general principles of law (e.g., to the constitution).

Medical schools often use problem-based instruction (Hmelo, 1994; Williams, 1992). This often takes the form of simulated patients (simulated either on paper, by an actor, or by a computer) who provide information about some symptoms. After that, it is up to the students to know what questions to ask of the simulated patients and decide where to go from there. Students also have to define their own learning goals that guide the acquisition of any new content they might need in order to better understand the patient's problems.

Another way to organize instruction around problem solving is to create student projects (e.g., Dewey, 1933). An excellent example is the Discover Rochester project discussed by Collins et al. (1991). In this project, eighth-grade students who were at risk of dropping out of school spent one day each week exploring aspects of their hometown—Rochester, New York—from a scientific, mathematical, historical, cultural, and literary perspective. Working in groups, the students conducted their own research on topics such as industry, weather, theater, and employment. On the basis of their research, they developed multimedia exhibits for the Rochester Museum and Science Center. The exhibits included text, audio, graphics, maps, and music. Students also studied the reactions of people to their projects and refined them based on the feedback they received.

Authentic Problems and Informal Learning

Many people argue that curricula organized around authentic problems create experiences that are more similar to the kinds of informal learning that take place in daily life (e.g., Bransford & Heldmeyer, 1983; Brown, Collins, & Duguid, 1989). This becomes especially significant in the context of observations that students who perform poorly in school often seem to learn well in informal learning environments (e.g., Holt, 1964).

Our colleague, Otto Bassler, sent us an article written in 1944 by Corey that provides an informative contrast between learning in formal settings and learning in the context of meaningful problems. Entitled "Poor Scholar's Soliloquy," the article is written from the perspective of an imaginary student (we call him Bob) who is not very good in school and has had to repeat the seventh grade. Many would write Bob off as having a low aptitude for learning. But when you look at what Bob is capable of achieving outside of school, you get a very different impression of his abilities.

Part of the soliloquy describes how teachers do not like Bob because he does not read the kind of books that they value. Bob's favorite books include *Popular Science,* the *Mechanical Encyclopedia,* and the Sears and Wards catalogues. Bob uses his books to pursue meaningful goals. He says, "I don't just sit down and read them through like they make us do in school. I use my books when I want to find something out, like whenever Mom buys anything second hand I look it up in Sears' or Wards' first and tell her if she's getting stung or not" (Corey, 1994).

Later on, Bob explains the trouble he had memorizing the names of the presidents. He knew some of them, like Washington and Jefferson, but there were 30 altogether and he never did get them all straight. He seems to have a poor memory. Then he talks about the three trucks his uncle owns and how he knows the horsepower and number of forward and backward gears of 26 different American trucks, many of them diesels. Then he says, "It's funny how that diesel works. I started to tell my teacher about it last Wednesday in science class when the pump we were using to make a vacuum in a bell jar got hot, but she said she didn't see what a diesel engine had to do with our experiment on air pressure so I just kept still. The kids seemed interested, though" (Corey, 1944).

Bob also discusses his inability to do the kinds of word problems found in his textbooks. Yet he helps his uncle make all kinds of complex plans when they travel together. He talks about the bills and letters he sends to the farmers whose livestock his uncle hauls and about how he made only three mistakes in his last 17 letters—all of them commas. Then he says, "I wish I could write school themes that way. The last one I had to write was on 'What a Daffodil Thinks of Spring,' and I just couldn't get going" (Corey, 1944).

Bob ends his soliloquy by noting that, according to his dad, he can quit school at the age of 15, and he feels like he should. After all, he is not getting any younger and he has a lot to learn.

Bob's soliloquy is as relevant to the 1990s as it was to the 1940s. First, it provides a useful contrast between typical instructional practice and learning that occurs in the context of meaningful problem solving. Second, it highlights the fact that many students seem to learn effectively in the context of authentic, real-life activities, yet have great difficulty with the decontextualized type of instruction common in most schools.

Of course, not everyone is lucky enough to have an uncle like Bob's who, in effect, gives him an apprenticeship in everyday problem solving. Throughout the years, a number of educators have explored ways to recreate some of the advantages of informal learning by changing typical instructional practice. These explorations have often resulted in the development of problem-first curricula such as *The Adventures of Jasper Woodbury* series.

DESIGN PRINCIPLES FOR THE *JASPER* SERIES

The *Jasper* series represents an example of problem-based learning that has been modified to make it more usable in K–12 settings. These modifications include the use of a story format to present problems, plus the use of embedded data and embedded teaching to seed the environment with ideas relevant to problem solving. *Jasper* is also designed to set the stage for subsequent project-based learning. Its overall goal is to help students transform mere facts into powerful conceptual tools. In Chapter 2, we discussed *The Right Angle* as an example of transforming facts into tools.

Seven Initial Design Principles for *Jasper*

In previous publications, we have discussed seven design principles that characterize each adventure in the *Jasper* series (see Table 3.1). These design principles mutually influence one another and operate as a Gestalt rather than as a set of independent features of the materials. For example, the narrative format (principle

TABLE 3.1
Seven Design Principles Underlying The *Jasper* Adventure Series

Design Principle	*Hypothesized Benefits*
1. Video-based format	A. More motivating. B. Easier to search. C. Supports complex comprehension. D. Especially helpful for poor readers yet it can also support reading.
2. Narrative with realistic problems (rather than a lecture on video)	A. Easier to remember. B. More engaging. C. Primes students to notice the relevance of mathematics and reasoning for everyday events.
3. Generative format (i.e., the stories end and students must generate the problems to be solved)	A. Motivating to determine the ending. B. Teaches students to find and define problems to be solved. C. Provides enhanced opportunities for reasoning.
4. Embedded data design (i.e., all the data needed to solve the problems are in the video)	A. Permits reasoned decision making. B. Motivating to find. C. Puts students on an "even keel" with respect to relevant knowledge. D. Clarifies how relevance of data depends on specific goals.
5. Problem complexity (i.e., each adventure involves a problem of at least 14 steps)	A. Overcomes the tendency to try for a few minutes and then give up. B. Introduces levels of complexity characteristic of real problems. C. Helps students deal with complexity. D. Develops confidence in abilities.
6. Pairs of related adventures	A. Provides extra practice on core schema. B. Helps clarify what can be transferred and what cannot. C. Illustrates analogical thinking.
7. Links across the curriculum	A. Helps extend mathematical thinking to other areas (e.g., history, science). B. Encourages the integration of knowledge. C. Supports information finding and publishing.

2), the generative design of the stories (principle 3), and the fact that the adventures include embedded data (principle 4) makes it possible for students to learn to generate subgoals, find relevant information, and engage in reasoned decision making. The complexity of the problems (principle 5) helps students deal with this important aspect of problem solving and the use of video (principle 1) helps make the complexity manageable. The video format also makes it easier to embed the kinds of information that provide opportunities for links across the curricula (principle 7). The video is also important because it makes complex mathematics problem solving accessible to students having difficulties with reading. The triplets of related adventures (principle 6) afford discussions about transfer. These design principles are described in more detail elsewhere (CTGV, 1991). Similar sets of design principles are applicable in many curricular domains, including science and literacy (CTGV, 1990; McLarty et al., 1990).

Scaffolds for Learning

The seven initial design principles were developed in order to adapt case-based and problem-based learning to K–12 classrooms. In settings such as business school, medical school, and law school, learners have considerable skill and knowledge that they can draw on. In K–12, students need scaffolds in order to succeed (e.g., Vygotsky, 1978, 1986).

Aspects of each *Jasper* adventure that help scaffold learning and transfer include the visual format, presenting information in the form of a story, presenting embedded data that support reasoned decision making, and presenting role models that motivate students. Scaffolds for transfer include the video-based analog and extension problems that accompany each adventure, plus the encouragement to have teachers extend the *Jasper* experience by working with thematically related projects that involve their community.

After we developed and tested the first several *Jasper* adventures, we began to include embedded teaching scenes within the adventures in order to provide students with models of how to approach particular types of problems. In addition, we included teaching tools that teachers could use to help students grasp concepts that were particularly difficult to teach.

In general, the evolution of the *Jasper* project has involved an increasing realization of the value of providing scaffolds that place complex problem solving within all students' reach.

SUMMARY

Jasper represents an example of curriculum design that is closely related to case-based, problem-based, and project-based learning. The goal of each of these approaches to curriculum design is to teach content and skills in the context of attempts to solve authentic problems. These approaches are different from others, such as curricula for teaching general thinking skills and curricula that first present facts and principles and then present applications problems for students to solve.

General thinking-skills curricula typically attempt to minimize the need to acquire new content knowledge and, instead, concentrate on general strategies that are presumed to apply across a wide variety of content areas. Programs such as these can be very useful for students. Nevertheless, the *Jasper* series attempts to help students acquire not only skills, but also powerful conceptual ideas.

Typical text-based curricula involve the presentation of facts and principles followed by applications problems that usually appear at the end of each chapter. In Simon's (1980) terminology, applications problems are designed to help students conditionalize their knowledge so that it will be accessed when needed. Nevertheless, typical uses of applications problems frequently result in knowledge that remains inert.

A number of professional schools in law, business, medicine, and educational leadership are using varieties of case-based, problem-based, and project-based instruction (e.g., Barrows, 1985; Bridges & Hallinger, 1995; Hmelo, 1994; Williams, 1992). These curricula were specifically designed to help students acquire knowledge that prepared them for action rather than remained inert.

We view *Jasper* as an example of problem-based learning that has been adapted to fit the K–12 curriculum. *Jasper* problems include a number of scaffolds that are designed to seed the environment with ideas, and models that can help students learn to solve the *Jasper* challenges and deepen their understanding as they extend their thinking to *Jasper* analogs and extensions, plus projects that are relevant to the local community.

4

Initial Work on Instruction and Assessment

Our goal in this chapter is to explore issues of instruction in the context of *Jasper* and discuss our initial attempts to assess the effects of instruction on learning and transfer. As noted earlier, when we first developed *Jasper* we hoped that it would help transform the nature of teaching and learning that took place in classrooms. Instead of a major emphasis on the transmission of knowledge from teachers to students, our vision was one of students and teachers collaboratively exploring the *Jasper* environments, generating questions about important issues to be explored, searching for data that were relevant to these issues, and engaging in conversations as different groups of students communicated their thinking to one another.

The *Jasper* adventures were especially designed with an eye toward cooperative learning. When working in cooperative groups, students have opportunities to discuss, explain, and compare their ideas to those of their peers (e.g., NCTM, 1989; Palincsar & Brown, 1984, 1989; Vygotsky, 1978). Groups of students can also monitor one another and, in the process, help keep each individual from getting too far off track. Of course, groups of students sometimes fail to work together in a cooperative manner (e.g., Cosden, Goldman, & Hine, 1990; Goldman, Cosden, & Hine, 1992; Hine, Goldman, & Cosden, 1990; Salomon & Globerson, 1989). One of our hopes was that the availability of shared problem-solving environments such as *Jasper* would enhance the probability that group work would be a success.

Overall, the types of activities that we wanted our materials to support were consistent with recommendations suggested by the NCTM Commission on Standards for School Mathematics (1989). The NCTM's suggestions for changes in classroom activities include more emphasis on complex, open-ended problem solving, communication, and reasoning; more connections from mathematics to other subjects and to the world outside the classroom; more uses of calculators and powerful computer-based tools such as spreadsheets and graphing programs for exploring relationships (as opposed to having students spend an inordinate amount of time calculating by hand). In proposing a more generative approach to mathematics learning, the NCTM stated: "... (t)he mathematics curriculum should engage students in some problems that demand extended effort to solve. Some might be group projects that require students to use available technology and to engage in cooperative problem solving and discussion. For grades 5–8 an important criterion of problems is that they be interesting to students (p. 75)."

In this chapter, we discuss our initial efforts to understand and study how *Jasper* was used in classrooms and how its use affected learning and transfer. We discuss several types of studies:

1. A series of well-controlled baseline and intervention studies that explored the effects on transfer of *Jasper* instruction compared to more traditional instruction that focused on the same content.
2. A series of observational studies that helped us see the wide range of instructional strategies that could be used with *Jasper*.
3. A study involving *Jasper* sites in nine different states that allowed us to assess the effects of *Jasper* on problem solving and attitudes toward complex challenges and mathematics.
4. Studies designed to find ways to increase even further both the depth of students' understanding and the flexibility of their abilities to transfer. Each of these areas is discussed further.

BASELINE AND INTERVENTION STUDIES

In several articles (CTGV, 1993a 1993b; Van Haneghan et al., 1992), we discussed experiments that were designed to explore issues of instruction that compared *Jasper* with more traditional approaches. Several of our experiments involved baseline studies where, prior to any instruction in *Jasper*, sixth-grade students who scored in the eighth and ninth stanine on standardized tests of mathematics achievement were asked to solve *Jasper* problems. The students had a very difficult time.

We expected even the high-achieving students to have difficulty because traditional instruction tends not to prepare students for complex problem solving. We also found that the more we helped students define the subproblems necessary to solve the *Jasper* problems, the better they performed. Figure 4.1 shows the performance of college students and sixth graders at Levels 1, 2, and 3 of prompting, where Level 3 prompts provided the most structure by breaking the overall *Jasper* problem into simpler one- and two-step word problems. Students perform much better at Level 3 than at Levels 2 and 1. These data show that students had the mathematical knowledge necessary to solve the *Jasper* problems, but had difficulty identifying and defining subproblems on their own.

The experiments just described were baseline studies that did not involve instruction in *Jasper*. A number of our experiments were designed to assess how different approaches to instruction affected transfer. In particular, we asked whether the ability to transfer to new, complex problems, would be influenced by instruction that focused on complex problems such as those in *Jasper*, versus instruction that involved the same concepts as *Jasper* (e.g., distance, rate, and time) yet were organized around typical one- and two- step word problems found in most mathematics curricula.

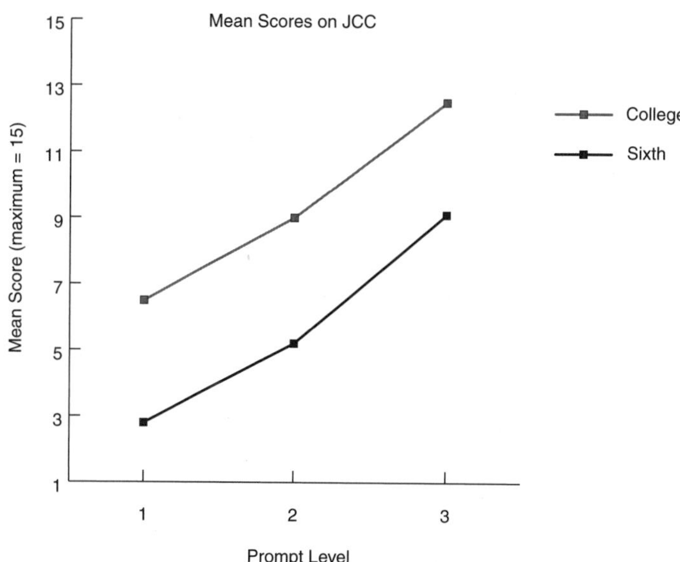

FIG. 4.1. Data on baseline problem solving at three levels of prompts.

Our expectations were consistent with the principle of transfer-appropriate processing (e.g., Bransford, Franks, Morris, & Stein, 1979) and led us to predict that the best way to learn to deal with complexity is, in fact, to deal with complexity. Due to the visual format of the *Jasper* problems, we also assumed that the complexity would be manageable by students in the fifth and sixth grades. And we hoped that students who worked in the context of *Jasper* would also be able to solve word problems on distance-rate-time even though they had not practiced on these.

Transfer Study I

In our first study of instruction and transfer, participants were fifth graders from a high-achieving mathematics class. They were assigned to *Jasper* instruction or Word Problem instruction groups. Before and after their respective instruction (instruction took place in four, 1-hour sessions), groups were given several tests to assess learning and transfer. One test was designed to tap students' mastery of the solution to *Journey to Cedar Creek* (*JCC*). Not surprisingly, students in the *Jasper* group scored much better on the mastery test. Students in the Word Problem group had seen the adventure, but they had not solved it. Instead, they solved one-and two-step word problems that involved the same concepts as the overall adventure.

We were most interested in the effects of *Jasper* versus Word Problem instruction on transfer to new, complex problems. The transfer problem we used was video-based and its solution was isomorphic to the JCC challenge. It told the story of a character named Nancy who buys a houseboat and must then decide if she can get the boat home before sunset without running out of fuel. The boat has the same problems as Jasper's cruiser in JCC—it has a small temporary fuel tank and its running lights do not work. The solution has the same structure as JCC although the data were different; it involves consideration of the same subproblems and has the same outcomes.

Students watched the transfer video and then solved the problem while talking aloud. The initial question was general and asked students to decide if Nancy could make it home (i.e., Level 1). Subsequent Level 2 questions prompted students to consider three of the subgoals (time home, fuel home, and money).

The analyses of the total scores indicated that *Jasper* students achieved much higher transfer scores than the Word Problem students. Overall, the performance after instruction of the fifth graders in the *Jasper* group was as good as college students in a *JCC* baseline study who had not received instruction in *Jasper*. Details can be found in CTGV (1993a); Goldman, Vye, et al. (1991); and Van Haneghan et al. (1992).

It is also important to note that we gave all our students posttests on one- and two-step word problems similar to those practiced by the Word Problem group—word problems that involved the same basic distance-rate-time concepts as the *Jasper* problem. Both groups did very well on these problems; however, a number of the students in both groups were at ceiling on the test, making it difficult to draw firm conclusions about how much the groups had learned.

Transfer Study II

We used the preceding instructional design (i.e., *Jasper* instruction vs. word problem instruction) in a second study that involved a different test of transfer. This time the transfer problem was the *Jasper* video, *Rescue at Boone's Meadow*. In contrast to the Nancy transfer problem, *RBM* does not share specific mathematical procedures or the same goal organization as *JCC*, but *RBM* and *JCC* do share elements of a general trip-planning schema. For example, several elements from *JCC*, specifically time and fuel considerations, are relevant to the *RBM*. We predicted positive transfer on those elements of the problem that overlap from the first planning adventure (*JCC*) to the second one (*RBM*). Other aspects of *RBM* are quite different from *JCC*. In particular, *RBM* includes issues of optimizing travel time by considering multiple possible routes, pilots, vehicles, and other factors. These issues of optimization are not present in the *JCC* adventure. For this aspect of problem solving, we did not expect to see positive transfer from *JCC* to *RBM*.

As in Transfer Study I, high-achieving fifth graders were randomly assigned to either a *Jasper* or a Word Problem instruction group. The lesson plans used in Transfer Study I were used for each group, respectively. Again, prior to and following instruction, students were administered a series of tests designed to test mastery of *JCC* and transfer.

The *RBM* transfer test was used in a think-aloud interview format. We analyzed the interviews by looking for elements associated with finding and testing feasible routes (i.e., range, payload, landing, and time), and elements associated with optimization of routes (i.e., were multiple routes, vehicles proposed, and were time estimates compared). When we computed a total score for each student, we found that *Jasper* students scored significantly higher than Word Problem students, indicating that *Jasper* students explored more of the *RBM* solution space than Word Problem students.

We examined this effect further by looking at the percentages of students who mentioned, attempted, and solved the feasibility constraints. These data are presented in Fig. 4.2. We expected that *Jasper* students would show positive transfer from *JCC* to *RBM* on the time and range subproblems. The range subproblem shows evidence of this effect in terms of the number of students attempting and solving; the time problem does not, although the only student to successfully solve the time problem was in the *Jasper*-instructed condition. In addition to these specific transfer effects, data also indicated that a greater number of *Jasper*-instructed students mentioned, attempted, and solved the payload problem. Because issues of payload were unique to *RBM*, these data suggest that *Jasper*-instructed students may have learned a general heuristic from *JCC*, that is, generate possible constraints on plans and test against them.

We also looked at the extent to which students attempted to optimize their solution. As noted earlier, we did not expect to see group differences in this aspect of problem solving because *JCC* instruction does not focus on generating and evaluating multiple plans for purposes of optimization. The results confirmed this expectation: 33% of the *Jasper* students and 41% of the Word Problem students generated only one plan for rescuing the eagle. Furthermore, although most students in both groups tried to determine how much time their plan or plans would take, in both groups, less than half of the students who generated more than one plan compared the time estimates associated with their plans to decide which was fastest (CTGV, 1993a).

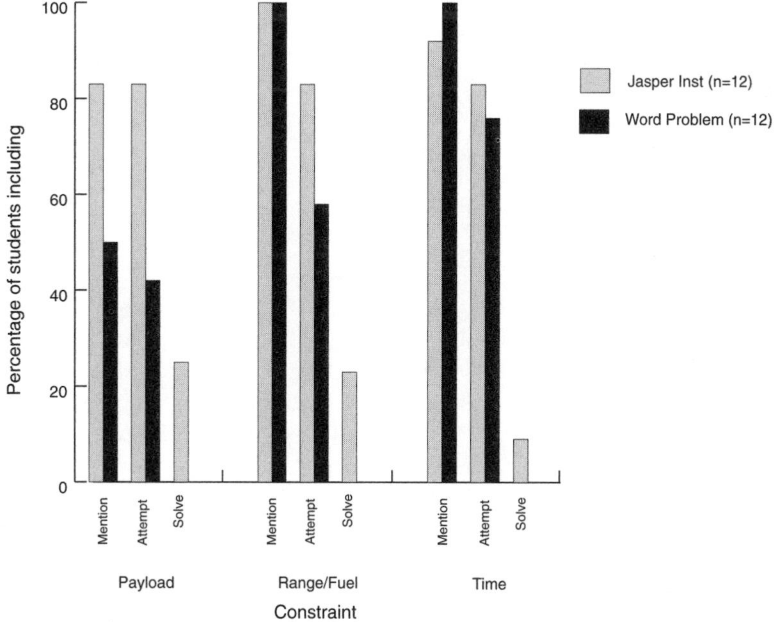

FIG. 4.2. Transfer data from *JCC* to *RBM*.

Transfer Study III

In a third study, we assessed the effects of solving *Rescue at Boone's Meadow* on students' abilities to solve similar types of rescue problems (Goldman, Williams, Vye, Bransford, & Pellegrino, 1993). Students in the experimental group solved *RBM* and then saw the optimal solution and compared it to their solutions. Students in the comparison group watched *RBM* and then saw the optimal solution. Experimental and comparison groups included students who were either skilled in mathematics as indicated by achievement tests or less skilled.

Both groups received two types of near-transfer problems. The first one caused them to have to consider an alternative route: "Suppose the ultralight cannot land at Hilda's because it is flooded. But there is another gas station at Mason's (see Fig. 4.3). What's the quickest way to rescue the eagle without going to Hilda's and how long will that take?"

In solving the Mason analog, the experimental group that had previously solved *RBM* was more likely than the comparison group to generate complete and feasible routes. This was true for both skilled and less-skilled mathematics students. Data are shown in the upper panel of Table of 4.1.

A second problem on route planning involved changing the speed of the ultralight from 30 to 20 miles per hour. The optimal plan with this change actually remains the same as the original. *Jasper*-instructed students were more likely than

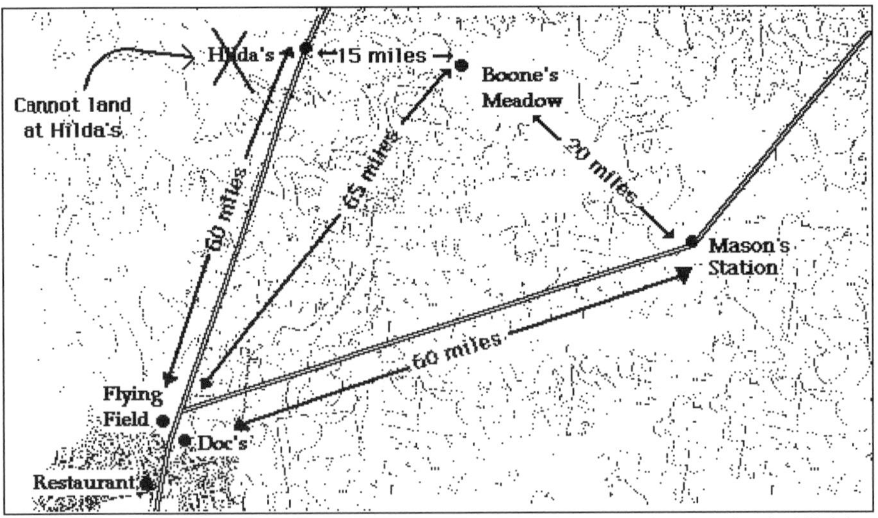

FIG. 4.3. Mason's problem.

TABLE 4.1
Data for Transfer Study II

Percentage of Students Providing Complete and Feasible Routes: Mason Problem		
	Jasper Instructed	*Comparison*
Skilled	*75%*	*50%*
	(n = 12)	*(n = 12)*
Less skilled	*64%*	*29%*
	(n = 11)	*(n = 14)*
Complete and Feasible Routes: Problem 2.		
	Jasper Instructed	*Comparison*
Skilled	*83%*	*58%*
	(n = 12)	*(n = 12)*
Less skilled	*45%*	*7%*
	(n = 11)	*(n = 14)*
Complete and Optimal Route: Problem 2.		
	Jasper Instructed	*Comparison*
Skilled	*83%*	*25%*
	(n = 12)	*(n = 12)*
Less skilled	*18%*	*0%*
	(n = 11)	*(n = 14)*

comparison classes to generate both complete and feasible routes and complete and optimal routes. Data are shown in the middle and lower panels of Table 4.1.

Studies of Group Versus Individual Problem Solving

We have also had opportunities to study *Jasper* in the context of individual versus group instruction. For example, Barron (1991) compared the performances of students who attempted to solve *Journey to Cedar Creek* either individually or in pairs. She found that pairs of students performed much better than individuals.

Barron then attempted to assess how much each individual student had learned by presenting them with subsequent transfer problems that they were asked to solve individually. On these individually administered transfer tests, only some of the students who had initially worked in pairs outperformed students who initially worked individually. These tended to be the students whose achievement scores in mathematics were high. The results suggest that group problem solving is beneficial for students, but that not all students will immediately transfer from doing well in a group to being able to do well individually. Barron's study was of a relatively short duration. With more experience solving a variety of problems, it is reasonable to expect more positive benefits of working in groups on individual achievement. Results presented in the next chapter involve longer term studies and demonstrate positive benefits of working with *Jasper* on individual problem solving and achievement.

A number of additional studies also shows that groups tend to solve *Jasper* problems much better than individuals (e.g., CTGV, 1994; McNeese, 1992; Vye, Goldman, et al., in press). In addition, students ranging in age from fifth grade to college almost always prefer solving *Jasper* problems in groups rather than attempting to solve them individually.

Groups are especially likely to generate a wider range of possible solutions to problems than are individuals (CTGV, 1993b; McNeese, 1992; Vye, Goldman, et al., in press). Of course, there are also individual differences among groups, with some performing much better than others. Vye et al. (in press), studied the reasoning processes of students working in pairs to solve the *Jasper* problem *The Big Splash* and found that more successful problem solving was associated with more coherent argument structures in problem-solving dialogues. In coherent arguments, students' searches for data and calculations were highly goal-directed rather than simply hit-or-miss. In addition, students in the successful pairs were more likely to offer explanations for their claims as well as explanations about counterclaims offered by the other member of the dyad.

OBSERVATIONAL STUDIES OF DIFFERENT APPROACHES TO INSTRUCTION

The preceding experiments involved relatively well-controlled baseline and intervention studies designed to explore issues of learning and instruction. However, we also wanted to explore the use of *Jasper* in real classrooms. How would the instruction look when teachers used *Jasper*? We had the opportunity to visit the classrooms of a number of teachers. They introduced us to many instructional techniques for teaching with *Jasper* that we had never anticipated. Many of the instructional techniques we observed were better than anything we had ever imagined. A few were worse than we had ever imagined. All were informative.

Opportunities to see *Jasper* used in so many ways helped us realize that the relationship between curriculum design and instruction was far from an exact science. The good news was that our approach to curriculum design allowed great flexibility with respect to instruction. This was also the bad news.

The Concept of Affordances

It became helpful to us to view the effects of curriculum materials on instruction from the perspective of Gibson's (1977) concept of affordances. Gibson noted that different features of the environment afford activities for particular organisms such as walk-onable, climbable, swimmable, and so forth. Similarly, different types of instructional materials afford different kinds of learning activities (Jenkins, 1979). Some materials may lend themselves to protracted problem posing and formulation whereas others may structure the situation completely, leaving little to do but add up the numbers. For example, traditional word problems typically provide the goal and only those numbers needed to solve the problem and, hence, afford computational selection. In contrast, the *Jasper* series affords students opportunities to create problem structure as they solve the problem, potentially leading to more opportunities for group interactions that support generative learning (CTGV, 1992b).

The concept of affordances does not guarantee that particular types of activities will happen. Surfaces can be walk-onable without anyone walking on them; they can be climbable without climbers and swimmable without swimmers. Similarly, the affordances built into the *Jasper* materials provided no guarantee that they would be perceived and used.

Dimensions of Instructional Models

We found it useful to focus on three dimensions of instructional models that help characterize how teachers used *Jasper* in their classrooms (CTGV, 1992b). The first dimension dealt with assumptions about the sequencing of content and tasks in the curriculum. At one end of this dimension is the extreme reductionist view that all components of a skill must be mastered before the components can be assembled into the skill they comprise. At the other end is the view that components are meaningless unless students understand them in the context of the composed skill.

A second dimension dealt with assumptions about the value of making errors and floundering with a task. At one end of this dimension is the assumption that errorless learning is ideal; at the other, that important lessons of learning occur only when students make errors or reach impasses and are then helped to correct their initial misconceptions (Borasi, 1987, in press; Clement, 1982; Minstrell, 1989; Schank & Jona, 1991; Van Lehn, 1990).

A third dimension dealt with assumptions about the teacher's role in the learning process; the dimension runs from authoritative provider of knowledge to a resource who may sometimes be consulted by the students and, at other times, might even become the student whom others teach.

In specifying these dimensions, we purposely provided the extremes. We noted that points along these dimensions may be actualized in different combinations by different teachers and by the same teacher in different situations. The values along these dimensions define particular instructional models. We discussed three such models in CTGV (1992b), yet noted that many others are possible. These three provide contrasting cases of capitalizing on the affordances of the *Jasper* series and are, thus, illustrative of the importance of the instructional model in determining classroom learning activities.

Example Model 1: Basics First, Immediate Feedback, Direct Instruction

One model of instruction that many people have suggested to us is what we call the basics-first model. People who recommend this model feel that the *Jasper* adventures provide an excellent application for practicing one's skills. However, they assume that *Jasper* should be used only after students acquire all the necessary sub-skills and subconcepts. Thus, if an adventure involves decimals, measurement, time, and so forth, proponents of the basics-first model argue that each of these areas should be taught prior to working on a *Jasper* adventure.

In many existing curricula, basic concepts and skills such as these are taught in workbook or computer-based drill-and-practice environments that present the materials in an out-of-context format. Teaching usually follows a direct instruction model wherein teachers (or the authors of the materials) explain the concepts and demonstrate how to do the problems that exemplify the particular sub-skill. A particular sub-skill is considered to be acquired when the student can supply correct answers to the problems. Students practice doing these problems until accurate performance is demonstrated.

In essence, the basics-first teaching model is one in which students are shown how to do problems exemplifying particular sub-skills; these problems are then practiced until the student accurately answers them and then the next sub-skill is introduced in the same way. When the *Jasper* series is used in classrooms operating under this model of instruction, few of the generative activities uniquely afforded by the *Jasper* adventures are realized. Because they see their role as one of providing students with knowledge, teachers operating under this model tend to structure the solution for students and walk them through it, occasionally asking them to supply the facts needed to solve the problem.

On the three dimensions of content sequencing, feedback, and role of the teacher, the decontextualized basics-first model of teaching stands in direct contrast to the anchored instruction approach that we described earlier in this chapter and elsewhere (e.g., CTGV, 1990; see also Brown, Collins, & Duguid, 1989). By helping students understand the nature of real-world problems that are inherently interesting and important, a major goal of anchored instruction is to help students understand why it is important to learn various sub-skills, and when they are useful. In our view, the basics-first model does not provide students with enough opportunities to find and formulate problems on their own. In addition, basics-first curricula often lead to misconceptions about the nature of mathematics. When mathematics is discussed by practicing mathematicians it becomes clear that it is a science of order and pattern finding that is much more interesting and creative than the mere computation of numbers (e.g., see NCTM, 1989; Schoenfeld, 1985, 1989).

In criticizing the basics-first teaching model we are not dismissing the importance of developing proficiency in sub-skills. In fact, we have devoted considerable attention to understanding how to arrive at fluent arithmetic skills and how this process might be enhanced (e.g., Bransford, Goin, et al., 1988; Bransford, Goldman, & Vye, 1995; Goldman, Mertz, & Pellegrino, 1989; Goldman, Pellegrino, & Mertz, 1988; Hasselbring, Goin, & Bransford, 1988). We encourage teachers to use *Jasper* as an anchor for developing fluency for basic concepts and procedures, such as figuring out elapsed time, fuel consumption per unit time, and cost per unit.

However, unlike the basics-first model, we advocate the use of basic exercises in conjunction with work on *Jasper*.

Data we have collected indicate that problem-solving experiences are extremely important. For example, even when students become quite good at sub-skills, they often remain poor at assembling the sub-skills for purposes of solving problems unless they have had the opportunity to explore complex problem environments (e.g., Hasselbring, Sherwood, et al., 1988; Van Haneghan et al., 1992). Similarly, the opportunity to watch students explore problems such as *Jasper* helps teachers identify and correct important misconceptions involving both concepts and procedures (e.g., Goldman & CTGV, 1991). In addition, the opportunity for students to work in groups, and eventually to define and research their own issues related to the *Jasper* adventures, helps reinforce the idea that the teacher is not the sole proprietor of all knowledge. Because it is very difficult for anyone to know everything about a *Jasper* adventure, students get the opportunity to see models of their fellow students and teachers as learners and information finders. Such models are not apparent when the major classroom activity is to memorize concept definitions and engage in computational drills.

Example Model 2: Structured Problem Solving

A second model of instruction that has been suggested to us focuses on the need to help students minimize errors and feelings of confusion. We call this the structured problem-solving model. It differs from the basics-first model in that the introduction of complex problems is not delayed until the basic mathematics skills have been mastered; rather, the complex is introduced in parallel, or slightly asynchronously, with the more basic. Thus, this model capitalizes on the potentially motivating features of having students see complex situations in which their sub-skills might be used.

An important feature of the structured problem-solving model is the attempt to eliminate errors and feelings of confusion on the part of the students. Thus, instead of beginning instruction by having students attempt to generate the kinds of subgoals that must be considered and to then figure out how to evaluate options (e.g., in order to help Emily find the fastest way to rescue the eagle), the teacher prepares a set of worksheets that specifies possible rescue plans and guides students through the processes of evaluating these plans. The greater the degree of guidance, the higher the probability that the students will not make errors.

Figure 4.4 includes examples of some structured exercises that can guide students through a set of possible solutions to *Rescue at Boone's Meadow*. In the full set of exercises, eight possible routes are provided; some are not feasible, others are feasible but require a lengthy amount of time. Students consult the episode (either the video or a storyboard form of it) to fill in the data that are left out of the route description. On the basis of the data, they make decisions regarding feasibility and comparative speed of one route versus another (e.g., the time it takes for Emily to fly from CC-B-H and back to CC compared to Larry's flying CC-H-B-H and driving

PLAN I
Emily thinks that the quickest way to rescue the eagle would be for Larry to fly from Cumberland City to Boone's Meadow and back the same way. Will this plan work and if so, how long will it take?

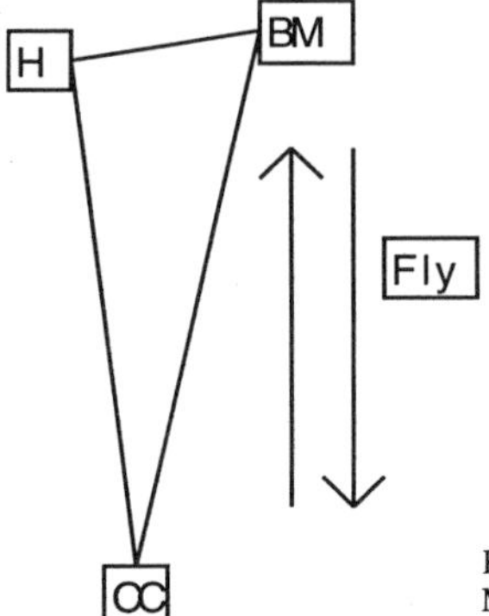

KEY: CC = Cumberland City; BM = Boone's Meadow; H = Hilda's

Is there enough landing area at Boone's Meadow?
Emily first wanted to figure out if Larry would have enough space to land at Boone's Meadow. The vet said that most planes need about ________ feet of runway, and that Boone's Meadow was half of that distance. That meant that the runway at Boone's Meadow was ____ feet long.
Emily remembered that Larry had told her that the ultralight needed ___________ yards of runway to land. Changing this to feet she found that the ultralight needed ______ feet to land.

Can the ultralight land at Boone's Meadow?
YES NO (circle one)

Will the plane have enough gas?
Next Emily wanted to figure out if the plane would have enough gas to fly the route. To answer this question she first had to figure out how far the plane could fly on 1 tank full of gas.
Emily knew that the plane could fly __________ miles on 2 gallons of gas. With this she calculated that the plane could fly __________ miles on 1 gallon of gas. Emily also knew that the gas tank held _________ gallons of gas. From this information, Emily calculated that the plane could fly ___________ miles on a full tank of gas.
To decide if the plane would have enough gas to fly the route, Emily next had to determine how far the plane would have to travel. She knew that the distance between Cumberland City and Boone's Meadow was _____ miles. She calculated that the total distance to Boone's Meadow and back to Cumberland City would be ___________ miles.

Can the plane travel from Cumberland City to Boone's Meadow and back the same way without running out of gas?
YES NO (circle one)

DO YOUR CALCULATIONS IN THE SPACE BELOW

FIG. 4.4. Example of structured exercises for *Rescue at Boone's Meadow.*

back to CC from Hilda's). The errors that these materials eliminate are those involved in constructing the routes and determining the factors that need to be considered in evaluating each route.

We have used structured exercises, such as these, in an experiment designed to compare their effects to a situation in which students have to generate the routes and the factors that need to be evaluated (see Model 3, next). Our observations of classes of students using these worksheets make clear that, even when students sit in groups (with one worksheet per group), the interactions among them are minimal and are confined to fact-finding and computation. Not surprisingly, we see little evidence of subgoal generation and of the kinds of monitoring that, in less structured situations, are necessary to keep discussions on track.

Overall, the strong point of the structured problem-solving model is that students only work on correct plans; the trade-off is that they do not engage in problem generation and monitoring. We noted earlier that an important part of everyday problem solving is the ability to generate the subgoals necessary to achieve one's objectives. Based on assumptions about transfer-appropriate processing (e.g., Bransford, Franks, Morris, & Stein, 1979; Morris, Bransford, & Franks, 1979), we believe that the best way to develop such abilities is to allow students to engage in generative learning activities. A model for teaching that emphasizes generation is discussed next.

Example Model 3: The Guided Generation Model

Our third model of instruction is consistent with the composite teaching examples for *Rescue at Boone's Meadow* that were discussed earlier. We think that it is a more powerful teaching model than Models 1 and 2 because it emphasizes the importance of generative activities on the part of students. Meaningful generation most frequently occurs in relatively complex situations where the subgoals necessary for solution are not prespecified, so this teaching model attempts to make maximum use of the affordances present in the *Jasper* series. The use of cooperative groups helps make the generative learning model feasible, in part because students tend to keep each other from going too far wrong. Nevertheless, we also noted earlier that teachers sometimes provide guidance to students. In addition, they often adopt the role of learner—especially when students are allowed to explore issues that are suggested by the *Jasper* adventures (e.g., what do spoilers on the wing of a plane do? When did eagles become endangered?). Teachers will probably not know the answers but can attempt to help students learn how to find out for themselves. Overall, we hope to establish a community of inquiry or learning that includes students, teachers, and others as well (e.g., Brown & Campione, 1994; Lipman, 1985; Scardamalia & Bereiter, 1991).

A guiding concept for the kind of teaching and learning that we envision for Model 3 is the concept of *scaffolding*. The term comes from Vygotsky (1978), who emphasized the importance of social support for learning provided by parents, peers, and others. He defined the zone of proximal development as the region wherein students could exceed performance levels they could reach on their own with the right kind of help or scaffolding. Ultimately, the goal is to be able to remove the scaffolds and enable students to proceed on their own.

We find that, at least for their first *Jasper* adventure, all of our teachers supply some degree of structure that helps students begin to generate subgoals and plans for reaching them. Nevertheless, it is rare to find the degree of structuring shown in Fig. 4.4 (see Model 2, previously described). The structuring that our experienced teachers provide is much less restrictive than the structure discussed under Model 2.

Teachers have also helped us find and study ways to adapt the complex *Jasper* adventures to the needs of students with different degrees of preparation. For example, imagine that students do not yet know how to multiply decimals. There are ways to help them solve the *Jasper* problems using other means (e.g., instead of dealing with 1.5 hours, students can deal with 60 minutes and 30 minutes and then combine them). In other cases, teachers have helped us see that options can be built into *Jasper* adventures. For example, when working with teachers to develop *The Big Splash*, we discovered that some wanted to have their students calculate volume (in this case the volume of a circular pool), whereas others did not. To accommodate these requests, we built options into the challenge. One was to use the estimate of the volume of the pool suggested by the owner of the pool store. A second was to check the accuracy of this estimate by using information about the diameter and depth of the pool.

A particularly interesting example of teacher-provided support was shown to us by Nancy Johnson, a teacher who taught *Rescue at Boone's Meadow* to first graders. She did not expect these students to deal with the entire problem. Nevertheless, by handing out a map and manipulatives that represented a standard for distance, Johnson was able to help the students figure out the time and distance to rescue the eagle, given a particular route. One group of students was even able to determine that the plane would need extra fuel.

Overall, our observations suggest that there are multiple ways to use *Jasper*, and that teachers need the freedom to adapt it to their own teaching styles. Nevertheless, we encourage teachers to stay as close to Model 3 as possible. It is this model that is illustrated in the *Jasper* teaching video that accompanies this book.

THE NINE-STATE IMPLEMENTATION PROJECT

In the summer of 1990, the Chancellor of Vanderbilt University, Joe B. Wyatt, arranged with corporate and educational partners in Tennessee and eight surrounding states to develop a field trial of the *Jasper* series. (At that time, only four adventures were available: *Journey to Cedar Creek, Rescue at Boone's Meadow, The Big Splash,* and *A Capital Idea*). The goal of the trial was to explore how a program such as *Jasper* might fit into different educational settings, and to begin to understand the kinds of ongoing technical and pedagogical support that teachers would desire when working with *Jasper*. We also wanted to understand how *Jasper* would fit with various standardized assessments used in different states, and we wanted to include some of our own assessments that mapped directly into the goals of *Jasper*. We explained to the teachers and corporate representatives that our philosophy with respect to most of the state assessments was "Do no harm." In contrast, we hoped to see gains on assessment instruments that more directly reflected the potential benefits of working with *Jasper*. By the same token, we warned that the first year of trying out a new program such as *Jasper* can be difficult, so we might not find any measurable benefits at all.

Developing Relevant Assessments

As noted in earlier chapters, the goals for learning that underlie the *Jasper* series emphasize the importance of helping students—all students—learn to become independent thinkers and learners rather than simply become able to perform basic computations and retrieve simple knowledge facts (e.g., Bransford, Goldman, & Vye, 1991; Bransford, Sherwood, Vye, & Rieser, 1986; Goldman, Pellegrino, & Bransford, 1994; Resnick, 1987; Resnick & Klopfer, 1989; Scardamalia & Bereiter, 1991; Schoenfeld, 1988, 1989). An especially important consideration is that students must learn to identify and define issues and problems on their own rather than simply respond to problems that others have posed (e.g., Bransford & Stein, 1984, 1993; Brown & Walter, 1990).

Because we were dealing with multiple sites in nine different states, we could not visit sites to observe in classrooms and conduct think-aloud interviews with students as they solved problems (see earlier in this chapter for studies that involve think-aloud interviews). Therefore, we developed paper-and-pencil instruments for assessing three aspects of our implementation: classroom instructional activities, student outcomes, and teachers' reactions to the implementation. These are briefly discussed next (additional details are provided in CTGV, 1993a; Pellegrino et al., 1991).

Classroom Instructional Activities

Our information about ways in which *Jasper* was implemented in classrooms is based on teacher self-report, artifacts that we received (e.g., newspaper articles, letters, etc.), and a very small number of on-site observations of actual *Jasper* classes. There was wide variation in how teachers implemented the instructional model, especially regarding the use of large and small group generative activity. In some classes, problem solving was mostly teacher-driven and students' activities were mostly focused on fact-finding. In others, problem solving was more consistent with the guided generation model we discussed previously.

All classes completed the two trip-planning adventures; most also completed one of the business plan/statistics adventures, and five classes completed both of the business plan/statistics adventures. In general, students spent approximately 1 week's worth of class time watching and solving each adventure. For most classes, these activities took the place of time that would normally be devoted to word problems.

There were a number of innovative activities implemented by the teachers. For example, a number of classes planned field trips around the topics and events in the trip-planning episodes. Two classes in Arkansas went on a field trip to a small airport where they watched a pilot flying an ultralight. It turned out to be a different model than the one in *Rescue at Boone's Meadow* and the students immediately barraged the pilot with questions about payload, fuel capacity, and so forth. Several classes took the business-plan model depicted in *The Big Splash* and devised their own plan to raise money for their school by selling snacks to other students. The students made enough money to finance a trip to a Civil War site in a neighboring state.

Other unanticipated activities included strategies for informing the community about *Jasper*. These provided important models for our own dissemination efforts and played a key role in the evolution of our thinking regarding learning communities. For example, a number of the teams made presentations to various groups in their local communities, including parents, other teachers, school and district administrators, local media, local and state government officials, and members of the corporations supporting the implementation. The teams frequently used the technology to make their presentations.

Assessments of Student Learning

Four test instruments (Basic Math Concepts Test, Word Problem Test, Planning Test, and Math Attitudes Questionnaire) were developed and used to examine the effects of the *Jasper* program. Scores from comparison and *Jasper* students on these measures, along with the standardized achievement test scores, form the basis of the analyses. Comparison classes were chosen by each school system so that, as much as possible, they were equivalent to experimental classes in terms of student demographics and achievement levels, and experience and teaching quality of the teachers. The four instruments were administered to students by their teachers during the first 3 months and the last month of the 1990–1991 school year. Students were also given midyear Word Problem and Planning tests as progress checks.

Basic Math Concepts. We wanted to assess changes in students' knowledge of basic math concepts because the solution to *Jasper* subproblems required students to use basic concepts such as units of time and distance, area, decimals, fractions, and so forth. Nevertheless, the *Jasper* program that we implemented did not include extended instruction in these math concepts; therefore, we did not expect the *Jasper* groups to do any better than the comparison groups. In fact, an alternative hypothesis that we considered was that time spent on *Jasper* was time taken away from basic math instruction, so scores of students in the *Jasper* classrooms might actually show less of an increase during the school year than scores of the matched comparison students. With few exceptions, the overall finding was that the *Jasper* groups and the matched comparison groups improved during the course of the year, and that both groups improved at the same rate. This pattern was observed for content-area problems representing area/perimeter/volume, decimals, and decimal-fraction conversions (Pellegrino et al., 1991).

Word Problems. Although they are not a primary target of the *Jasper* program, word problems constitute a typical measure of children's problem-solving performance. We were interested in determining whether the *Jasper* students would be better able to solve word problems that involved content related to the material presented in the *Jasper* adventures. We created one-step and more complex two-step and multistep word problems that tested students' abilities to solve trip-planning (*Jaspers* 1 and 2) and business-plan-related (*Jaspers* 3 and 4) word problems. Various sets of problems were included in the beginning-of-year, midyear, and year-end test batteries. A description of the item types appears in Pellegrino et al. (1991).

Our word-problem test can be viewed as a test of the near transfer of the problem-solving skills developed in solving the *Jasper* adventures. We expected that the *Jasper* students would do better than the comparison students on these word problems, particularly on the more complex two-step and multistep problems. The data indicate that aggregate pretest scores were equivalent for *Jasper* and comparison classes and that, at posttest, the performance of students in the *Jasper* classes was superior for all three problem types. As indicated in Pellegrino et al. (1991), this general effect held for each individual site that we examined.

Planning (Generation) Problems. We noted earlier that the *Jasper* program focuses on the importance of helping students learn to plan, a process that involves generating the subgoals necessary to solve complex problems. Therefore, we created experimental planning problems that assessed higher level planning and subgoal comprehension. One of the planning problems (shown in Fig. 4.5) is a multistep

Jill lives in Carson City. She wants to drive her car from her house to a friend's house in Meridien. As shown on the map, Jill can take the road from Carson City to Johnstown and Johnstown to Meridien. Her car is filled with gasoline and ready to go. There is a gas station in Carson City, Ceymore, and Meridien, but there is not one in Johnstown. Jill plans to leave on her trip at 8:00 in the morning.

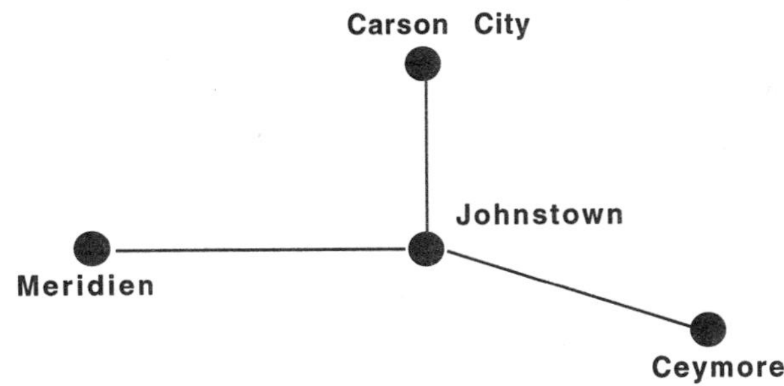

Top-Level Planning Challenge: What does Jill need to think about to figure out how long it will take her to make the trip?

Subgoal Comprehension Problem: Jill divides the distance from Carson City to Meridien (120 miles) by the speed she will drive (60 miles per hour). Why does she do this?

FIG. 4.5. Example of a planning problem.

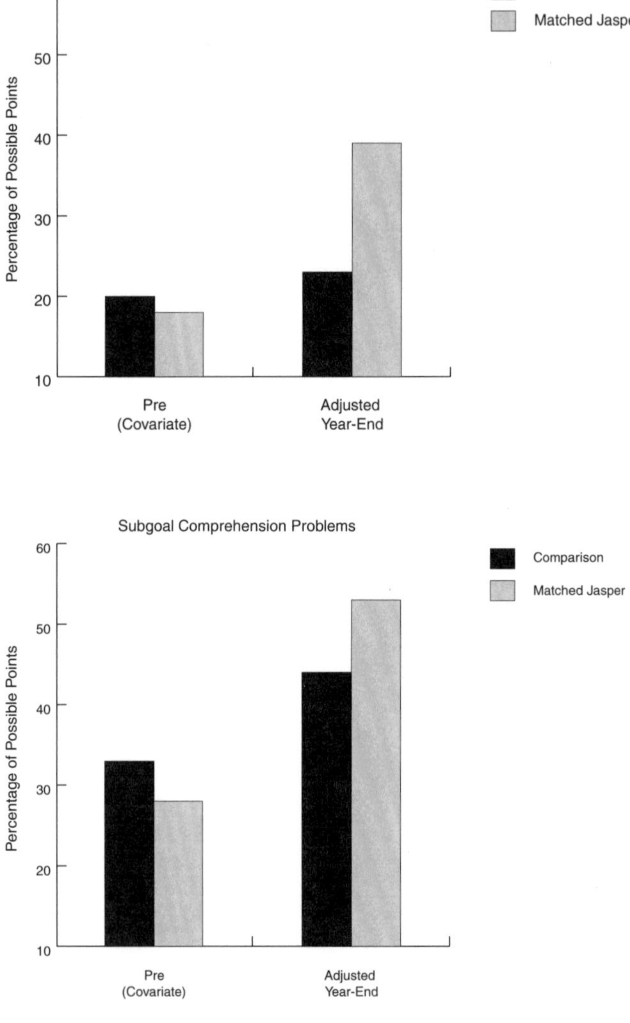

FIG. 4.6. Pretest and posttest data on planning problems. Pretest was used as a covariate in the analysis of the year-end data.

trip-planning task. A top-level planning question was presented first. This question requires students to generate the subgoals that need to be considered in planning the trip. In addition to top-level planning questions, we asked subgoal comprehension questions. Each of these questions shows calculations related to accomplishing a specific subgoal; the student's task is to explain why it is useful to do this calculation. The planning tests also included calculation questions where the students computed the answers to individual subgoals.

As illustrated in Fig. 4.6, all children had considerable difficulty with the planning and subgoal comprehension components of these problems at the beginning of the year. However, students from the *Jasper* classrooms scored much higher at year-end than the students from the comparison classrooms on both the planning and subgoal comprehension questions. The *Jasper* students did slightly better than the comparison students on the calculation scores, but this effect only approached significance.

Attitudes. An important question to be asked about any approach to instruction is whether it helps educators win the battle but lose the war. It is not difficult to imagine programs that provide a great deal of practice that helps students perform well on specific tests yet, at the same time, manages to convince the students that they never want to study that area again. Because of this concern, we wanted to assess changes in students' attitudes toward mathematics and problem solving rather than only assess changes in problem-solving skills.

Considerable research has demonstrated a strong relationship between math achievement and students' feelings toward math (e.g., Fennema & Sherman, 1977; Meece, Wigfield, & Eccles, 1990). The findings suggest that, above and beyond ability, feelings about the usefulness of math, math self-confidence, and patterns of attributions for success and failure can strongly affect how well students learn math. In prior classroom-based research with the *Jasper* program, teachers and students have reported that the *Jasper* program makes mathematics more enjoyable and that students better understand the usefulness of math (Van Haneghan et al., 1992). To more formally assess the effects of the *Jasper* program on attitudes, students were given a questionnaire at the beginning and the end of the school year that assessed their level of agreement or disagreement with statements about a variety of attitudes about mathematics. We hypothesized that students in *Jasper* classrooms would show more positive changes in attitudes about mathematics from the beginning of the school year to the end of the school year, as compared to students in the comparison classrooms.

An important aspect of attitude research is assessing the basis on which students attribute the causes of their success or failure in mathematics. Such research focuses on whether students view the cause for success and failure as being internal and changeable versus external and unchangeable. To this end, we included a number of items in our attitude questionnaire that asked students about the factors to which they attribute success or failure. Because attributional style has been shown to be a more stable construct than attitude, we did not expect to see substantial changes as a result of the *Jasper* instruction.

Students' math attitudes were assessed with a 35-item questionnaire. The items were selected to cover a broad range of constructs that can be grouped into three general categories. Table 4.2 presents examples of the general categories and specific subscales. Results confirmed our prediction for attitudes. On four of the five Attitudes Toward Math scales, *Jasper* students showed significantly improved atti-

TABLE 4.2
Math Attitude Scales

Scales	*Examples Item*
Attitude Toward Math Scales	
Math ability	I am better in math than most students in my grade.
Math anxiety/self-confidence	Math tests scare me (–).
Math utility	I see lots of uses for math outside of school.
Current interest in math	Math is less interesting than it used to be (–).
Feelings about challenging problems.	I like the challenge of solving complex problems that involve mathematics.
Attribution Scales	
Beliefs about ability	You can't really improve how well you do in math (–).
Attributions for success and failure	When I do well in math it is because I am lucky (–).

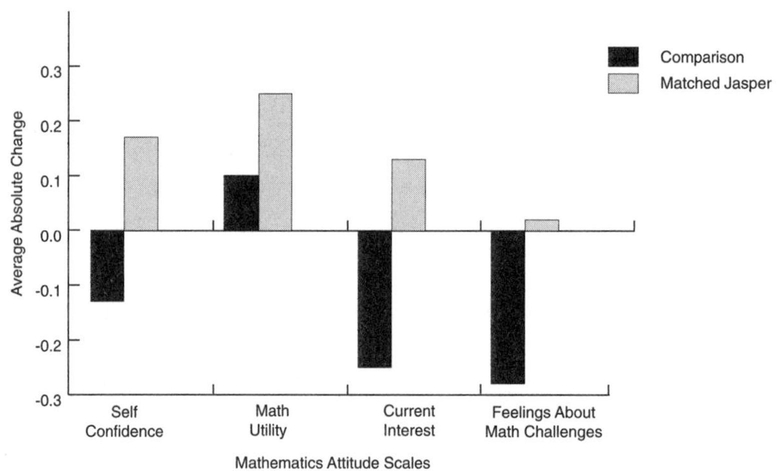

FIG. 4.7. Pre- to posttest changes in attitude scales.

tudes as compared to the comparison group (see Fig. 4.7, which illustrates changes in attitudes from pretest to posttest). *Jasper* students showed less anxiety toward mathematics, were more likely to see mathematics as relevant to everyday life, more likely to see it as useful, and more likely to appreciate complex challenges. On the two attribution scales, the scores were largely unchanged across time for both the *Jasper* and the comparison students.

Veteran Teachers' Comments About Jasper

In addition to quantitative data, the *Jasper* Implementation project yielded a great deal of qualitative data from teachers and parents. These data were collected after the teachers had taught *Jasper* for a year. With one exception (to be discussed later), the responses to *Jasper* were very positive. Some of the positive comments were as follows:

> Teacher #12: "We see every day that kids do not relate math to reading or reading to English or reading to social studies. They're all separate subjects.... *Jasper* helped them to see that math is real life situations.... It was really fun to see them relate to different situations at school and on field trips. They'd say 'This would make a good *Jasper* problem.'"
>
> Teacher #8: "Well the children themselves are the best salesmen. The kids would go home so excited and (the parents would say) 'I've got to find out about this *Jasper*. It is all my kid talks about ...' We wrote letters to the new fifth graders coming up–giving them tips so it will make their year better. In all of them, I was looking over them, they wrote about *Jasper*: 'Just wait until you get to *Jasper*. It's not just that it's fun, you'll learn so much.'"
>
> Teacher #2: "If you have any way of getting to (my) kids in high school, you'll find that they remember those four *Jasper* episodes. They may not remember anything else that we did that year but they'll remember ... those episodes because it did hit them and it did make an impact on them this year."

Teachers also shared with us information from parents. A letter from one of the student's parents appears here:

> I just wanted to let you know how much working with the Jasper math program has meant to X. We feel not only have his math skills improved but his interest is unending. X describes Jasper as situations that really occur "because you see them happen and then have to decide what to do—It's real!" When I asked him why he found it so much fun he said, "Because you could watch it instead of having to read and you get to work together and discuss ideas in a group."
>
> Previously X felt math was unimportant and boring. He even attended summer school in order to improve his basic skills. X never before wondered about situations or how to do certain types of problems. Most recently he wanted to know how to find the area of a hexagon and the volume of a triangular prism. I asked him if he was studying this in school, and he said no, but he might need to know it sometime.
>
> I believe his curiosity in math has been sparked as a result of working with the Jasper program. The badges he has earned are among his most prized possessions. X has already said that he can't wait to get to the middle school next year and see the new Jasper programs there.
>
> Thank you so much for all your time and efforts. I know you and many others have spent numerous hours bringing this program to our school and ensuring its success. Please extend our appreciation to all those involved. In our opinion, the results are benefits of the Jasper program and will continue long after X leaves fifth grade.

Effects of Jasper on Low- and High-Achieving Students

Almost every teacher mentioned that the *Jasper* adventures had a very positive effect on students who traditionally did poorly in mathematics classes.

For example:

> There was a little boy in my class who was not a very good math student. In fact he was not a very good student at all. He was a real sweet boy, and I had him sitting in the front of the class, but that still didn't seem to help him get motivated towards school or towards math. He was in a group with a little girl who was a straight A student and both of the children came up to me and were arguing back and forth. The little boy thought you were supposed to subtract and the girl was just so sure you should multiply, and all the other kids in the group were listening to the A student. When they asked me what they were supposed to do, I told the A student that she should listen to the little boy more often because he was right. And he was all excited and she was all surprised and they went back to the group and reported, and the other kids seemed to have a new respect for this little boy and he got really motivated and by the end of the school year he really had turned into a math whiz and he was a B student by the end of the school year—a B math student.

We heard many stories similar to this one. Teachers had several hypotheses about reasons for the effects of *Jasper*. One was that many students who were academically less successful in math were also poor readers and *Jasper* removed the reading barrier. Another was that there was a great deal of information to notice in a *Jasper* adventure and this gave students a chance to contribute to group problem solving even if they were not great at mathematics. For example, one boy became a group hero because he was the only one to notice that a crucial place to visit in *Journey to Cedar Creek* closed at 5:30 p.m.

A number of teachers suggested a third reason why less successful students were able to contribute to group problem solving: Students who were traditionally successful in math could not dominate everything. With typical word problems, the academically advanced students usually came up with the answer very quickly. With *Jasper* problems, it is impossible for anyone (at least anyone we have met) to solve the problems all at once.

We have heard from many different sources that high-achieving students often did not like *Jasper* at first because they could no longer be the primary stars in class. This bothered us at first, but we eventually realized that it was a good lesson for these students. Most real-world problems are complex and require collaboration. Learning to value collaboration at an early age seems to be highly positive. Interviews with students often reveal statements such as the following:

Student 1: In math we're usually on our own doing a worksheet or something.
Student 2: Yeah!
Student 3: In this [Jasper] we were working in groups and we have to work together and share our ideas.

Student 2: And we had to be more respectful for other people, what they had to say and what they thought, so it helped our cooperation.

Jasper and Community Building

Several of the teachers noted that they attempted to help parents and community members see the value of *Jasper* by inviting them into the classroom, showing them an adventure, and asking them to solve it (usually in groups). The students in the classroom acted as experts who guided the adults when they went down erroneous paths. Thanks to our teachers, we have tried this idea in our own presentations to business leaders, principals, and others—always with excellent results.

Jasper and Follow-on Projects

Teachers also emphasized that the *Jasper* adventures suggested a variety of hands-on activities that were engaging to students. For example, a number of classes used information from the business-plan adventures to generate enough money to take an educational trip—and they used their trip-planning skills to plan it. These types of extension activities represent our ultimate goal for the *Jasper* series. The videodisc adventures are an intermediate step; they make it easier for teachers to begin to experiment with new approaches to instruction (e.g., ones that emphasize projects rather than an array of decontextualized drills), and they provide a common ground for further discussion by students, teachers, and parents (e.g., see CTGV, 1996a).

Teachers' Comments About Our Tests

A negative comment about the *Jasper* Implementation Project was universally expressed by every one of our *Jasper* teachers. Their students grew to intensely dislike our assessments. They did not mind the pretests that much, but midyear testing and the prospect of posttests took their toll. Here are some representative quotes from teachers about our tests:

> Teacher #4: "My kids, as much as they liked *Jasper*, as much as they begged for *Jasper*, they finally told me: 'If I have to take another test on *Jasper* I don't want to see another *Jasper*.'"
>
> Teacher #3: "The reaction of our students when they saw anything come in from Vanderbilt that was in a brown envelope or box was 'another test!'... You could see them when they started out—most of them were pretty good, they'd think and then they would get tired. You could see them just filling pages or leaving a lot of it blank."
>
> Teacher #9: "It seems to me that we're really asking kids to do something strange when we've introduced this wonderful technology and we've gotten them involved in the video experience ... Then you give them this test that's on paper."
>
> Teacher #7: "For children who can't read very well ... they feel like giving up before they even try."

These quotations represent only a sample of negative reactions by our teachers, and their statements are much more forceful when one can hear the emotion behind them rather than merely read them in print. The result was a reassessment on our part of formats for assessment. It seemed clear that giving students opportunities to test their mettle was important for teachers as well as students. Was it possible to do this in a way that seemed less like being tested and more like participation in some type of challenging event? Our exploration of this question led to the *Jasper* Challenge series, which is discussed next.

THE *JASPER* CHALLENGE SERIES

The *Jasper* Challenge series used teleconferencing technology to create a public performance arena for *Jasper* classrooms (CTGV, 1994). The Challenge series linked classrooms together through live interactive shows that allowed students to test their mettle with respect to the *Jasper* adventures and their extensions. We called our challenges SMART Challenges, where SMART stood for Special Multimedia Arenas for Refining Thinking.

In our initial SMART Challenges, students and teachers worked with a *Jasper* adventure as a starting point. They prepared much as one prepares for a speech, a business meeting, a musical performance, or an important football game. Students were then given the opportunity to compare their ideas, projects, and performances to those of peers from around the country, and to receive feedback and suggestions for improvement. Overall, the SMART Challenges contained the following features:

1. Solve one of the *Jasper* adventures;
2. Solve relevant analog and extension problems (these were originally presented as part of the preparation for the challenge series rather than as a part of *Jasper* per se); and
3. Participate as part of a larger community in a public performance arena created by technologies such as satellite uplinks or cable TV augmented by phone bridges that allow audio interaction.

Some of our experiences with SMART challenges are discussed next.

Initial SMART Challenges. The initial SMART Challenges were cast in the form of game shows conducted online. Students played the at-home audiences and called in their responses to the studio from which the program originated. The basic task for the students was to evaluate the performances of individuals featured on the game show. For example, our Pick The Expert game show was modeled after "What's My Line?" A panel of experts answered questions based on *Rescue at Boone's Meadow*; students decided which panelist was the true expert. To do so, they had to use knowledge they had acquired by completing the *Rescue at Boone's Meadow* adventure and a set of video-based analog and extension problems that prepared students for the challenge by engaging them in what-if thinking (e.g., what if Emily had faced a headwind of 10 mph when she attempted to rescue the eagle?). The information needed to distinguish among the experts should have been acquired through solving the adventure and the analog and extension problems.

A second game show format, Rate That Plan, built on the mathematical and problem-solving skills associated with the business-plan adventure *The Big Splash*. In *The Big Splash*, Jasper's young friend, Chris, wants to help his school raise money to buy a new camera for the school TV station. The Rate That Plan game show included presentations of three plans for raising money at a school fun fair. Students had to decide which plan they thought was best. They phoned in the class vote but also filled out individual response sheets with their explanations for their choice.

Reactions to the Initial SMART Challenges. The reactions to each of our initial SMART Challenges were highly positive and in marked contrast to the reactions we had received to the written measures we had used in the Implementation Project. Teachers reported that the discussions following the uplinks were spirited and were motivated by the opportunity students had to compare their answers to those of peers across the country. A number of the teachers felt that the discussions were especially helpful to students who had originally missed flaws in various plans because it helped them improve their understanding of key concepts (e.g., random sampling) that were necessary in order to create effective business plans. Others indicated that students enjoyed the opportunity to learn something new rather than merely repeat already acquired skills.

SMART Challenges II. Although our initial challenges were highly popular with students, teachers, and community members, we saw considerable variability in data collected about students' individual performances. Our data indicated that some students appeared to have learned a tremendous amount from preparing for the Challenge whereas others had learned relatively little. We tried to understand why these differences existed. One possibility was that the concepts were simply too difficult for many of the students. Another possibility that seemed more plausible was that some of the teachers had not adequately prepared their students for the challenges. This might have been due to a lack of time, a lack of interest, or perhaps an inadequate understanding of some of the concepts required for the preparation. In order to explore these possibilities, we decided that the next step in our research should be to keep a better eye on what happened in classrooms.

Our observations revealed considerable variability in the way that teachers attempted to help their students prepare for the SMART Challenges. In some cases, students were adequately prepared; in other cases, they were not. In addition, only some of the teachers helped students reflect on their experiences with the SMART Challenges in ways that would be expected to lead to improved learning and transfer in the future. These observations helped us realize a fundamental limitation of the SMART Challenges that we had developed. Basically, they involved only summative assessments—assessments that occurred at the end of the learning cycle rather than during learning. In order to help teachers and students prepare for SMART Challenges, we needed more of an emphasis on formative assessment. The topic of formative assessment is discussed in the next chapter. First, we discuss some additional research that had a major effect on the redesign of Jasper to increase its benefits.

INCREASING THE DEPTH OF UNDERSTANDING AND FLEXIBILITY OF TRANSFER

Our experiences in classrooms, and with the nine-state Implementation Project and initial SMART Challenges, led us to formulate a good news-bad news story. The good news was that we and the teachers were seeing many positive benefits from *Jasper.* The bad news was that these benefits were not as great as we felt they could be. We became especially concerned with the flexibility with which students could transfer their thinking to new situations. Although the data discussed earlier showed promising evidence of transfer, we became worried that it was still somewhat restricted.

One way to characterize our concern was from the perspective of Dunker's (1945) work on functional fixedness. He noted that problem solvers would often follow a learned solution procedure even when a simpler one was possible. In Dunker's terms, the problem solvers remained functionally fixed.

As an example of functional fixedness, imagine providing students with a new variant of the *Rescue at Boone's Meadow* problem—a variant that allowed them to successfully rescue the eagle by flying directly to Boone's Meadow and back rather than needing to take the more circuitous route needed in the original solution. Would students spontaneously generate this simpler solution, or would they remain functionally fixed? We individually administered problems such as these and discovered that a number of students showed evidence of functional fixedness; for example, they did not fly directly to Boone's Meadow and back. Instead, they followed Emily's original route. These and other experiments convinced us that their thinking was much less flexible than we wanted it to be.

In other cases, it was clear that students could learn a strategy for solving a *Jasper* adventure without acquiring a deep understanding of important concepts related to the strategy. For example, students could successfully solve *The Big Splash* without understanding issues about sampling needed for subsequent problem solving. Across a number of studies and classroom observations, it became clear that we needed to encourage students to reflect on possible perterbations of cases and problems in order to deepen their understanding and make their problem solving more flexible. Visually based what-if analog and extension problems were added to each *Jasper* adventure in order to fulfill these goals. What-if analog problems were created by reusing the setting, characters, and objects of the videos and perturbing the values of one or more of the variables. Extension problems extended students' thinking from the adventure to other contexts (e.g., from planning a rescue in an ultralight to planning for Lindbergh's trip across the Atlantic). Specifically, analogs and extensions were designed to accomplish several purposes:

- help students develop flexible knowledge representations and enhance transfer and generalization of complex problem solving, particularly analogical transfer;
- help students develop better understanding of key mathematical principles embedded in the *Jasper* adventures, and
- help students make connections between the adventures and the thinking and planning that took place in many historical and contemporary events.

Analog and Extension Problems in *The Big Splash*

As an example of the benefits of adding analog and extension problems to the *Jasper* adventures, consider work conducted by Schwartz, Goldman, Vye, Barron, and the CTGV (in press). One of the key concepts in *The Big Splash* is the concept of a representative sample. In the adventure, Chris takes a representative sample of students by sampling every sixth student in the cafeteria line at school. Other information in the video indicates that there were 360 students in attendance on an average day. Thus, Chris took a one-sixth sample of students in a situation where all classes of students in the school were present and had an opportunity to be included in the sample.

Table 4.3 shows what-if analog problems for the representative sample concept.

The analog questions in Table 4.3 change the size of the sample and the context of sampling. Teachers encourage students to consider both sample size and sampling context in assessing their confidence in the procedure.

The instructional goals for these analogs include helping children understand two important characteristics of representative samples:

1. The sample needs to be representative of the entire population and drawn in an unbiased manner.
2. The sample needs to be large enough to give reliable results.

Table 4.4 shows the pre/posttest instrument used to assess the benefits of working with *Jasper* analogs. The items required the students to select among two alterna-

TABLE 4.3
Analog Problems for Representative Sample Concept

How much confidence would you have had in Chris' data if he had administered the questionnaire in the following ways?
1. To every fifth student who entered the school building on Monday morning.
2. To 1 of the students in his home room.
3. To every 6th student who attended a Saturday swim meet.
4. To every 40th person who entered the school cafeteria.
5. To every 3rd person who entered the school cafeteria.
6. To all the teachers in the school who then predicted how many children would want to participate.

tives and explain the basis for rejecting the nonselected alternative. Pretests were given after students solved *The Big Splash* but before they worked on analogs. Students (sixth graders) were then provided three days of instruction that dealt with the representative sample analogs, as well as others dealing with sample size. We then administered the posttest. The pre-post design allowed us to address the effects of the representative sample and sample size analogs on students' understanding of the two important characteristics of representative samples.

In addition to examining the percentage of correct selections (Fig. 4.8), we also looked at the explanations students gave for why they did not choose the less preferred option. We were particularly interested in whether the responses reflected an increased understanding of biased versus unbiased samples and of the need for

TABLE 4.4
Pre- and Postintervention Assessment

Amy is doing a fun fair booth. She decided to do a survey to estimate expected revenue.

Information provided about Amy's school:

- 400 students at the school in grades 1, 2, 3, and 4.
- 100 students in each grade, 5 classes per grade.
- At lunch time, all the students in the school line up in the cafeteria line with their classes.

Amy needs your help. Here are some methods she is considering. Tell Amy which method would be better to use. Then tell her what is wrong with the method she should not use.

Illustrative Representative Sample Items

Who to sample

Amy thinks she'll give out 200 surveys. She thinks about
A) Giving surveys to all of the kids in grades 1 and 3.
B) Giving surveys to half of the kids in grades 1, 2, 3 & 4.

Which should Amy choose? A B (circle one)
What is wrong with the method she should not choose?

Method of Selection
Amy thinks about:
A) Asking the first 20 and last 20 students in the line.
B) Asking every 10th student in the line.

Which should Amy choose? A B (circle one)
What is wrong with the method she should not choose?

Amy thinks she will:
A) Ask the first 60 kids in the cafeteria line.
B) Put all the students' names into a hat, shake it up, pull out 60 names, and give the survey to those 60 kids.

Which should Amy choose? A B (circle one)
What is wrong with the method she should not choose?

Sample Size:
Amy thinks she will:
A) Give a survey to 20 kids in the cafeteria line.
B) Give a survey to 70 kids in the cafeteria line.

Which should Amy choose? A B (circle one)
What is wrong with the method she should not choose?

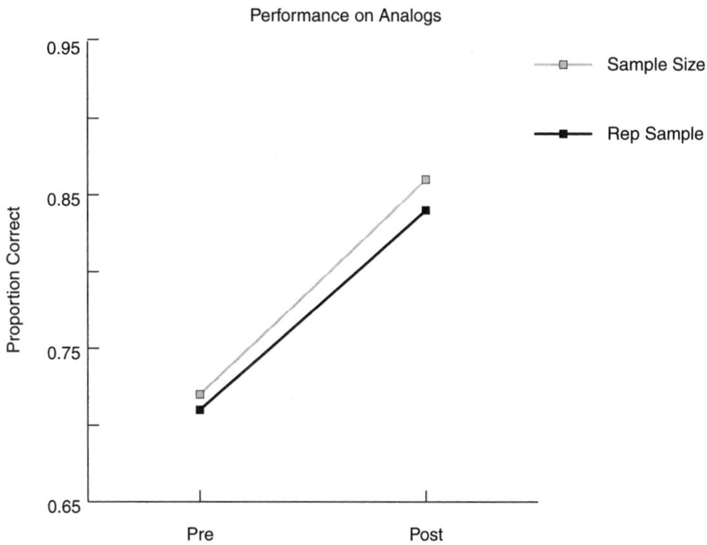

FIG. 4.8. Performance on representative sample and sample size items before and after instructional uses of analogs.

a large enough sample to give reliable results. These responses were quite revealing of what students did and did not understand.

An increased emphasis on fairness was evident in responses to items dealing with how to choose a sample. For example, in choosing between the first and last 20 students in a line versus every 10th student, there was a substantial increase in the percentage of students who mentioned fairness or variety in the explanations of their choices: from 38% at pretest to 61% at posttest. That is, increasing numbers of children explained that all the types of people in the school should have an equal opportunity to be in the survey rather than just the classes at the front and back of the line. It is interesting to note that there was also a computational misconception reflected in the explanations: At pretest, 36% of the students indicated that the two procedures would give different total numbers of students in the survey; this percentage declined to 24% at posttest.

Students' responses to another item that dealt with the method of selection indicated that they had very definite ideas about fair or procedurally just methods. These ideas differed from those often accepted by statisticians for producing unbiased samples. For example, on the item that compared the first 60 students in line with drawing names from a hat, students tended to reject the hat procedure because it did not ensure equivalence from all grades. This is evident in the following explanation for rejecting the hat: "She might pull out all 1st grade names and so it will be up to the 1st graders." At pretest, 44% of the students responded in this manner. However, because many students did not think selecting the first 60 in line was a very good selection method either, 46% of the students provided pragmatic reasons for their choices, such as "It takes too long" (to pull names out of a hat) and "It wastes time."

After the analog instruction, there was a greater tendency to accept the hat procedure. Explanations emphasized fairness and variety in the population, for example, "Don't choose (line) because you want to make sure you have all grades." At posttest, 56% of the students provided this type of explanation. Pragmatically based explanations decreased correspondingly to 29%. However, even at posttest, students rejected other randomization methods that statisticians would generally accept as generating an unbiased sample. For example, students rejected a procedure where students were excluded on the random basis of the last digit of their phone number. This method of selection was rejected on the grounds that it unfairly excluded people from a chance to be in the sample. The students did not like any method of selection that excluded students from the sample on the basis of preexisting attributes, even if those attributes had been assigned randomly.

One other item dealt with sample size by specifically comparing asking 20 versus 70 students to do the survey. The analog instruction resulted in increased understanding of the need to have a large enough sample, as the data in Fig. 4.8 indicate. The quantitative improvements on the sample size item were accompanied by a shift to a concentration on the explanations that mentioned sample size from 48% at pretest to 63% at posttest. An example of this type of explanation is, "If she only gives it to 20 kids she won't have a large enough number to work with."

Overall, studies of analog instruction indicate that working with the representative sample analog items improves students' understanding of key characteristics of representative sampling beyond what they had understood from just solving the adventure. Additional discussion is provided in Schwartz et al. (in press).

Combining Declarative and Procedural Knowledge in Problem Solving

Our work with students attempting to solve analog and extension problems also helped us discover an aspect of everyday problem solving that is possible to simulate in a *Jasper* environment but not in typical textbook environments that present students with sets of unrelated word problems at the end of each chapter. Everyday problem solving often involves multiple opportunities to solve the same or similar problems (Lave, 1988). In addition, people can take problem-solving shortcuts by combining declarative, factual knowledge with procedural knowledge. For example, imagine having solved the *Jasper* problem in *RBM* and realizing that it took approximately 2½ hours for the ultralight to fly from Cumberland City to Boone's Meadow to Hilda's. You are now asked about the flight time of an ultralight that travels at a speed of 60 mph. You can solve this problem without even remembering how far the plane had to travel. All you need to know is that the original time was 2½ hours at 30 mph and that the new speed is twice as fast. Therefore, the flight time is cut in half.

Studies by Williams, Bransford, Vye, Goldman, and Carlson (1992) showed that students initially have difficulty knowing when to use declarative knowledge and when to recompute based on new variables. With training on analog problems, the ability to combine declarative and computational knowledge improved a great deal (e.g., Williams, 1994; Williams, Bransford, Vye, Goldman, & Hmelo, 1993; Williams et al., 1994).

SUMMARY AND CONCLUSIONS

Discussion in this chapter focused on our initial attempts to assess the effects of working with *Jasper* on students' learning and transfer. Several types of studies were discussed.

One line of research involved a series of well-controlled baseline and intervention studies designed to assess the effects of working with *Jasper*. The baseline studies assessed the degree to which sixth graders who scored high on standardized tests of mathematics could solve *Jasper* problems. Data indicated that they had a great deal of difficulty unless we helped them structure the problem space by breaking the complex problem into simpler problems. These findings suggest that high-scoring students had the knowledge and skills necessary to solve the *Jasper* problems, but lacked the skills to begin with a complex problem and identify and define important subproblems on their own.

Another series of studies compared learning and transfer that resulted from opportunities to work with *Jasper* versus opportunities with the same concepts in the context of simpler one- and two-step word problems. Data indicated that experiences with *Jasper* produced a much-higher ability to transfer to new, complex problems.

A second line of research involved observations in classrooms of teachers' uses of Jasper. The good news from our observations was that our *Jasper* adventures provided a great deal of flexibility with respect to teaching styles. This was also the bad news.

A third line of research centered around the nine-state *Jasper* Implementation Project. Our goal was to do no harm with respect to standardized tests of mathematics achievement, plus assess the potential value-added of working with *Jasper* on measures of complex problem solving and attitudes toward mathematics. We found strong advantages for *Jasper* in both of these domains. Teachers who had taught *Jasper* also provided valuable information about the effects of their series on their students.

We also found that students and teachers tired of our paper-and-pencil assessments. This motivated us to attempt the *Jasper* SMART Challenge Series that allowed students and teachers to test their mettle. Students and teachers were extremely excited by this experience.

A fourth line of research focused on the issue of helping students deepen their understanding of the mathematical concepts underlying *Jasper* and, in the process, develop a more flexible ability to transfer to new problems. This research led us to redesign the *Jasper* series by adding video-based analog and extension problems to each adventure. Studies showed that opportunities to work on analogs and extensions had strong effects on students' understanding and abilities to solve new problems that they confront.

Overall, the studies in this chapter deal primarily with the summative assessment that occurs at the end of some unit of instruction, and much less with the ongoing formative assessment that provides feedback to students and teachers as they proceed with the learning process. Issues of formative assessment are discussed in Chapter 5.

5

Explorations of Formative Assessment

The initial approaches to instruction and assessment discussed in Chapter 4 focused primarily on summative assessment—on assessment of what students had learned after they completed some unit of instruction. The more we observed in classrooms, the clearer it became that assessment needed to be ongoing. This meant that we needed to make students' thinking visible so that they could receive feedback from their peers and others (e.g., Peterson, Fennema, & Carpenter, 1991). Without feedback, learning is extremely difficult, if not impossible. Effective uses of feedback provide opportunities for formative assessments—they are formative because they affect the actions of those trying to learn and teach.

A CLASSIC STUDY OF FEEDBACK

One of our favorite examples of the importance of feedback comes from an experiment by Thorndike (1913), who practiced drawing a line that was exactly 4 inches long. He practiced hundreds of times and never improved. The reason was that he was blindfolded. He could never receive feedback about his actions, so he never knew the length of the line he had just drawn. Eventually Thorndike removed the blindfold and was able to see how close each line he drew came to 4 inches. He quickly mastered his goal. His conclusion was that, without feedback, it is difficult to know how to adjust one's practice in order to improve.

At first glance, feedback opportunities seem abundant in typical classrooms. Students receive grades on tests and papers, teachers provide feedback about students' oral answers, students receive report cards. However, there are a number of reasons why these opportunities for feedback are not sufficient for students to learn effectively; the result is that students are often in a position analogous to Thorndike while blindfolded. For example:

1. Grades on tests, essays, and report cards usually come too late for students to engage in online revisions of their thinking (analogous to Thorndike receiving a grade after 100 blindfolded attempts).

2. Grades usually provide information only about right versus wrong answers; they are rarely accompanied by information about how to improve in particular areas (analogous to someone telling the blindfolded Thorndike only that his attempts were either right or wrong).

3. Students typically do not have access to standards of performance and, hence, cannot attempt their own self-assessment. Sometimes they set their standards too low; most times, they must wait for someone else to give them feedback. In contrast, once Thorndike removed his blindfold, he had access to a standard (the perfect 4-inch line) and could judge his progress for himself.

4. There are many missed opportunities for providing feedback in classrooms—especially in the context of helping students learn to engage in complex performances such as understanding important content rather than memorizing it, setting learning goals, writing with clarity, taking responsibility for seeking feedback, and so forth. Unlike Thorndike's clearly visible attempts to draw lines, the processes underlying these complex activities tend to remain invisible. In essence, students attempting to improve their abilities to engage in complex performances are often in the position of Thorndike when he was blindfolded.

Students must especially learn to actively seek feedback on their own so that they can monitor their progress, and they must learn to reflect on their learning processes so that they can continually improve. This includes a need to set clear goals so that they will know when they are on- versus off-track. Many classrooms that provide lots of feedback (especially ones that use computer-based integrated learning systems) do so in ways that make students depend on others rather than help them develop their own self-assessment skills.

SMART PROGRAMS AND FORMATIVE ASSESSMENT

A focus on the importance of formative assessment led to a reformulation of our SMART Challenge series that was discussed in Chapter 4. As noted there, SMART stands for Special Multimedia Arenas for Refining Thinking. However, we began to realize that our initial SMART challenges fell short of the goal of refining thinking. They provided materials for learning and a big event that was motivating. However, they failed to provide systematic opportunities for helping students prepare for the big event by allowing them to test their mettle, receive feedback, and have opportunities to revise.

The new goals of the SMART Challenge series became one of creating opportunities for students and teachers to obtain feedback about their solutions, gain access to resources to help them revise, and showcase examples of well-articulated reasoning. Table 5.1 summarizes the design principles used to develop the *Challenge* programs.

The Challenge Programs

Four *Challenge* programs were created around the *Jasper* adventure *The Big Splash*. We knew from our previous research that there were a number of statistical concepts

TABLE 5.1
Design Principles for *Jasper Challenge* Programs

Principles Guiding the Development of Jasper Challenge Programs
1. Engaging programs with an authentic purpose
2. Built-in opportunities for revision and chances to improve
3. Use of authentic audiences (the learning community) to energize learning
4. Showcase student explanations to communicate standards
5. Stimulate discussion through sharing ideas across classrooms
6. Communicate values of self-assessment and reflection
7. Introduce new conceptual tools to teachers and students that support sensemaking

that were often difficult for students to grasp, so we created our programs to address these concepts. Each program focused on a different part of the problem-solving process in *The Big Splash*. The first program was a general introduction, the second program focused on expenses, the third focused on revenue, and the fourth focused on a set of analogous problems that had to do with sampling.

Table 5.2 summarizes the content of the four programs that complemented *The Big Splash* episode. The organization of each program is described next, with the content of the second *Jasper Challenge* show used to instantiate the general descriptions.

Program Content and Organization

Each SMART program was composed of four major segments called SMART Lab, Roving Reporter, Toolbox, and The Challenge. The programs were hosted by a character named Steve, a young man with an exuberant, zany personality who welcomed the students to each show, interacted with another character in Toolbox, interviewed students as the Roving Reporter, and delivered The Challenge at the end of each show. SMART Lab and Roving Reporter relied on data from students in classrooms that were participating in the *Jasper Challenge* series and constitute the *Jasper* learning community. The four segments of the shows comprising the *Jasper Challenge* series are discussed next.

SMART Lab. The focus and purpose of SMART Lab was to provide feedback to students about decisions they had made in the course of their work on *The Big Splash*. This was accomplished by having students respond in writing to a series of questions about their work. The responses of all students participating in the learning community (approximately 100 students) were then summarized and represented graphically or in a table that was shown as part of the show. The host of SMART Lab was a young woman named Denise. She explained the graph or

TABLE 5.2
Summary of the Contents of the *Jasper Challenge* Shows for *The Big Splash*

Show	*SMART Lab*	*Roving Reporter*	*Toolbox*	*The Challenge*
1	• Student attitudes toward complex problem solving	• Introduction to students, teachers, and principals in learning community	• Discussion of use of bar graphs to display data	• Watch *The Big Splash* • Begin work on expenses • Generate itemized list
2	• Method of pool filling	Student explanations of:	• Timelines to compare plans	• Revise plan for pool filling
	• Total Expenses	• Pool filling method • Itemized expenses • Timelines	• Computer animation illustrating relation of rate of water flow to time to fill pool	• Revise itemized expenses • Draw a timeline for your plan • Estimate total revenue
3	• Revised pool filling method • Revised total expenses • Best ticket price choices • Estimations of total revenue	Student explanations of: • Best ticket price • Total revenue • Pie charts • Revised plans	• Part-whole representation illustrating extrapolation from sample to whole population • Computer animation illustrating cumulative frequency to determine best ticket price	• Revise estimate of revenue • Evaluate Huckster plans • Take several samples of size 60. Think about whether, if Chris took another sample of 60, his estimate would be the same
4	• Flaws in Huckster plans	Student explanations of:	• Estimates of total revenue graphed based on 100 samples of size 15, 60, and 90	• Prepare for The Big Challenge • Evaluate each plan and identify flaws
	• Reliability of samples	• Critiques of Hucksters	• Use of above graphs to discuss reliability of sample estimates in relation to size	
	• Monte Carlo data for sample size 60	• Why 60 is a good sample size		• Choose the "best" plan

table to students, provided some commentary about the range of responses, and posed some questions designed to encourage the students to think about the reasonableness of various alternatives.

For example, in the second show, Denise used a computer to graphically display students' responses, reproduced in Fig. 5.1 and on the accompanying CD-ROM. This graph illustrates the percentage of students who selected various options for filling the pool that would be used with the dunking machine. Denise described each axis and then reported the percentage of students selecting each plan. She commented that some students were quite creative and chose to combine methods for filling the pool, such as using the school hose plus the water truck from the pool store. Denise next showed a graph that related the most commonly calculated total expenses for each plan chosen. She explained that there were so many estimates, even for the same plan, that she just graphed the total expense that was most frequently calculated for each. After summarizing the data, Denise warned that these total expenses were not necessarily correct, and she questioned whether there should be so many expense estimates for the same plan. She suggested that it might be time to double-check and see if there might be expenses that were missed, extra expenses that did not need to be there, or calculational errors.

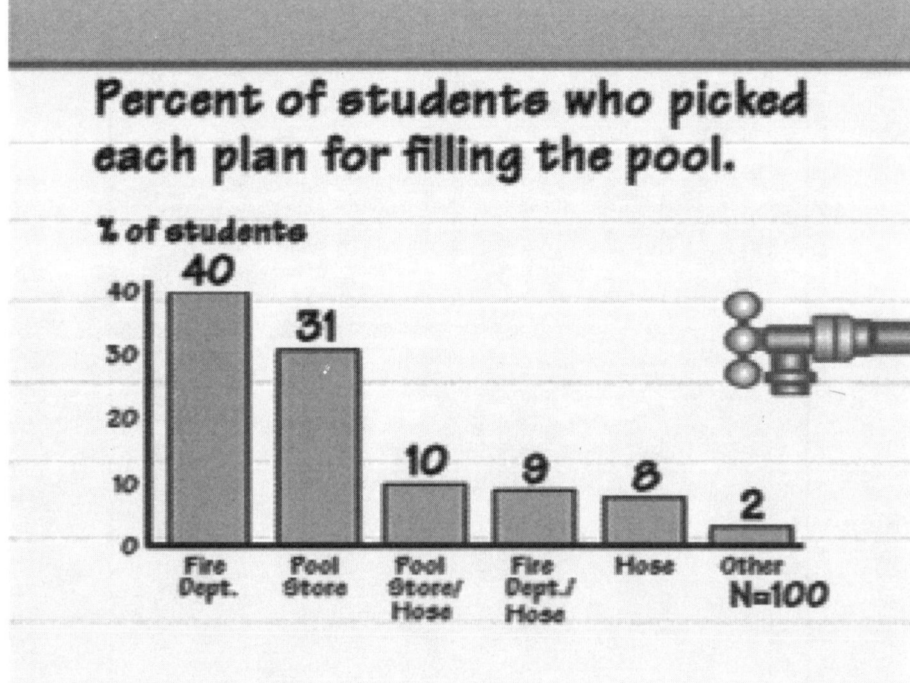

FIG. 5.1. Data from SMART Lab program.

Roving Reporter. In Roving Reporter, video clips were shown of Steve interviewing various students in the learning community about the problem solving they have been doing. Teachers nominated students who they thought were doing an exemplary job. The purpose of this segment was to showcase student reasoning and provide an opportunity for members of the learning community to react to various ideas. For example, in the second show, Roving Reporter featured 10 different interviews of students describing the plan they had generated for filling the pool and their expenses. One student provided the following rationale for his group's decision to use the fire department:

> Because we thought that the school hose would take too long and the pool, the pool store would probably cost and we didn't want to waste the money and we thought about the fire department having to go out on a call but it pumps 1000 gallons a minute, an um, and there are 2500 gallons in the pool so its going to take 2 minutes, 2 and a half minutes. I don't think they'll be called in that 2 and half minutes and its not going to take that long to pump it out, plus they get it for free.

This particular rationale sets a nice context for asking students if they could begin to quantify the amount of risk associated with relying on the fire truck to bring the water. One of the analogous problems for *The Big Splash* reminded students of the data on number of calls and false alarms per week that was provided in the adventure. Through what-if thinking and using additional data in the analogous problems, students could begin to think about differentially risky situations.

Other students featured in the second show rejected using the fire department, feeling that the plan entailed too much risk. Another group outlined in detail their plan for using the school hose plus the pool store, thereby minimizing both risk and cost, as well as ensuring that the pool could be filled by the fair's starting time.

Toolbox. Toolbox was hosted by a character named Dave whose specialty was generating visual representations to aid problem solving. Steve visited Dave in each show and engaged Dave in conversation about the problem solving in *The Big Splash*. Dave provided ideas for visual representations that could be conceived as tools for thinking, problem solving, and communicating. We chose visual representations for a number of reasons, including their usefulness for revealing patterns and communicating mathematical ideas in a nonprocedural manner. Toolbox was not designed to give away solutions but, rather, to provide scaffolding for students' conceptual understanding of the mathematics and problem solving. Many of the tools also suggested ways for students to revise their solutions.

In the second show, Toolbox began with Steve asking Dave if he had any pictures or diagrams that would help determine the best plan. Dave suggested a timeline. In the course of completing the timeline, they realized that they needed to determine how long it would take to fill the pool using various pool-filling methods. Dave used his computer to dynamically illustrate fill time as a function of the rate of water flow, as shown on the accompanying CD-ROM. A still of this representation is shown in Fig. 5.2. As the computer showed the number of gallons filled in 30-second

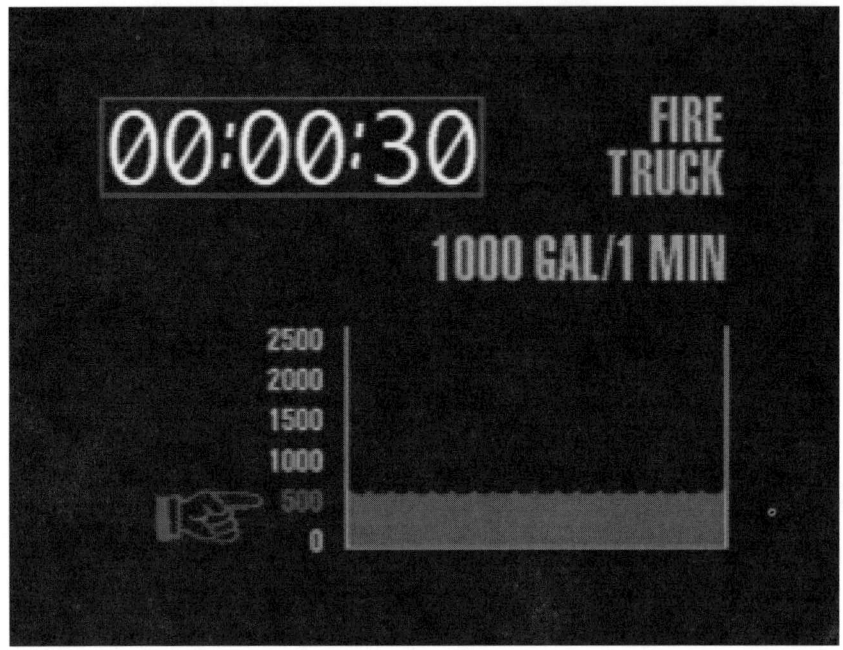

FIG. 5.2. Scene from a dynamic tool in Toolbox program.

increments, Steve made a table to record the results. The segment ended with Steve wondering about alternative ways to fill the pool and suggesting to the audience that they think about it.

The Challenge. Each show ended by giving the students a new problem-solving challenge to focus on. These challenges were delivered by Steve and included a challenge to revise their work based on feedback they had just received. A second part of the challenge was to begin work on a new part of the problem. In the second show, shown on the accompanying CD-ROM, students were to reconsider their plan for filling the pool, revise estimates of total expenses, and begin working on estimates of the total revenue they could expect on the day of the fair. Steve suggested they draw a diagram to help explain their estimates of total revenue.

A Culminating Event: The Big Challenge

As students worked with the SMART programs, they knew that they were preparing for a Big Challenge, which was to be a live, interactive event that challenged them to evaluate various business plans. The video portion of the event was broadcast live on our local PBS station. Interactivity was achieved by giving each participating class a cellular phone that students used to call in their critiques of a set of flawed business plans. In addition, each class was called by the host of the show and was asked to explain the class' analysis of a particular plan.

Students had prepared their responses in advance to all but one of the business plans. The novel plan provided students with the challenge of thinking on their feet during the live broadcast. After the plan was shown on the air, students had 10 minutes to call the TV station with an analysis of the flaw(s) in the plan. The students' answers were then summarized and the data were displayed on the show for all the students to see. For example, one plan involved a proposal for a can-crushing machine that would accept cans and give the depositor a few cents in exchange. The owner of the machine could then collect additional money when the cans were turned in for recycling. An estimate was given for how much money could be made with this business. The major flaw in this plan was in revenue estimation: The number of cans deposited during a 1-hour period on a Saturday morning were counted and generalized to 24 hours a day, 7 days a week, thereby providing an inflated revenue estimate.

A VALUE-ADDED STUDY OF THE *JASPER CHALLENGE* SERIES

To look at the added benefit of the *Jasper Challenge* programs for student learning and attitudes, a set of inner-city classrooms participated in a 6-week study (Barron et al., 1995). All classes followed the same curriculum (*The Big Splash* and related analogous problems) and all participated in The Big Challenge. However, approximately half of the classes received the *Jasper Challenge* programs and the other classes did not. Classes were matched within school on their previous year's mathematics achievement scores and then randomly assigned to one of two types of implementations (*Jasper-only* or *Jasper plus Jasper Challenge* programs).

Student Characteristics

The students and teachers who participated in this study were recruited from among the fifth-grade teachers and classrooms within two schools, yielding nine classrooms and 208 students. Instruction took the place of the regularly scheduled mathematics class. Of the nine classrooms, two were Chapter I mathematics classes. (The Chapter I program serves economically disadvantaged students who are experiencing academic difficulty.)

Sequence of Instruction

In preparation for The Big Challenge, students spent approximately 10 class sessions solving *The Big Splash*, six sessions on analogous problems, and two sessions evaluating business plans. All classes spent the same amount of time on each part of the problem as well as on the analogous problem activities. Students in the *Jasper-only* classrooms also received the challenges that were shown in the programs but they were in written form and delivered by project personnel.

Professional Development Sessions

At the beginning of the project, all teachers attended three 2-hour professional development sessions. The first professional development session provided an overview of *The Big Splash* and learning goals for students, and focused on solving the expenses challenge. The second session focused on revenue, and the third focused on the analogous problems. During these sessions, ideas for using visual representations to facilitate students' conceptual understanding and problem solving were discussed. These were the same representations that were featured in Toolbox. This was done to insure that all teachers were informed about useful conceptual tools, even *Jasper-only* teachers.

Findings

In the discussion that follows, we report our findings in three areas: student learning, student attitudes, and reactions to The Big Challenge. These represent summative assessments of our experiment to study the effects of formative assessment comprised of the *Jasper Challenge* series.

Student Learning

To look at the effects on students' knowledge of business planning and sampling concepts, an instrument focusing on those concepts was developed. It was administered to students at the start of the study and following The Big Challenge. The assessment items focused around a business planning scenario that was structurally identical to *The Big Splash,* although the cover story and the numbers were different. The scenario involved a student named Allison who wanted to have a booth at her school's fun fair. She decided on a game in which students fish for plastic ducks swimming in a pool. If they caught a duck, they received a prize. Several different question formats were used, including open-ended items, items that required manipulation of survey data, multiple choice items, and justification of multiple choice responses. A set of sample items is provided in Table 5.3. Four different measures of student learning were derived from this assessment instrument.

Composite Measure of All Concepts. The business planning assessment included a set of 16 multiple-choice questions that covered topics such as selecting an appropriate sample size, using an appropriate sampling method to obtain a representative sample, vocabulary, planning, and recognition of a distribution that would result from taking 100 samples of size 15 versus 100 of size 80.

As illustrated in Fig. 5.3, all students gained relative to their pretest performance. However, the *Jasper-plus* students who had received the four *Jasper Challenge* programs gained significantly more. Interestingly, univariate analyses of each of the 16 individual items revealed significant effects of time for each item, but no interactions. Given the advantage of the *Jasper-plus* group on the composite score,

TABLE 5.3
Assessing Student Learning

Example Items from Business Planning Test
Extrapolation
From the 80 students she surveyed, Allison determined the best ticket price and how much money she would make by charging this ticket price. She should multiply this amount by ___ in order to figure out total revenue. Explain your choice.
(a) 8 (b) 6 (c) 4 (d) 5
Survey Method
What do you think would be the best way for Allison to give out her survey?
Explain your answer.
(a) give it to all her friends (b) give it to every third person in her home room (c) give it to every fourth person on her school bus (d) give it to every fifth person at the school assembly
Sample size
Allison decided to give a survey to a sample of students at her school to find out how many people might be willing to buy a ticket to her "Fishing for Prizes" game. There are 400 people who go to her school. How many people would you tell her to get to complete her survey?
(a) 10 (b) 80 (c) 200 (d) 300

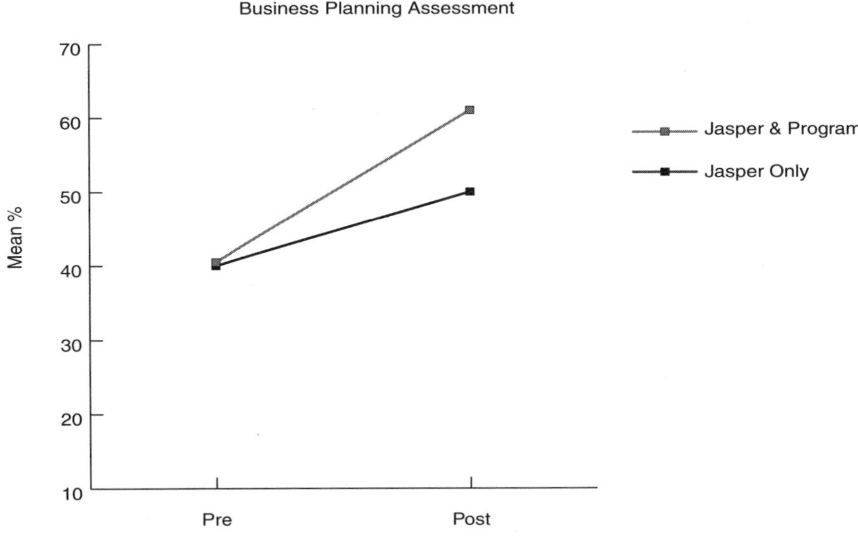

FIG. 5.3. Overall data for *Jasper* Only vs. *Jasper* Plus.

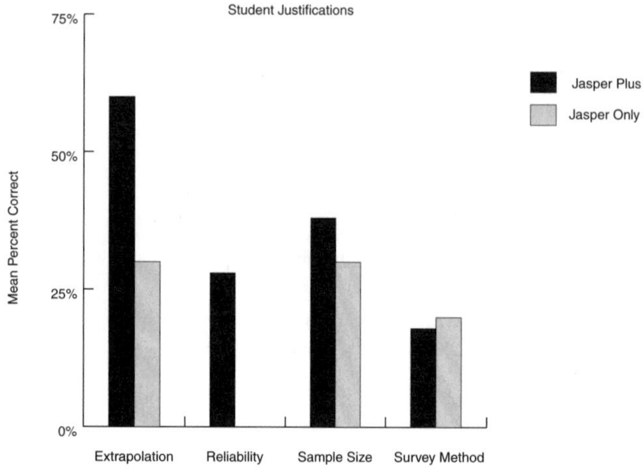

FIG. 5.4. Accurate justifications for correct answers.

the absence of group × time interactions on the individual items suggests that the advantage for the *Jasper-plus* group was a general one, rather than specific to one content area.

Justification of Answers. For a subset of the multiple-choice items just described, students provided written justifications for their answers. Figure 5.4 shows the proportion of students who had selected the correct answer and were able to provide a correct justification for their choices. There was a tendency for students in the *Jasper-plus* group to more frequently provide correct justifications for their correct answers. On the first two items represented in Fig. 5.4, we found that students who had received the programs were significantly more likely to correctly justify their selected answers. On these items, the percentage of students in the *Jasper-plus* group who justified their answers correctly was twice as large as the percentage of students in the *Jasper-only* group. These items had to do with extrapolating from the sample to the population and the reliability of the information generated from different sample sizes. On the remaining items, the group differences were not significant.

Generation of Elements of a Good Business Plan. In an open-ended planning question, students were asked to generate as many ideas as they could to help Allison develop a good business plan. Responses were scored for the presence of a number of different elements such as suggesting she estimate income, determine expenses, evaluate time, and use a survey. Our analyses suggest that more students indicated the need to think about expenses and income at posttest than at pretest, regardless of group. However, the likelihood of suggesting that Allison use a survey was significantly greater in the *Jasper-plus* group than in the *Jasper-only* group at posttest. The idea of using surveys with a sample of a population to generate information about the entire population is one of the big ideas that we especially wanted students to begin to understand.

Using Survey Data to Estimate Revenue. Students were given a set of survey data that Allison had hypothetically collected. The data consisted of the number of students who were willing to pay each of three prices for a ticket to her booth; this was analogous to the data Chris had collected in *The Big Splash*. To determine the best ticket price, students needed to use the notion of cumulative frequency to figure out how many students would buy tickets at each price. In order to estimate total revenue on the day of the fair, they needed to extrapolate these survey results to the whole population. On the assessment instrument students were asked to do three things with the Allison data. First, they were asked to use it to determine the best ticket price. Second, they were asked to estimate total revenue for the school, based on a given ticket price. Third, they were asked to determine the number of people who would buy tickets if she charged a particular price. A composite score was created that summarized students' performance on these three problems. Overall, the test was quite difficult. As Fig. 5.5 shows, both groups of students improved from pre- to posttest and there was no difference at posttest between the groups. Students in both instructional groups learned how to work with survey data that was similar to the data presented in *The Big Splash*.

In summary, our results showed a value added for *Jasper* plus *Jasper Challenges* compared to *Jasper* alone. On some specific measures, such as using data to determine the best ticket price and to estimate total revenue for the school, both groups did equally well. On the score for the overall transfer test (Allison's business plan), the *Jasper* plus *Jasper Challenges* group performed better than *Jasper* alone. Overall, students in the *Jasper* plus *Jasper Challenges* were more likely to give correct answers, and more likely to effectively justify these answers. In addition, they were more likely to spontaneously think to collect data from a representative sample of respondents to make inferences about the larger population.

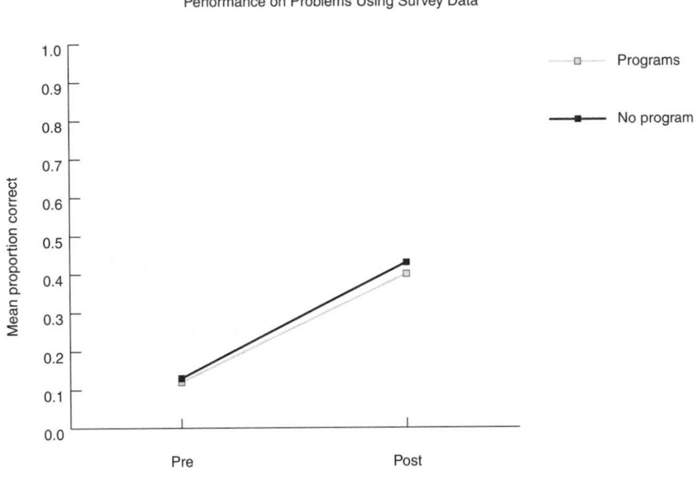

FIG. 5.5. Using survey data composite score.

Student Attitudes

In addition to examining the effect of the *Jasper Challenge* programs on student learning, we were interested in whether these programs might impact student attitudes. We adapted an instrument we had previously developed to measure attitudes related to solving episodes in *The Adventures of Jasper Woodbury* (CTGV, 1992c, 1994; Pellegrino et al., 1991). In the present context, we focus on the results of four scales: interest in business planning, confidence in business planning, anxiety about complex mathematical problem solving, and belief in the value of knowing what other students are thinking.

The results of our analyses indicated that the students who participated in SMART (*Jasper-plus* students), as compared to the students in the *Jasper-only* group, showed significantly greater positive changes in attitudes on two scales: interest and confidence in business planning. Both groups reported decreases in anxiety about complex mathematical problem solving and increases in the perception that knowing the thinking of other students is helpful.

Student Reactions to The Big Challenge

Following their participation in The Big Challenge, we asked students to fill out a 17-item questionnaire in which they used a Likert scale, ranging from 1 to 6, to rate how much they agreed with a particular statement. These questions included topics such as how much they enjoyed the show, how prepared they felt, how confident they felt, how much they enjoyed listening to other students explain their answers, and how they liked the characters in the show. Significant differences between the students who had and had not received the *Jasper Challenge* programs were found on five items. These items and their means are listed in Table 5.4. There were no differences on the remainder of the items. Both groups of students enjoyed

TABLE 5.4
Reactions to The Big Challenge

Significant results		
	Means	
Items	*Jasper-only*	*Jasper-plus*
I felt prepared for *The Big Challenge*.	4.43	5.17
I thought the Challenge questions were easy.	4.19	4.73
I would like to participate in another program like this one.	4.78	5.40
I liked hearing other students explain their thinking on TV.	4.71	5.11
It would have been more exciting to have all the questions be about plans we had never seen before.	3.46	4.44

the characters and style of the show and enjoyed hearing other students explain their answers. The finding that students in the *Jasper-plus* implementation felt more prepared suggests that there may well be value added by the *Jasper Challenge* series in terms of students' self-confidence with respect to performances that reach into the wider community or that deal with a larger mathematical arena. This is an important goal if we want students to enter the broader community as productive and willing mathematical thinkers.

ADDITIONAL STUDIES OF FORMATIVE ASSESSMENT

We have conducted a number of additional SMART studies. Some have involved replications in the context of *The Big Splash*, but we dropped the comparison groups because all teachers wanted the SMART challenges (e.g., Barron, Mayfield-Stewart, Schwartz, & Czarnik, 1996; Vye, Barron, Belynne, & Till, 1996).

Additional studies have involved the use of SMART with other *Jasper* adventures. One set of studies involved *Blueprint for Success*, where students are asked to design a playground. In order to solve the adventure, students must learn about drawing to scale, plus how and why to present top, front, and side views of all of their equipment. They must understand concepts such as area, perimeter, volume, and ways to optimize area given a perimeter of a fixed length. They must also be sure that all requirements for safety are met.

The *Jasper Challenge* programs developed for *Blueprint for Success* were similar to the ones discussed earlier involving *The Big Splash*. For example, students saw data collected from others in SMART Lab, received information about just-in-time tools from Toolbox, and were able to hear other students' explanations of actions and choices in Roving Reporter (which we renamed Kids-online for reasons discussed later).

Changes in the Design of SMART

Our work with SMART in the context of *Blueprint for Success* also involved some changes in format in order to make the SMART concept more feasible to use on a broad scale.

Changes in SMART Lab

In our original work with *The Big Splash*, we had displayed data collected from the classrooms participating in the *Challenge* series. This involved considerable effort to collect data, summarize it in graph form, and show it during the program. For *Blueprint*, we decided to create a SMART Lab that did not rely on collecting data from the students watching the program. Instead, students were informed that they were seeing data collected from a sample of students who had solved *Blueprint*. Examples of data presented during SMART Lab included scatterplots of other students' swing set designs that specified relationships between the desired height of the swing set from the ground and the length of its legs (see Fig. 5.6 and the accompanying CD-ROM). Students were also helped to see problems with various designs; for example, designs where the length of the legs of the A-frame swingset were assumed to be the same height as the swing set (see Fig. 5.7). This was a very common design flaw for many students. Seeing the SMART Lab encouraged them to rethink their designs and revise.

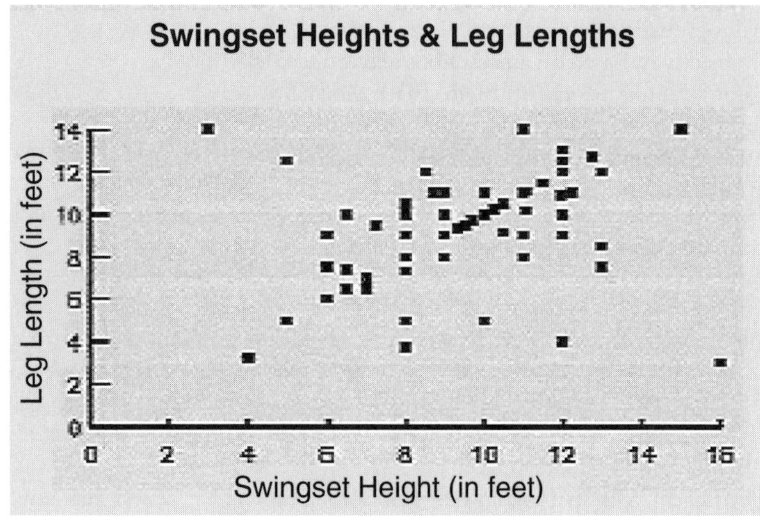

FIG. 5.6. Scatter plot data.

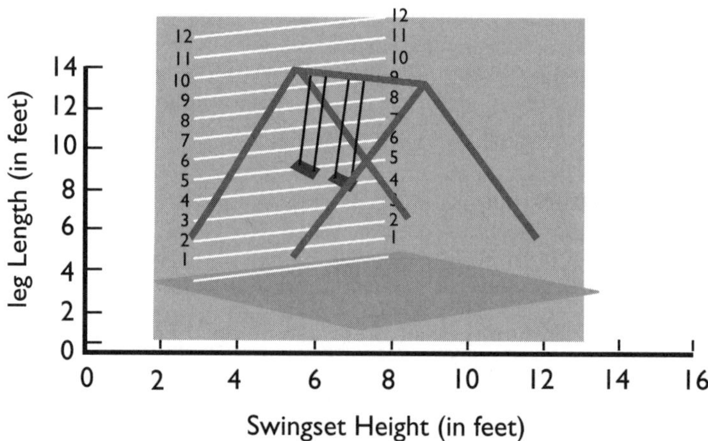

FIG. 5.7. View of swing set where desired height equals length of legs.

We found that students responded extremely well to SMART Lab despite the fact that it did not include their personal data. Teachers encouraged students to plot the data for their class and compare it to the sample data shown in SMART Lab. (It is noteworthy that Internet technology now makes it feasible to collect data from participating classes and display that data, so future SMART Challenges can use the original model of SMART lab if they wish. We say more about moving SMART to the Internet in Chapter 7.)

From Roving Reporter to Kids Online

The SMART Challenges organized around *Blueprint for Success* also changed Roving Reporter to Kids Online. In Roving Reporter, students who were actually participating in the challenge were interviewed and then shown via video during the next program. Needless to say, this was a very time-intensive task. Our change to Kids Online was analogous to our change with respect to data in SMART Lab: We videotaped interviews with students (actually actors) that students in the classroom then viewed and discussed as a class. For example, a student might give a presentation of his or her current thinking about the design of a swing set or a sandbox and then ask for feedback (see the accompanying CD-ROM). Students in the classroom would discuss the presentation for strengths and weaknesses. We designed the presentations to model positive aspects of how to present (e.g., effective uses of visuals) yet contain some errors in thinking that needed correcting. Students in the classroom were very motivated by Kids Online.

SMART Resources on Interactive CD-ROM

A third change we made when designing the SMART Challenges to accompany *Blueprint for Success* involved a decision to make the resources from SMART more easily accessible by the students and teachers in the classroom. The SMART programs for *The Big Splash* had involved linear programs shown on videotape. This made it cumbersome for them to rewind. In SMART *Blueprint*, we made the SMART resources available on CD-ROM, complete with an interface that made it easy to access particular parts of the program. We still encouraged teachers to show each *Jasper Challenge* program in a linear fashion so that the whole class would share a common context (anchor). However, students then had access to the CD-ROM resources in their classroom. They were encouraged to use these as needed as they rethought their designs and wanted guidance about revisions. The availability of the interactive CD-ROM turned out to be extremely valuable. Some examples of the resources available on the CD are discussed next.

Some Examples of Resources for Blueprint. Draw Like an Architect showed different views of playground equipment. Students and teachers could visualize what a swing set, slide, and sandbox looked like when viewed from the top, front, and side (see Fig. 5.8 and the accompanying CD-ROM). We developed this tool

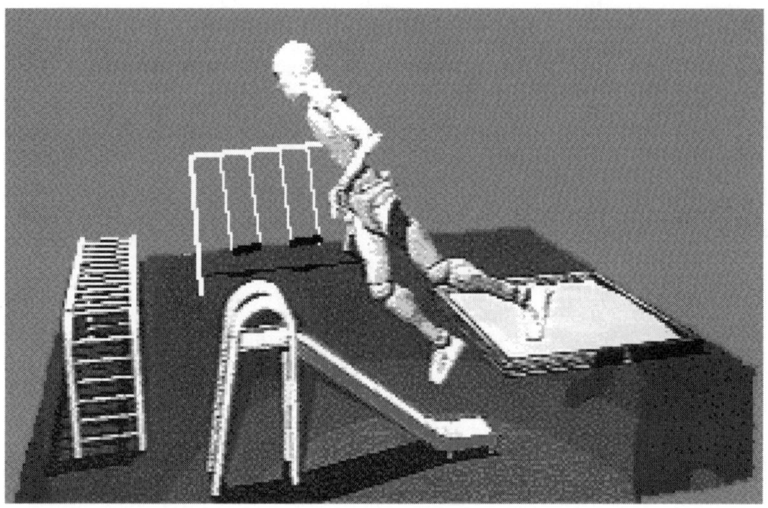

FIG. 5.8. Visual tool to help students imagine what a swing set, slide, and sandbox look like when viewed from the top, front, and side.

because students had a very difficult time with such visualizations and teachers had a hard time communicating the relevant information to them.

A second visual resource was designed to promote students' understanding of the use of graph paper to draw to scale. In our prototype, a person was represented at several different levels of scale (see Fig. 5.9 and the accompanying CD-ROM). This progression helps students understand key representational issues.

A third visual resource helped students see how to use graph paper as a ruler (see Fig. 5.10) in order to facilitate drawing diagonals to scale. The tool was not presented as if it were a worksheet assignment; instead, it was introduced as something that students could use if they wished.

Tools for Teachers

As we developed the CD-ROM resources for the classroom, we faced the problem of efficiently directing students to resources. For example, we encouraged teachers to have students create designs (blueprints) for swing sets in order to make their thinking visible. By looking at the designs, teachers could assess what each student understood and where he or she needed further help. But the task of repeatedly assessing the quality of students' blueprints takes a great deal of time.

To help the teachers with this process, we designed and tested a computer-based tool for assessing students' blueprint designs. The purpose of the tool was to help teachers focus on important features of students' drawings, assess these features, and provide appropriate feedback to help students revise their work. Figure 5.11 shows one of the computer-based rubrics used to assess students' use of scale in their drawings.

FIG. 5.9. Visual tool to promote understanding of the use of graph paper to draw to scale.

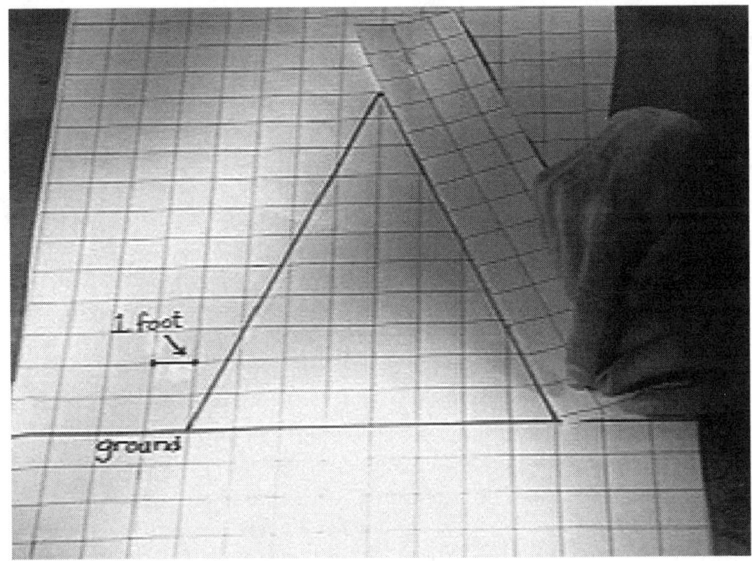

FIG. 5.10. Visual tool to help students make a graph paper ruler to measure lengths in scale drawings.

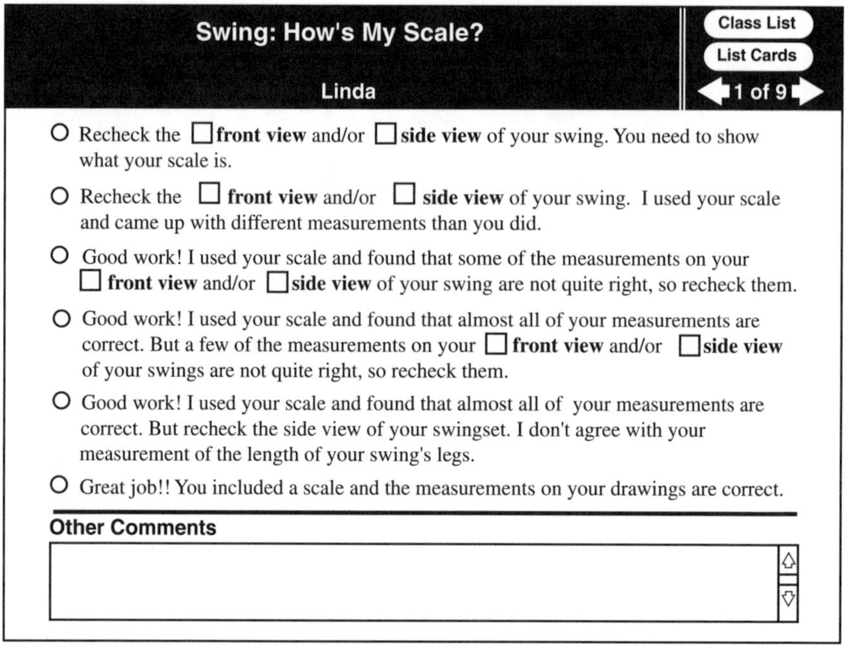

Swing: How's My Scale? Linda	Class List / List Cards / 1 of 9

- O Recheck the ☐ **front view** and/or ☐ **side view** of your swing. You need to show what your scale is.
- O Recheck the ☐ **front view** and/or ☐ **side view** of your swing. I used your scale and came up with different measurements than you did.
- O Good work! I used your scale and found that some of the measurements on your ☐ **front view** and/or ☐ **side view** of your swing are not quite right, so recheck them.
- O Good work! I used your scale and found that almost all of your measurements are correct. But a few of the measurements on your ☐ **front view** and/or ☐ **side view** of your swings are not quite right, so recheck them.
- O Good work! I used your scale and found that almost all of your measurements are correct. But recheck the side view of your swingset. I don't agree with your measurement of the length of your swing's legs.
- O Great job!! You included a scale and the measurements on your drawings are correct.

Other Comments

FIG. 5.11. A HyperCard program for helping teachers give feedback about blueprints.

The suggested feedback contained in the assessment tool is relatively general, but it alerts students to key concepts and provides suggestions for resources that can be used to garner more information. By providing this type of feedback, students assess their own work and diagnose their own particular errors.

Examples of the Benefits of Working With *Blueprint for Success*

We have used a number of measures to assess the effects of *Blueprint for Success* plus the SMART *Jasper Challenges* (Barron et al., 1996; Bransford, Zech, Schwartz, et al., 1996; Zech et al., in press). Teachers all wanted to be in SMART, so we could not find a non-SMART comparison group. Nevertheless, we have multiple sources of data about what students learned over time. All students were from inner-city schools that typically did quite poorly in mathematics.

We devised an overall test of geometry concepts relevant to SMART *Blueprint*—concepts such as area, perimeter, volume, and drawing to scale. The test is difficult, especially for fifth graders. Data illustrated in Fig. 5.12 show gains on the geometry test for two different groups of students who participated in SMART in 1994 and 1995. Data in Fig. 5.13 show gains by achievement level for the 1994 group. There were no interactions with achievement levels, indicating that students at all levels of initial achievement gained equally well. Similar results were found for the 1995 group.

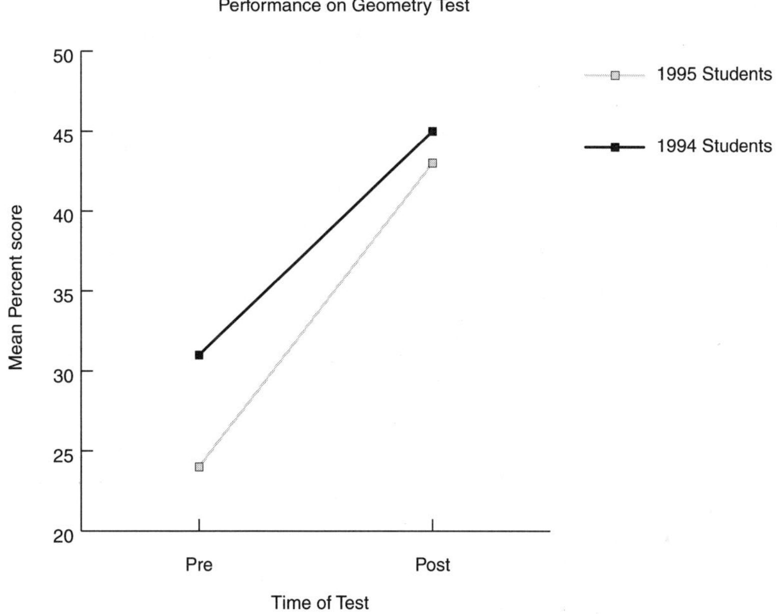

FIG. 5.12. Overall performance by 1994 and 1995 students.

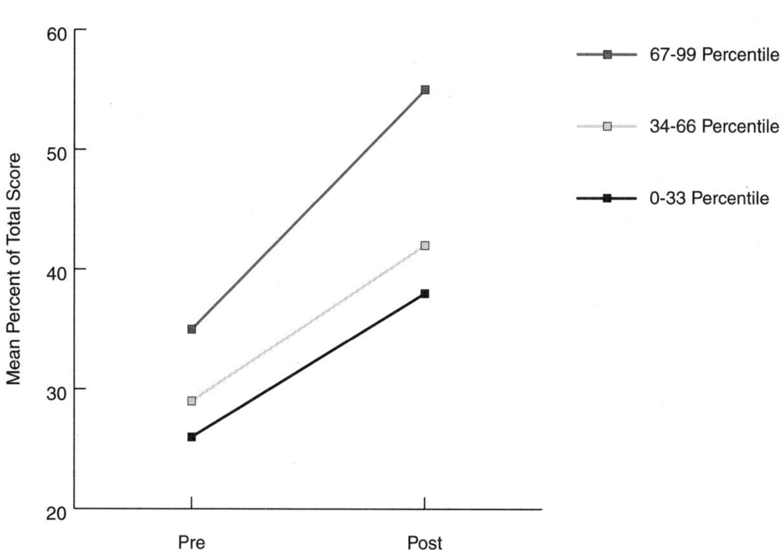

FIG. 5.13. Performance by 1994 students in each of three mathematics achievement groups.

We also devised measures to assess changes in students' understanding of scale drawings and blueprints. On both a pretest and posttest, we asked 106 students to make drawings of a chair—drawings that would be precise enough for a builder to build it. The pre- and posttest drawings for each student were shown to reviewers with no designation as to which drawing was from the pretest and which was from the posttest. Reviewers compared the drawings on the dimensions of scale, realistic measurements, and types of drawings included to convey accurate measurements (i.e., front view, side view, top view). Based on this analysis, reviewers were able to correctly classify each student's pretest versus posttest drawings in 97% of the instances. In short, almost everyone improved.

Data from our studies also showed that students and teachers made extensive use of teaching tools that were available as resources. Some of the resources were embedded teaching scenes from *Jasper*, some were on the SMART CD-ROM, and some were in the form of peers, teaching, and handouts. Observations indicated that, after accessing appropriate resources, students often created designs that were considerably more advanced than they were prior to using the tools. In addition, when we interviewed students about their work in designing a playground for the challenge in *Blueprint for Success*, students often referred to these resources as they explained the revisions they had made in their work (see Fig. 5.14).

From Problems to Projects

Our experiences with SMART Challenges have also allowed us to study some advantages of moving from problem-based to project-based learning (Barron, 1996). In most of our SMART studies, students began with problem-based learning (e.g., *Jasper* and its analogs and extensions plus SMART programs relevant to the problem). After working in the problem-based environment, students got the opportunity to work on actual community-based projects that had real consequences for their everyday world. For example, after working with the challenge of using data to create a business plan for *The Big Splash*, students have had opportunities to gather data relevant to their school that would allow them to create a business plan to present to the principal or other outside party. Plans based on good data and well-reasoned arguments were actually implemented. Thus, students in one set of SMART classrooms created business plans that enabled them to eventually sponsor a fun fair for their entire school (Barron et al., 1996). In another case, students working on *Blueprint for Success* eventually earned the right to try their hand at designing a playhouse to be put into preschool environments. Well-designed playhouses were actually built and donated in the students' names.

Studies of Problem- and Project-based Learning

One reason for beginning with problem-based learning and then moving to projects is that the opportunity to work on shared, concrete problems such as *Jasper* enhances the quality of students' subsequent projects. The problem-based environ-

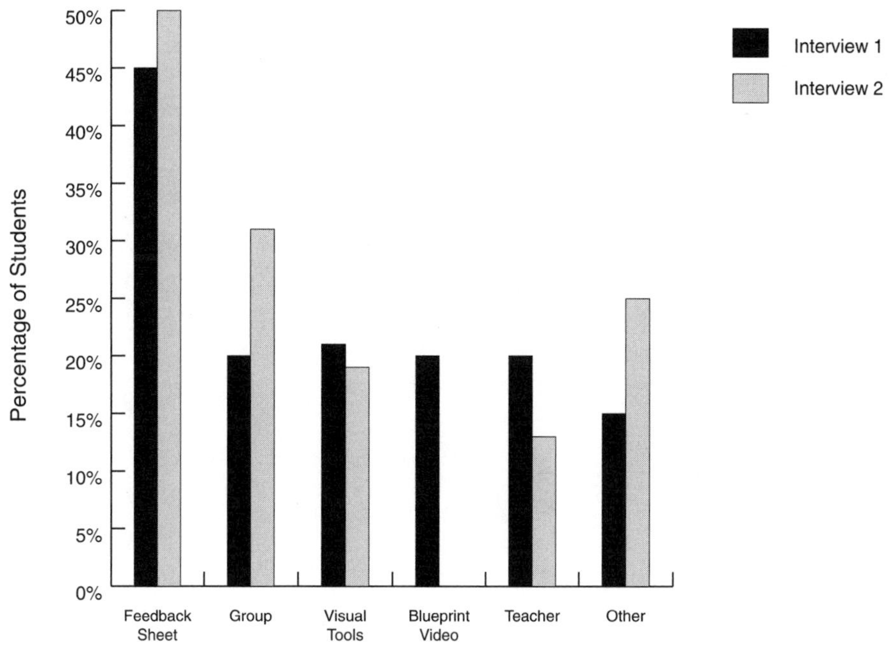

FIG. 5.14. Percentage of students who reported using different resources to revise their swing set designs.

ment provides a common ground for communication that helps students' subsequent conversations because they can refer to common referents. These environments also help students develop collaboration skills, in part because they provide opportunities for different students to notice different things about the anchor problems. Students, therefore, learn to appreciate the contributions of their peers. The scaffolds built into the *Jasper* adventures (see Chapter 3) also help students who lack the background knowledge necessary to successfully complete various projects.

A study by Moore et al. (1996) illustrates how even a brief opportunity to engage in problem-based learning can facilitate the quality of subsequent projects. Two groups of students were asked to work in small groups to create a business plan for a fun fair to be held at their school. They were to think up a fun-fair event that would be of interest to their fellow students and present data showing that there was indeed interest. In addition, they were to explain the expenses involved.

Students in both strands of the experiment spent 1 hour discussing and then writing up their business plans. Students in the experimental strand had a prior experience of first attempting to solve *The Big Splash* over three class periods; students in the comparison strand did not have this problem-based experience.

Data were analyzed from a number of perspectives. For present purposes, we present data from a condition where judges, blind to the experimental condition, looked at the written plans for the school fun fair and rank-ordered them in terms of quality. Results are illustrated in Fig. 5.15. Plans written by the group that first received problem-based learning were generally of much higher quality than were plans from the project-based-only group.

Students' Reflections on the Importance of Their Experiences

A second reason for encouraging both problem-based and project-based curricula is that the combination appears to be very beneficial to students. We assessed this idea by interviewing sixth-grade students who had been involved in problem-

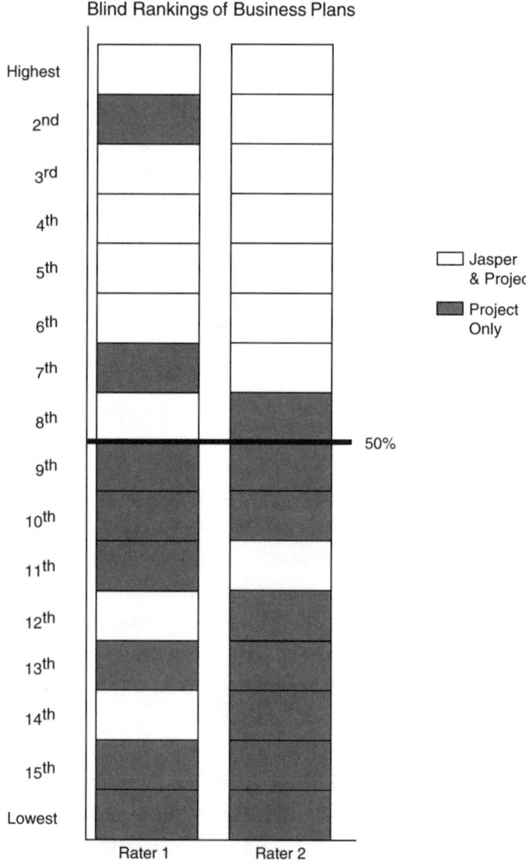

FIG. 5.15. Data comparing project-based to problem plus project-based learning.

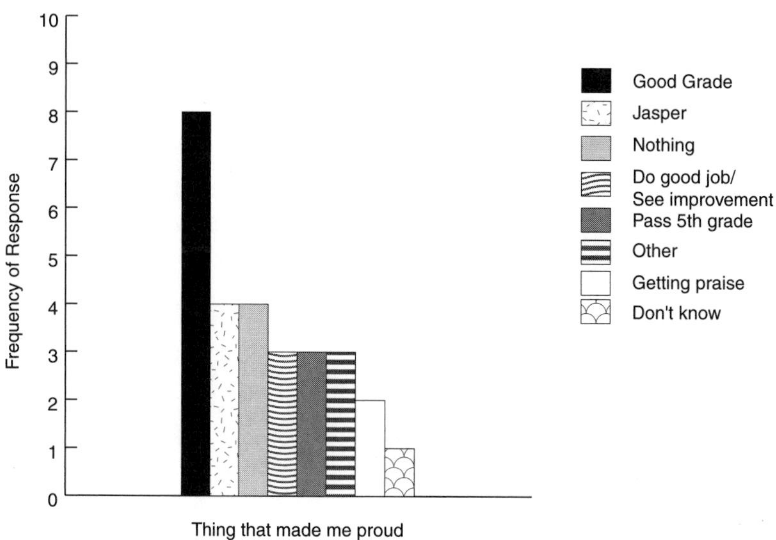

FIG. 5.16. Responses to "Did you do anything in gr. 5 that made you feel proud?"

plus project-based learning during the fifth grade. During the first half of fifth grade, they had solved *Blueprint for Success* and then designed playhouses that were actually built and donated to the community. During the last half of fifth grade, they had solved *The Big Splash* and then created business plans for events to include in a fun fair for their school—a fun fair that was actually held.

Our interviews were conducted by people who were not associated in the students' minds with Vanderbilt University or the fifth-grade *Jasper* projects. The interviewers began by asking students to think about last year when they were fifth graders and describe things that made them feel proud and creative. Interviewers also asked them to name things that they would like to do again. The results were extremely interesting. For each question asked, the answer provided by the majority of students was "*Jasper*" (which in their minds included the projects that followed *Jasper*). Results are illustrated in Figs. 5.16, 5.17, and 5.18.

It is instructive to note that different students answered "*Jasper*" to each of those questions—the data do not simply come from a small subset of students who said "*Jasper*" to everything. Across the three questions noted, more than 50% of the students spontaneously mentioned *Jasper* as something that was very special to them in fifth grade. When students were explicitly asked about *Jasper* later in the interview, nearly all said that it was a very important experience for them.

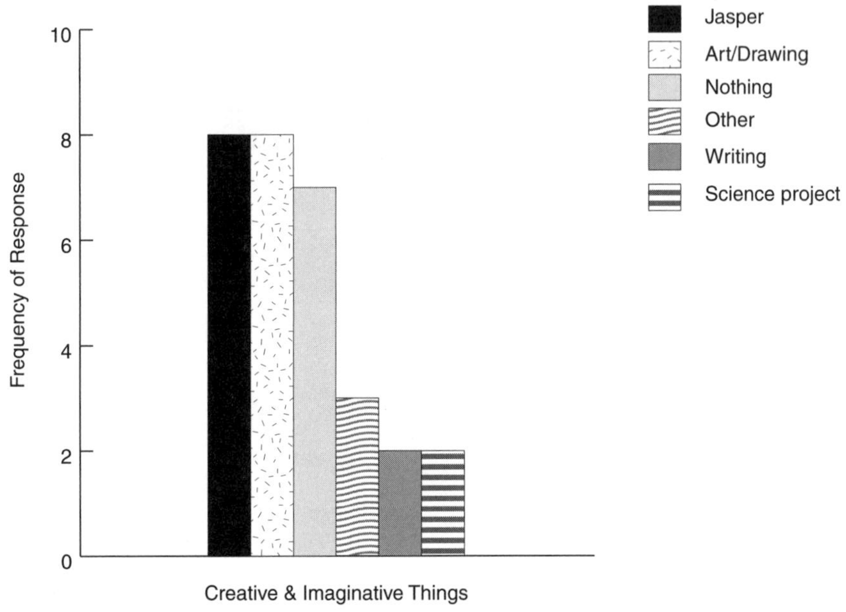

FIG. 5.17. Responses to "Did you do anything where you used your creativity and imagination?"

EXPANDED INSTRUCTIONAL MODELS OF *JASPER*

Our experiences with the effectiveness of SMART Challenges have prompted us to rethink our recommendations for instruction surrounding all the *Jasper* adventures. We are not yet able to provide teachers with SMART Challenges for all of the *Jaspers* (although we are working on ways to do this by using the Internet). Nevertheless, data from SMART have prompted us to recommend that teachers provide students with multiple opportunities to Identify problems to be solved, Develop plans, Act on them, Receive feedback and Revise as necessary. We call these I DARE cycles. They are designed to help make students' thinking visible so that it can be analyzed, tested, and refined both by the students themselves and by teachers and peers.

I DARE and *Rescue at Boone's Meadow*

Our early work with *Jasper* (see Chapter 4) did not explicitly emphasize multiple I DARE cycles. When solving *Rescue at Boone's Meadow* (where the ultralight is used to rescue a wounded eagle), for example, we encouraged teachers to let students brainstorm, work out their best plan in a group, present their plan to the rest of the group, and then discuss the strengths and weaknesses of different plans. This approach worked well and resulted in very encouraging transfer data (e.g., CTGV, 1992c; Van Haneghan et al., 1992). Nevertheless, student learning can be strengthened with an explicit emphasis on I DARE.

A typical I DARE cycle for *RBM* might begin with brainstorming problems and possible plans and then asking groups to try one plan at a time. For example, they might have Jasper walk to Hilda's with the eagle and then drive. How long would this take? Because the time would be quite long (over 5 hours), students can be encouraged to try a different plan.

A second plan might be to fly the ultralight straight to Boone's Meadow (where Jasper and the eagle are waiting) and then fly straight back. This is a great plan if it is possible, but it is not. The plane cannot hold enough fuel to get there and back without breaking the limits of its payload.

A third plan might be to fly to Boone's Meadow and bring along an extra gallon of gas to refuel there. Then the flight could go from Boone's Meadow to Hilda's and from Hilda's to Cumberland City. This plan will work, but students might be encouraged to think about even faster plans. (For example, since the ultralight's maximum speed is only 30 miles per hour, it is faster to drive from Hilda's to Cumberland City in a car or truck along the road. There are no roads linking any of the other points.)

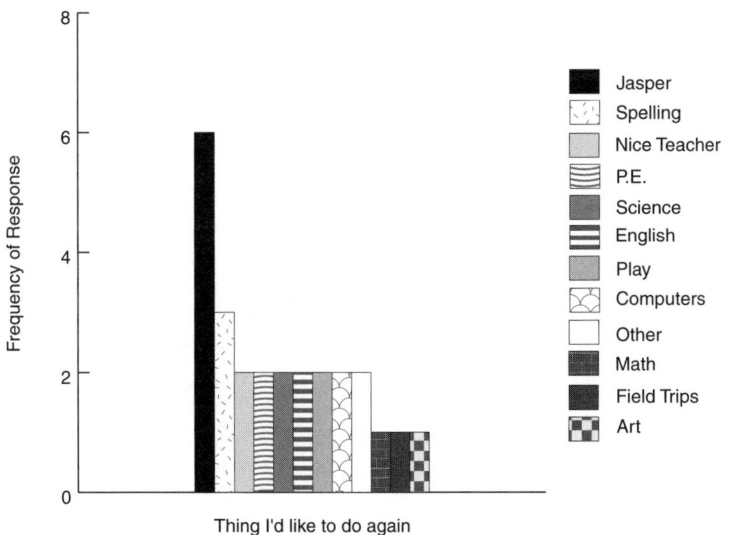

FIG. 5.18. Responses to "What would you like to have a chance to do again?"

A major advantage of emphasizing multiple I DARE cycles is that students have numerous opportunities to determine trip time, fuel consumption, and payloads. This helps them develop levels of competence and confidence that are less likely to develop if students only choose one plan and work it through.

I DARE cycles can also be illustrated in the context of *Blueprint for Success,* even when it is solved outside the context of SMART. We encourage teachers to provide students with multiple I DARE opportunities by first helping them design and receive feedback about swing sets, then slides, then sandboxes, and finally the shape of the fence for the playground.

I DARE and Smart Tools

Our work with Smart Tools also makes extensive use of I DARE cycles. For example, in *Working Smart,* students are challenged to create a set of Smart Tools that will allow them to easily solve large classes of problems. Initially, students have a very difficult time creating Smart Tools that are appropriate to a particular class of problems. They need multiple chances to create tools, test their mettle, and revise them so that they work effectively. After several I DARE cycles, students' abilities to create effective Smart Tools increase rather dramatically (e.g., see Bransford, Zech, Schwartz, et al., 1996).

Software Support for Feedback and Revision

We are also continuing to develop software that helps students learn by engaging in multiple I DARE cycles. For example, Biswas and Crews of Vanderbilt's Computer Science Department have taken the lead in helping us develop *Jasper Adventure Player* software that provides multiple opportunities for feedback and reflection. For example, the software illustrated in Fig. 5.19 provides coaching to students as they attempt to solve *Jasper* adventures such as *Rescue at Boone's Meadow.* Students enter their solution strategies and receive opportunities to see simulations of the effects of their decisions. If the plane runs out of fuel, it crashes. If the flight time has not been adequately determined, the plane does not land in the right place. Overall, the software provides a convenient workspace for keeping track of steps and calculations, plus a simulation component that the student can use at various points in the problem-solving process. The software also provides coaching when students need prompts to think about ways to optimize their plans. Students can also use the software to change the variables in the problem (e.g., the capacity or speed of the ultralight) in order to create analogous problems for others to solve.

Crews, Biswas, Goldman, and Bransford (in press) studied the effects of the *Jasper Adventure Player* on student learning. One group of students saw the *Jasper* adventure and then worked with the *Adventure Player* software with all its functions intact (full system). A second group also worked with the software, but its simulation and coaching functions were disabled (core system). Data indicated that these functions had powerful effects on students' problem-solving performances. For example, students who received the full system made few errors in solving *RBM* (Fig. 5.20).

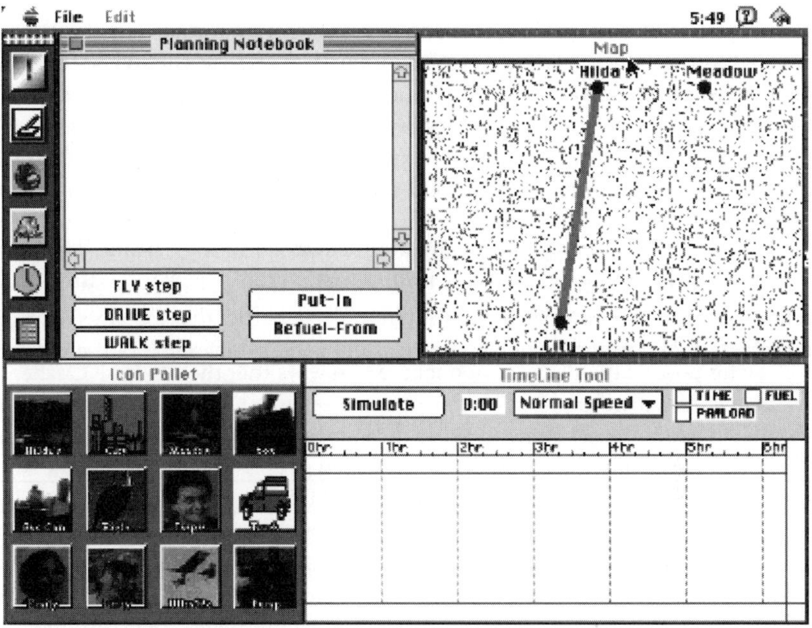

FIG. 5.19. A screen from the *Jasper Adventure Player* software.

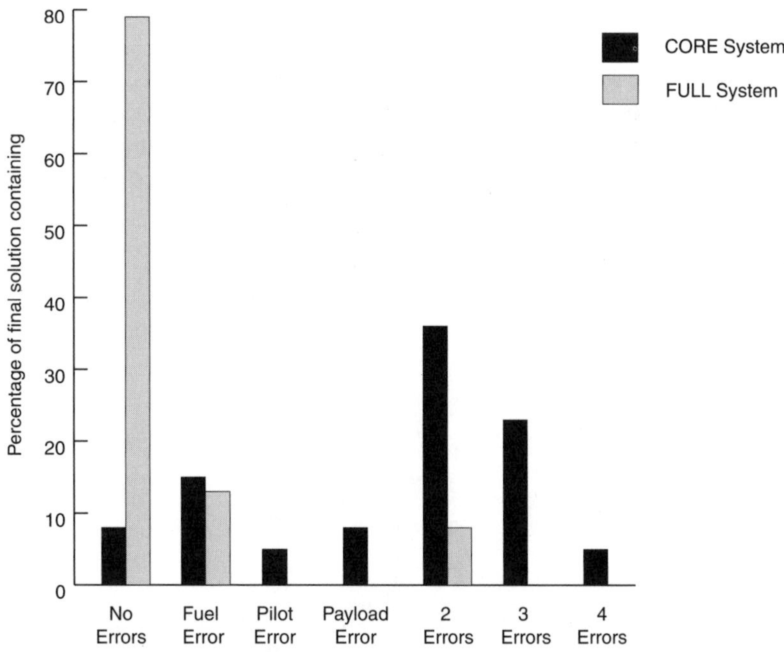

FIG. 5.20. Percentage of errors in students' final *RBM* solutions.

The full system also helped students optimize their solution plans (Fig. 5.21). The findings illustrate the importance of seeing simulations of one's plans and receiving coaching when workable plans were still not optimal (in terms of taking the least amount of time to get the eagle to the vet).

SUMMARY AND CONCLUSIONS

Our focus in this chapter was on the importance of feedback for learning. This point seems obvious, but opportunities for feedback are often absent in classrooms. A focus on formative assessment attempts to rectify this situation and, in the process, increase students' learning.

A major portion of our discussion focused on ways that the SMART Challenge series moved from an emphasis on summative assessment to formative assessment. We devised a number of studies to assess the value added of SMART. Data indicate that it increases student learning when compared to classrooms that had the same content and instruction but did not receive SMART.

We also discussed the value of extending problem-based instruction such as *Jasper* with project-based instruction that is tailored to the local community and has real consequences. The quality of students' projects can be enhanced when they first have opportunities to engage in problem-based curricula. Data also indicate that projects are very important. When students were asked to look back on their previous year in school, their participation in projects is spontaneously mentioned as having been very important to them.

Work with SMART has prompted us to emphasize the importance of formative assessment for all *Jasper* instruction, irrespective of the presence of SMART. Use of the I DARE cycle helps students learn more from their *Jasper* experiences because it provides multiple opportunities for students to test their mettle and revise as needed. Specially designed software (e.g., the *Jasper Adventure Player* software) also provides students with opportunities for feedback, and the feedback has clear effects on their problem-solving performance.

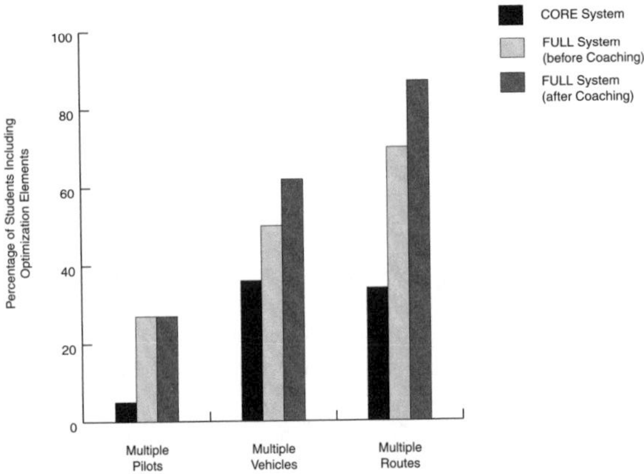

FIG. 5.21. Optimization by considering multiple plans.

6

Teacher Learning and the Importance of Learning Communities

Our goal in this chapter is to discuss the *Jasper* project from the perspective of teacher learning. We use the term *teacher learning* to refer to learning by teachers and learning from teachers. As we discuss later, both kinds of learning are facilitated by the development of learning communities where people feel free to share their concerns and ideas.

We noted in Chapter 1 that the major reason for creating *Jasper* was to encourage teachers to work with us to better understand learning in classrooms. This strategy worked extremely well. *Jasper* has brought us into contact with hundreds of outstanding teachers who have taught us invaluable lessons about teaching, learning, and classrooms as learning environments. They have also helped us better understand the challenges involved in implementing new programs such as *Jasper*—challenges such as understanding how to fit *Jasper* into their already-packed curriculum, changing their teaching and assessment practices to accommodate it, becoming comfortable with the technology involved in using it, and helping parents and other community members understand its value.

We begin with a discussion of our initial attempts to work with teachers and the lessons they taught us about the need to change our approach. We then discuss some of our own experiences as learners—experiences that helped us understand the challenges faced by teachers as they attempted to implement *Jasper*—challenges that highlight the need for ongoing support rather than for one-shot workshops. An emphasis on the need for ongoing support leads to an exploration of the concept of learning communities—communities that promote individual and group learning by creating a climate where people can share their ideas and concerns.

EARLY LESSONS ABOUT PROFESSIONAL DEVELOPMENT WORKSHOPS

One of our first major lessons from teachers occurred during the summer of 1990 as we prepared for the *Jasper* implementation project that involved *Jasper* sites in nine states. As discussed in Chapter 4, (see also CTGV, 1994) Chancellor Wyatt of Vanderbilt University arranged for a three-way partnership involving Vanderbilt, corporations, and schools in order to implement the *Jasper* series.

Ten corporations sponsored the implementation in 11 school districts distributed over nine states. Sixteen different schools participated: five inner-city schools, five suburban, and six in rural or small town locations. Eleven corporate representatives and 28 teachers (largely volunteers) attended a 2-week summer training institute at Vanderbilt.

Challenges of Preparation

As we prepared for the 2-week Summer Institute, we struggled with the challenge of being responsive to the diversity of needs and experiences of the teachers and corporate representatives who would attend the workshop. The corporate representatives brought varied backgrounds although all had information technology and computer expertise. Teaching experience of the teachers varied from 4 to 25 years and a variety of certifications and degrees held (including mathematics and nonmathematics teachers) were reflected in the group. Some taught in self-contained classrooms and others taught where instruction was departmentalized.

The classes that would be using the *Jasper* series were predominantly fifth and sixth grade, although two fourth-grade classrooms also participated. Intellectual abilities of the children ranged from mildly retarded to gifted, as described by the teachers.

We decided that approximately one-third of the Summer Institute time would be devoted to solving *Jasper* adventures and brainstorming teaching ideas and lesson plans; one-third to computer skills; and one-third to multimedia-related competencies (i.e., using scanner and audio recording equipment and software) that would allow teachers to help students conduct research relevant to themes in *Jasper* adventures (e.g., principles of flight, endangered species) and then make multimedia presentations for others to observe. To the degree possible, we decided to anchor the computer and technology skills training in the context of *Jasper* (CTGV, 1990). For example, we had participants practice word processing on lesson plans for a *Jasper* adventure; they used spreadsheets in solving the adventures. Additional details of the activities are provided in CTGV (1994, in press).

The Importance of Formative Assessment

In retrospect, our workshop would have been a disaster except for one decision: to conduct in-depth daily assessments of participants' feelings about the workshop (see the discussion of formative assessment in Chapter 5). At the end of each day, guardian angels (staff and graduate students from Peabody College at Vanderbilt) interviewed participants and asked them to fill out written sheets indicating what was working and what needed to be changed. Guardian angels then discussed issues with the participants. We made it clear that we wanted people to be brutally honest with the guardian angels. Our staff made a commitment to go over these assessments each day and make any necessary changes for the next day.

The feedback we received at the end of the first day was devastating. We were too academic. We used obscure terms that were hard to follow. We talked too much. Everyone wanted more hands-on experiences with *Jasper*, lesson planning, and software; then they wanted time to discuss these experiences. They didn't want to be lectured at.

We had done our best to tone down being academics. Our presentations on the first day represented the best use of multimedia we could muster. They included rich visual and auditory information and were sprinkled with humorous scenes and quotations. But, in retrospect, we have to admit that the teachers and corporate representatives were right. We were still telling and showing even though we were doing it with great multimedia support.

Luckily, the feedback indicated that the first day had not been an entire disaster. Everyone enjoyed the opportunity to watch a *Jasper* adventure and then solve it in groups. This allowed them to get involved rather than simply listen to and watch us present.

The next morning, the LTC staff began the workshop by summarizing the feedback from the previous day, apologizing for being so long-winded, and suggesting plans for revising the rest of the workshop. The reactions of the participants were extremely gratifying. The teachers were especially pleased that we had paid attention to their feedback. As we got to know them better throughout the course of the workshop, they confided that they were not used to being listened to—especially by academics.

Through their daily feedback, the teachers and corporate representatives helped us make a gradual transition from teaching by telling and showing to learning by doing and reflecting. Whether we worked on new *Jasper* adventures, software, or lesson planning, we began with generative activities and then had different groups present their ideas and discuss one another's perspectives. For example, we had groups generate their own lesson plans for a *Jasper* adventure and then showed video clips of others teaching *Jasper*. These images gave teachers contrast sets (to their own, self-generated images) that generated lively discussions. We also brought in local teachers who had taught *Jasper* to fifth and sixth graders. The teachers outlined what they had done and then answered questions. These sessions were very interactive and quite well received.

We carried the generative model into the multimedia training, too. As an Institute challenge, we asked each group of participants to prepare a *Jasper*-related multimedia project; on the last day of the Institute, each team presented theirs to the group. This proved to be very exciting for the participants. They were eager to share ideas with others at the workshop, but especially to have presentations that they could take back to their local communities to show principals, parents, community members, and students. The idea of making presentations became so important that we set up a staffed computer lab in the participants' hotel in the evenings. The lab was used with very high frequency.

Each team left the Institute with *Jasper* materials, a timeline for teaching each of four adventures and administering assessment instruments that we devised, and the expectation of receiving their equipment (with which they had worked at the Institute) within 2 weeks.

Skill Development

Figure 6.1 shows participants' evaluations of their own professional development during the 2-week Institute. As is obvious from the graphs, participants indicated significant improvement in skills related to technology, as well as having learned about teaching *Jasper*. Teachers also expressed concern about what would happen when they got back home and had all their regular responsibilities plus *Jasper*. It was this very concern that had led to the teaming of a corporate representative with each pair of teachers. We hoped that the corporate representative might provide assistance. We also hoped that each pair of teachers would be able to provide support for each other when they returned to their school campuses. We planned to bring teachers back together at the conclusion of the implementation year. Their insights from this reunion are summarized in the next section.

LEARNING FROM TEACHERS

We attempted to keep in touch with the teachers throughout the 1990–1991 academic year—through telephone conversations, America Online (an electronic network) and occasional visits to classrooms. During the summer of 1991, the majority of the teachers met with us in Nashville. They were interviewed individually and then invited to engage in group sessions. The teachers introduced us to a number of important ideas.

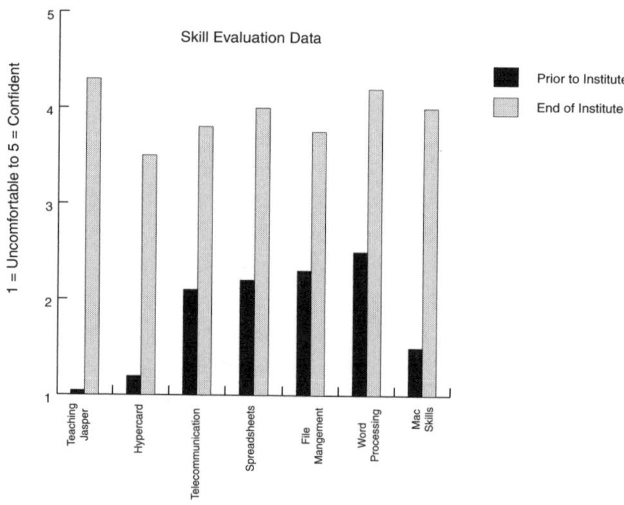

FIG. 6.1. Summer Institute participants' professional development.

Information About Students' Reactions to *Jasper*

First, teachers discussed their students' reactions to the *Jasper* adventures. Examples of the teachers' reports were discussed in Chapter 4 on assessment. Summaries of their insights include:

1. Most students were highly motivated to solve the *Jasper* adventures.
2. Students who were traditionally less successful academically often gained respect from their peers because they were able to make important contributions to problem solving.
3. Students who were traditionally successful academically could not dominate the class as easily because the problems were too complex. Some initially disliked *Jasper* for this reason but eventually learned to collaborate.
4. Parents and other community members learned to appreciate *Jasper* by watching an adventure, attempting to solve it (in groups), and being helped by the students.
5. Parents of many of the students mentioned that their children discussed *Jasper* at home and, in many cases, developed very positive attitudes toward the study of mathematics.
6. Students disliked our assessments but loved the *Jasper* Challenge series.

Multimedia Publications

Teachers also helped us understand why one component of our research project—the students-as-producers component—was less than successful. Our plan was to have students use the *Jasper* adventures as anchors for research on important topics that would culminate in multimedia products. For *Rescue At Boone's Meadow*, for example, students might choose to research eagles and other threatened or endangered species, principles of flight, the history of airplanes, the history of laws designed to protect animals, and so forth. We had also discussed the idea of students creating their own *Jasper*-like adventures that they could present to others. These could be paper-and-pencil or involve video taken by the students or other members of the local community.

Only a few classes ended up doing research related to the *Jasper* adventures or attempted to create their own *Jasper*-like adventures. The teachers helped us understand why. First, it was difficult for them to find time in the curriculum to add the research projects. It was hard enough to find the time to solve the *Jasper* adventures; most teachers used them instead of working on traditional word problems. However, there were few slots in the curriculum for extended projects. The teachers explained that more attention needed to be paid to curriculum planning if we wanted students to conduct extended projects and research.

A second reason why only a few classes engaged in *Jasper*-related projects was the time involved in finding resources that were appropriate for the research. Most school libraries did not have extensive readings on topics such as eagles and endangered species or principles of flight. To collect a set of readings took an enormous amount of time on the part of the teachers, and they were already overburdened by the need to create new lesson plans for teaching *Jasper*, plus explaining to parents and other members of the community what they were doing. This helped us realize that we needed to provide support not only for curriculum planning, but for curriculum materials as well.

A third reason why the research projects were often not completed was related to the technology expertise needed to use the *Jasper* multimedia publishing software that we had created. Teachers had received training on this software during the 2-week workshop in the summer. However, this training was very brief. In addition, for most teachers, there was a several-month lag between the training and the use of the software. Therefore, a great deal of relearning needed to take place. In addition, there were the usual glitches with the technology (the printer stopped working, etc.) that presented barriers to the teachers and discouraged them from relying on it extensively as part of their teaching plans.

In several of our sites, representatives from the local businesses that had sponsored the teachers served as technology consultants who helped the teachers use the software and fix any technology problems. We learned that this type of technology support is crucial for the success of any project. Without it, teachers make the choice to go with what is reliable for them. What is reliable is the use of worksheets, blackboards, and overheads. Unless they have support for help with technical breakdowns, many teachers will prefer to use these old, reliable technologies rather than continually risk breakdowns in their lessons because the modern technology does not work.

Uses of Electronic Mail

We had provided accounts to America Online and had expected a flurry of messages to us and to other teachers. However, the volume of electronic communication was quite low. A major reason was that teachers did not have phone lines in their rooms and, hence, could not connect to America Online unless they went someplace else—usually the teachers' lounge. This meant that they could not integrate long-distance electronic communication into their classroom teaching. In addition, it meant that they had almost no time to use the technology to communicate. This experience motivated us to see what would happen if teachers had access to a computer and modem at home.

Following the *Jasper* Implementation experiment, Chancellor Wyatt began the Vanderbilt Virtual School Project. Its goal was to connect teachers to an electronic network. In cities across Tennessee, businesses donated computers to teachers who could take them home and connect to the network with a modem. Under these conditions, we found that teachers' use of the electronic network increased significantly.

An interesting side note on this development involves a conversation with a colleague from another state who noted that the Vanderbilt Virtual School Project was wonderful but would not work in his part of the country. He explained that, in his state, the teacher's union would object to teachers having to extend their school day and do work in the evening. We noted that the teachers' use of computers at home was voluntary rather than mandatory, but he argued that the unions would still object. We hope this is not true.

Feedback About the *Jasper* Challenge Series

The teachers were extremely enthusiastic about the *Jasper* Challenge series. As noted in Chapter 4, the first *Jasper* Challenge took place near the end of the nine-state Implementation Project and was organized around students' experiences with *Rescue at Boone's Meadow*. It was projected by satellite and asked students to Pick The Expert from a panel of people who were all posing as experts on airplanes, headwinds and tailwinds, and principles of flight. Members of the panel each answered a series of questions from a game show host (character Larry Peterson in a tuxedo). At the end of the show, students voted on their choice of the real expert and phoned in their answers to our studio. A graph showing data accumulated over all the sites was then presented and students could see where they stood relative to all the others watching the show.

The teachers reported that their students were very excited by the *Jasper* Challenge. The fact that they were able to respond to the challenge and see data from other classes of students seemed to be an important part of their enthusiasm.

Feedback from teachers revealed three additional insights about the Challenge series. First, the Challenge series became a high-stakes event for the community that resulted in many things being done that might otherwise have taken much longer. For example, schools that were due to have satellite downlinks "some time soon" suddenly had them installed in time for the *Jasper* Challenge. Others forged links with local businesses that helped them arrange for downlinks or that supplied space for all the local classrooms to meet together to watch the *Jasper* Challenge. In one school, the prospect of being able to participate in the *Jasper Satellite Challenge* looked dim until a sixth-grade girl took it upon herself to call the governor of the state. She did not get through to him, but her actions generated enough attention to get a local TV station to run a story and also provide a portable downlink.

Second, many teachers noted that the Challenge helped unite them with the students because they all faced this outside challenge or common enemy. Teachers felt as much on the line as the students in helping everyone prepare. But everyone also understood that the overall goal was to learn rather than be evaluated.

Third, several teachers noted that they had not found enough time to help their students work through all the analog and extension problems necessary to prepare for the Challenge and their students had not done particularly well. This helped us see the need to place more emphasis on events that prepared everyone for the Challenge. As discussed in Chapter 5, our SMART Challenges eventually evolved into formative assessment opportunities designed to foster learning. In contrast, our initial *Jasper* Challenge was primarily a final, summative assessment event.

THE NEED FOR ONGOING FEEDBACK AND REFLECTION

Following the nine-state *Jasper* Implementation Project, we had numerous additional opportunities to collaborate with teachers. The most important message from all of them has been the need for ongoing support for learning in the form of feedback about their practices and opportunities for reflection and revision. The teachers were making hundreds of decisions daily and wanted to make the best decisions. In the absence of feedback and opportunities for ongoing discussion, they were unsure if they were making the right decisions. The fact that teachers emphasized this issue again and again helped us realize that the idea of cycles of feedback and revision discussed in Chapter 5 applied not only to students in classrooms but to all learners. The changes we were asking teachers to make were much too complex to be communicated succinctly in a workshop and then enacted in isolation once the teachers returned to their schools.

In retrospect, we have to admit that, initially, we only partially understood what the teachers were telling us about the need for ongoing support for learning. We did not truly appreciate what they were saying until we had a formative experience that placed us in the role of novices rather than experts. Throughout all our work with Jasper, we had been the experts. Our formative experience involved a new, collaborative project with other research groups that took us out of the expert role and made us novices who were trying to implement someone else's program. What we learned was unanticipated, humbling, and extremely important for all our subsequent work.

The formative experience occurred in the context of our participation in the Schools for Thought project (e.g., Lamon et al., 1996). This project arose from meetings sponsored by the James S. McDonnell CSEP program (CSEP stands for Cognitive Studies of Educational Practice). Participants in the CSEP program had each developed and studied individual school-based programs that data showed were quite effective (see Lamon et al., 1996; McGilly, 1994). Nevertheless, a number of CSEP grantees speculated that their results were limited by the fact that, at most, their programs involved only 60 to 90 minutes of a student's day. What would happen if individual projects were combined so that they would encompass the entire school day? Was it possible for teachers to endure a constructivist approach to curriculum, instruction, and assessment for their entire day? Would the different programs compliment one another or conflict?

For the first phase of the Schools for Thought project, the three programs we decided to combine were *Jasper*; the Fostering Communities of Learners (FCL) project developed by Brown and Campione (e.g., Brown & Campione, 1994; Lamon et al., 1996); and Scardamalia and Bereiter's Computer Supported Intentional Learning Environment (CSILE) project (Lamon et al., 1996; Scardamalia, Bereiter, & Lamon, 1994). Ultimately, the plan is to combine a number of additional, promising programs into the SFT project. Many are being developed in the context of CSEP (see Bruer, 1993; McGilly, 1994).

It is beyond the scope of this book to describe the FCL and CSILE programs (e.g., Brown & Campione, 1994, in press; Scardamalia et al., 1994). For present purposes, the important point is that our group in the LTC was suddenly placed in the role of novices whose job it was to integrate these programs with *Jasper* in order to implement SFT in two sixth-grade classrooms in Nashville. The lessons we learned were extremely valuable.

First, we were not total novices with respect to FCL and CSILE. We had attended 6 years of annual CSEP meetings where we heard about these programs as they developed over the years, and where they heard about the evolution of *Jasper*. In addition, we were friends with the program developers and, hence, frequently exchanged papers, phone calls, e-mail, and the like. We knew the theories that guided FCL and CSILE and we knew the data that showed why these programs were so useful. As a result, we could easily talk about FCL and CSILE. But we discovered a huge gap between this kind of knowledge and the ability to do FCL and CSILE on a day-to-day basis in the classroom. As we attempted to implement the two programs, we began to realize that we did not truly understand either of them.

We found ourselves saying the following when talking with the FCL and CSILE experts: "Enough about theory. Tell us what to do to make this work. How do we get started? What should we expect during the first several weeks of the program and how will we know that it's working? How do we monitor the learning of an entire classroom full of students who are working independently or in groups? How do we convince administrators and parents that this is going to be worthwhile?"

These are exactly the kinds of questions that teachers had asked us about *Jasper*. After one of our workshops with teachers, we remember commenting that, "the teachers aren't very theoretical." We wished that they would not focus so much on procedures. But we found ourselves doing exactly the same thing.

As noted earlier, the greatest lesson we learned was the need for ongoing discussion and dialogue with experts in FCL and CSILE. We usually did not know the kinds of questions to ask until we tried something in the classroom and encountered problems. In addition, the program developers often did not realize the need to explicitly explain something until they realized that we had done it wrong. This helped them make implicit assumptions explicit, but it required ongoing dialogue between them and us.

One example of the need for ongoing dialogue involved the use of CSILE in various classrooms. We used CSILE in our Schools for Thought sites as well as in some college classes at Vanderbilt. During one of their trips to visit us, Bereiter and Scardamalia looked at our databases and said, "This is good level I CSILE; now we need to work on Level II where we encourage dialogue that truly reflects knowledge building rather than simply knowledge telling." We had not realized that there were these levels and, hence, had not done anything to help students move beyond knowledge telling. Without feedback from the developers, we would have been satisfied with an implementation of CSILE that, in retrospect, was extremely weak. Similarly, by looking at our attempts to implement CSILE, Bereiter and Scardamalia were able to more clearly appreciate the need to help people understand differences between Levels I and II.

Another example of the need for ongoing dialogue involved our work with Brown and Campione's FCL. For our sixth-grade classes, we created a Mission to Mars unit that was designed to promote FCL-like activities such as focusing on the goal of working to accomplish an important consequential task such as making recommendations for a personed flight to Mars and back; using dilemmas (anchors) to get students to generate questions about what is needed to understand something like how and whether we can get to Mars; forming student expert groups to research answers to the questions they had generated; structuring collaboration by using activities such as reciprocal teaching (Palincsar & Brown, 1984) as a method for collaboratively exploring texts needed to conduct the research; and creating jigsaw groups composed of students from different expert groups who teach the others about their particular area of expertise, search for common issues across the groups, and help different groups edit and combine their individual group's research reports.

Everything seemed fine to us, but Brown and Campione helped us see things differently. First, we had not created a curriculum that was truly jigsawable so that each expert group needed input from the other expert groups in order to complete their tasks. Second, our reciprocal teaching sessions tended to focus only on text-level questions rather than higher level questions that helped students understand deep principles of the domain. Third, jigsaw groups formed to help students write about their work tended to focus only on grammar and spelling and failed to get at higher order issues of organization. Once these were pointed out to us, we were able to revise our approach. But without the opportunity for feedback and reflection, we would probably have continued in the belief that everything was fine. Our need for feedback was also informative to Brown and Campione because it helped them notice difficulties in interpreting their position—difficulties that had been invisible to them.

Our experiences with the Schools for Thought Project helped us more fully appreciate the accomplishments of the teachers who had attempted to implement *Jasper*. They lacked many of the advantages that were available to us in the Schools for Thought project. We had multiple opportunities to observe others' classrooms, discuss issues, and receive feedback from colleagues who were more knowledgeable about particular aspects of Schools for Thought.

Most of the *Jasper* Implementation Project teachers had access to one additional colleague in their school, plus a corporate representative in their community, but the only time they could meet was after school or on the weekends. Nevertheless, these local communities turned out to be very important. Teachers were able to support one another with respect to pedagogy; corporate representatives provided technology support, community support, and in many cases, even additional curriculum support.

When the Implementation Project teachers returned to Nashville to share their experiences after having tried *Jasper* for a year, they had valuable information to share with one another as well as with our research team. In essence, the teachers became a community of learners—a community that was united through its efforts to try a new approach to teaching that was organized around *Jasper*. This experience, plus our experiences with the Schools For Thought project, piqued our interest in the concepts of learning communities and learning organizations. What are their essential features? How can they be supported? This topic is discussed next.

THE DEVELOPMENT OF LEARNING COMMUNITIES

As previously noted, efforts to restructure one's teaching practices represent examples of complex learning that require ongoing opportunities for feedback and reflection rather than one-shot training workshops. A number of authors have begun to explore the organization of environments that support complex learning, and have called these learning communities or communities of learners (e.g., Brown & Campione, 1994; Cobb, 1994; CTGV, 1996a; Lin et al., 1995; Talbert & McLaughlin, 1993). Organizations that support ongoing learning have been called learning organizations(e.g., CTGV, 1996a; Senge, 1990). Not all communities are learning communities, and not all organizations are learning organizations. Data collected by Talbert and McLaughlin (1993) suggest that communities of teachers positively impact student achievement when they become learning communities. This makes it important to understand the social and organizational dimensions of communities that learn.

Our efforts to explore the concept of learning communities began with members of our group reading about the topic and discussing it. References such as those above were extremely helpful. Nevertheless, these authors were, of necessity, describing someone else's learning community; we wanted to find something that we could experience more directly. We eventually decided to use the readings as a guide for exploring a community that we experienced daily: our Learning Technology Center. Were we a learning community and, if so, what made us a learning community? If we could answer that question, we hoped to better understand how to help teachers develop learning communities of their own.

Studying Our Own Workplace

In Barron, Vye, et al. (1995), we discussed some features of our Learning Technology Center that appeared to be important for helping us learn from one another and make progress as a center. Seven features from this article are discussed next. We add an eighth feature that focuses on the kinds of beliefs and attitudes that help our community continue to work. Throughout our discussion, we compare the LTC's organization with the organization of typical classrooms in order to provide a contrasting case.

Anchored Collaboration Around Problems and Projects

The activities of the LTC are organized around shared problems and projects rather than around lessons presented by teachers. Our problems and projects almost always require the discovery of new knowledge. There is no right answer that someone is withholding from us and no single authority to whom we turn to tell us what is correct. In the process of pursuing goals relevant to our work, we engage in anchored collaboration and just-in-time knowledge acquisition. Anchored collaboration allows us to appreciate others' perspectives because people from different backgrounds bring unique perspectives to a common problem or project. This has a powerful effect on appreciating others' insights because it usually allows people to view a problem from new points of view.

Anchored collaboration also helps us define learning goals and engage in just-in-time knowledge acquisition. The knowledge may come from reading, from our own experimentation, or from visits by outside experts. Usually it comes from a combination of these sources. Our knowledge-acquisition activities are almost always a means to important ends rather than ends in themselves. And they frequently generate new foci for investigations.

Collaboration and Distributed Expertise

The LTC is a multidisciplinary group made up of cognitive psychologists, developmental psychologists, special education researchers, content specialists in areas such as literacy, mathematics, science, and public policy, and experts in computer and video design. Instead of assuming that everyone needs to know and learn the same thing (an assumption commonly found in many classrooms), we assume that no single individual is an expert in every area and explicitly acknowledge the importance of distributed expertise (e.g., Brown et al., 1993). By the same token, there is a great deal of knowledge (e.g., about work ethics, theoretical frameworks, uses of technology) that all of us share.

In the LTC, different individuals take the role of teacher or learner depending on the relationship between their expertise and the part of the project being worked on at any moment. Thus, instead of a fixed hierarchy of roles, our center is organized around a flexible structure where different individuals occupy leadership roles depending on momentary needs. Because any single project usually requires different leaders at different points in time, our projects are almost always multiply authored. We frequently reflect this by publishing as a group, namely, the CTGV.

Intrinsic and Extrinsic Motivation

Work at the LTC is based on a combination of intrinsic and extrinsic motivation. Almost everyone is interested in what they are doing and, hence, intrinsically motivated. Nevertheless, there are always aspects of a project that are taxing and mundane. Furthermore, there are many things that compete for one's time. Therefore, extrinsic deadlines play an important role in determining what gets accomplished within particular time frames.

The presence of important deadlines, and activities designed to meet them, contributes to an emotional climate that is far from steady-state and boring. In many classrooms, the only deadlines are tests that often involve a great deal of guessing about what to study. Our deadlines in the LTC tend to be much more self-defined than is true in most classroom contexts. We define the goals we are attempting to accomplish so preparation for meeting these deadlines is much less of a guessing game.

Connectedness to a Broad Community of Audiences

Our work would seem much less meaningful if we were our only audience. Much of the excitement, and most of the opportunities for new learning, come from interactions with diverse audiences that furnish us with new points of view. For example, we interact with fellow academicians, politicians, principals, teachers, students, parents, and business leaders. Each of these groups has very different perspectives, and each provides important points of view.

Our connections to broader communities also supply us with numerous models of ways to do things. For example, we often have opportunities to compare our responses to various grant solicitations to those of other academicians. And we have learned from observing how nonacademic groups (e.g., members of the business community) plan and communicate various ideas. No one ever forces us to copy their approaches. We have the freedom to choose whether or not to appropriate ideas from other groups that might help us better achieve our goals.

Frequent Opportunities for Formative Self-Assessment

Implicit in each of these points is the fact that we have frequent opportunities for formative self-assessment. By comparing our current thinking with others, and by subjecting our in-progress products to the scrutiny of others through reviews and presentations, we are able to continually find weaknesses and improve. This is very different from typical classrooms where the test at the end of the unit or year is usually summative and there are few real opportunities to revise.

The Use of Tools to Work Smart and Improve Efficiency

We could not do our work without the availability of tools that support productivity. Computer software for word processing and graphics, coupled with computer networks for collaboration, are elements that we absolutely need. Also necessary is software for planning, data analysis, and archiving. The tools that we use are used continuously. We do not simply learn a set, use them for awhile, and then learn a new set. This may be contrasted to classrooms where powerful tools are often missing. Even when they are present, they are often presented for a set of isolated lessons and never used again.

Support for Technology

It is important to note that there is a great deal of support for the technology tools we use. A number of individuals in our LTC are experts in particular aspects of technology and, hence, can help others who may need to learn something new or may be experiencing problems. Without this support, most of us would never attempt to use the tools that we find so valuable. In contrast, typical classrooms rarely have the technology for powerful tools, let alone the technical support needed to keep things going and growing.

Attitudes and Mental Models

Central to the collaborative spirit of the LTC is a model of being successful that emphasizes the role of being a learner as well as a knowledgeable expert. People who value professing their expertise more than they value learning something new are not good candidates for a collaborative group.

The importance of seeing oneself as a learner has prompted us to articulate two different models of what it means to be successful: an expert model and an accomplished novice model. We discuss each of these here.

The Expert Model. From the typical expert model perspective, reaching the level of the expert is the ultimate in success. A danger of this model is that people can fall into the expert trap. They assume that their role is to know all the answers rather than continue to learn.

The Accomplished Novice. An alternative to the expert model is something that we call the *accomplished novice* model. Accomplished novices appreciate the hard work required for them to have learned something very well. At the same time, they realize that what they have learned represents an extremely small part of all that is knowable. They view the idea of being successful as synonymous with being able to learn rather than with knowing all the answers. For them, becoming an accomplished novice is the ultimate sign of success.

We believe that the accomplished novice model of success has a very important effect on people's abilities to collaborate and learn from one another. Making the model explicit, and contrasting it with the expert model, helps people consciously evaluate their beliefs and attitudes. Based on our experiences, it is important to encourage teachers, researchers, and others who are attempting to collaborate to explicitly analyze their tacit models of being successful and discuss differences between the expert model and that of the accomplished novice. This helps provide a foundation for mutual trust, respect, and understanding. It also helps everyone appreciate others' strengths, and it gives people the freedom to make mistakes and, hence, continue to learn.

Understanding the Development of Professional Learning Communities

The study of our own learning community within the LTC has provided us with a way to think about features of learning communities that seem to be as important for teachers as they are for researchers. We consider these features in the next discussion.

Anchored Collaboration Around Problems and Projects

Schwartz and colleagues (1996) noted that attempts to restructure one's teaching can be viewed as a complex project-based activity involving real settings (classrooms) and real consequences (student learning). We noted in Chapter 5 that the quality of students' projects is enhanced when they can begin with problem-based learning that provides a common ground for discussion and collaboration. Similar principles appear to apply to adults. For example, beginning with problem-based curricula such as *Jasper* provides teachers with a shared context that they can refer back to as they discuss their own attempts to change their teaching and assessment practices. The *Jasper* teaching video that is on the CD-ROM accompanying this book provides an additional anchor for collaboration. Over time, teachers can then share their attempts to extend the problem-based curricula by helping their students carry out related projects in their own community.

Collaboration and Distributed Expertise

Ideally, professional communities include not only classroom teachers but also administrators, researchers, business leaders, and others. This provides a range of expertise that is invaluable. In addition, it can be extremely fruitful to encourage teachers to develop expertise in different areas rather than have each of them attempt to learn the same thing at the same time.

As an illustration, consider teachers learning about educational technology. Rather than ask everyone in a school to learn everything, one group might learn to make movies, one might learn to edit and compress movies, one might focus on sound, and so forth. People with different areas of expertise can then get together and share their knowledge (e.g., Brown & Campione, 1994). A focus on distributed expertise followed by sharing helps develop a sense of community because everyone teaches as well as learns.

Intrinsic and Extrinsic Motivation

Teachers who make the effort to improve their teaching practices are usually intrinsically motivated. Nevertheless, just like all of us in the LTC, they need extrinsic forms of motivation as well.

Real tasks with real deadlines are sources of extrinsic motivation that appear to be important for helping communities of learners move forward. Without real deadlines, it is easy to postpone personal and electronic meetings because everyone is busy and there is always something else to do. We noted earlier that the *Jasper* Challenge series provided a high-stakes event that included a deadline. This affected teaching schedules and schedules for the arrival of technology to support the Challenge series. Deadlines for meaningful tasks are very important for getting things done.

Connectedness to a Broader Community of Audiences

The prospect of facing real audiences is extremely motivating. Teachers who have worked with us have jelled as teams as they prepared presentations for other teachers who needed to learn how to teach with *Jasper*. Parents, administrators, and other members of the community are important audiences as well.

A task for teachers that has been particularly motivating has involved the creation of materials for other teachers about what it is like to teach with *Jasper*. *Jasper* teachers have responded to this task with brilliance and enthusiasm. Each *Jasper* videodisc includes video interviews with teachers who provide invaluable advice to new teachers. *Jasper* teachers are also featured in the *Jasper* CD-ROM that is included with this book. With multimedia and Internet technologies, teachers can create additional, inexpensive products that other teachers can use.

Frequent Opportunities for Formative Self-Assessment

We noted in chapter 5 that learners cannot improve without opportunities for feedback. In addition, there are important differences between providing feedback to people and having them seek feedback on their own.

Most teachers who have collaborated with us on the *Jasper* project have actively requested opportunities for feedback. Their ideal has been to have colleagues and other knowledgeable individuals visit their classrooms. An alternate plan is to ask others to watch videotapes of their teaching, or to react to their descriptions of their experiences and lesson plans. In all cases, the goal is to make their teaching practices as visible as possible so that others can provide feedback. This practice of making teaching and teaching decisions visible has not been the norm in schools. But it is extremely important for helping people change.

The Use of Tools to Work Smart

Teachers are often the last group to receive tools for working smarter. For example, when administrators think about computers for the schools, they usually think about computers for students, not teachers.

Our experience is that teachers welcome well-crafted tools, and that these tools can help them improve student achievement. *Jasper* and the SMART Challenge programs can be viewed as tools that enable teachers to accomplish goals that otherwise can be difficult to accomplish (e.g., present complex problems in a comprehensible and interesting manner; show dynamic visual representations that help students understand important concepts). In addition, in our work with SMART Challenges, we began to notice occasions where technology could help teachers improve their students' learning. Our software for providing feedback on students' blueprints in *Blueprint for Success* represents one example of tools we built for teachers (see Chapter 5). We developed similar software for evaluating business plans relevant to *The Big Splash*. We continue to attempt to identify and develop tools that help teachers increase their impact by working smart.

Support for Technology

A common mistake in providing technology for classrooms is to fail to provide adequate training and support for the teachers. Technology training needs to go beyond learning about the hardware. Teachers need to see how to integrate it with their curriculum. In *Jasper*, for example, we attempt to help teachers learn to use the technology in the context of mathematics. We also try to help teachers integrate *Jasper* with the rest of their mathematics curriculum.

In addition to training, teachers need ongoing support for technology. If their equipment fails, they need rapid access to help. Because they are extremely busy, they also need access to people who can help them stay abreast of new developments in technology. No business would put up with the way that technology tools tend to be introduced and supported in most schools.

Attitudes and Mental Models

Central to the development of professional learning communities is the attitudes people have about what it means to be a successful member. People whose primary mental model of success is to be the expert often have a hard time in learning communities. They become better able to learn when they move from a model of expert to a model of accomplished novice. This is often not an easy transition. For example, it can be difficult for veteran teachers to realize that it is okay not to have all the answers despite many years of teaching. It can also be difficult for researchers, administrators, and business leaders to move from the expert model to a model of accomplished novice. Many of these individuals are used to professing and are not particularly skilled at listening and learning. If they want to participate in a learning community with teachers, they must learn to value the wisdom of practice that teachers bring to the community. In our experience, this wisdom of practice represents a body of knowledge that is extremely valuable and important to learn.

Overcoming Constraints on Time

A key factor that constrains the development of professional communities involves constraints on time. Teachers are extremely busy. In the United States they rarely receive time for serious planning and collaboration with colleagues. It is very difficult to develop a learning community if there is no time to interact.

Whenever possible, we work with schools and districts to arrange for release time so that teachers can meet with one another at least several times per month. Meetings held after school hours are very difficult because teaching requires a level of vigilance that is extraordinarily high; hence, teachers are tired by the end of the school day. Meetings are much more productive if there is release time to hire a substitute for the teachers' classroom (many districts and schools have such funds in the professional development budgets). Hiring substitutes frees the teachers to meet during school hours.

Technology has the potential to enhance the development of professional learning communities, but only if it is used properly. We noted earlier in this chapter that providing *Jasper* teachers with access to electronic communication was less than successful. In retrospect, the reasons are clear. First, most teachers had no phone lines in their classrooms so they had very limited access to electronic mail. Second, even those who did have phone lines had almost no time to sit down and converse electronically with colleagues. They were too busy teaching. Third, there was no overall structure that drove the pace of electronic conversations. Teachers simply got onto the system when they had time. Often, they put out some general query or request and found that it was met with silence.

Having one's electronic message met with silence can be very disconcerting. The experience often leads to inferences that people do not want to talk about your issues. In reality, the silence usually stems from the fact that others are extremely busy. Creating some type of anchor or structure for conversations—complete with a time window for responding—is one possible way to help teachers use the potential that electronic communication provides. We are moving in this direction with our Internet Challenges, which include opportunities for teachers to compare notes about the challenges. This direction in our work is briefly discussed in Chapter 7.

The CD-ROM that accompanies this book shows scenes from *Jasper* in the classroom that is also designed to help teachers begin to form a learning community around *Jasper*. Teachers are first encouraged to solve a *Jasper* adventure in groups. They can then watch the teaching video and generate their own options for teaching with *Jasper*. When teachers communicate electronically about *Jasper*, they have a shared context for further inquiry.

SUMMARY AND CONCLUSIONS

Our goal in this chapter was to discuss *Jasper* from the perspective of issues of teacher learning and community building. One focus was on understanding the challenges faced by teachers as they attempt to incorporate new programs such as *Jasper* into their curriculum, and as they introduce new instructional opportunities to parents, administrators, and other community members. Another focus was on learning from teachers as they invented new ideas and provided feedback.

Our initial opportunities to learn from teachers arose in the context of our nine-state *Jasper* Implementation Project. The teachers provided us with clear feedback about the conduct of our workshop and, in the process, helped us practice what we preached about constructivist approaches to instruction. They also shared a number of important insights after having taught four *Jasper* adventures during the course of a year.

Teachers continued to invite us into their classrooms and help us understand challenges of *Jasper* instruction from their perspective. Their most important message was the need for ongoing support for feedback and reflection about their teaching practices. A formative experience helped us really appreciate the importance of the teachers' message; it involved the Schools for Thought (SFT) project that took us out of the role of being the experts and made us novices who had to learn how to teach in ways defined by others. This helped us appreciate the huge gaps between being able to talk about various programs and being able to actually do them day by day. One-shot training will not work. Instead, there need to be opportunities for ongoing dialogue.

The emphasis on ongoing learning prompted us to explore the emerging concept of learning communities and their implications for education. We analyzed our own workplace environment, the Learning Technology Center, from the perspective of a learning community. This analysis helped us appreciate how the structure of our center differs in critical ways from the structure of classrooms found in most schools.

The analyses also provide information relevant to the goal of helping teachers develop learning communities that provide ongoing feedback, information, and support for change.

7

Summary, Lessons, and Next Steps

Our goal in this chapter is to summarize the journey that the *Jasper* series has allowed us to take. We do so by discussing The LTC Framework, where LTC stands for Looking at Technology in Context (CTGV, 1996a). We then highlight key lessons learned from the *Jasper* experience, and discuss some of our next steps.

THE LTC FRAMEWORK

The LTC framework focuses on the intersection of the areas of technology, learning theory and educational practice. It does so by considering the matrix illustrated in Fig. 7.1.

The columns in the LTC Framework represent issues of educational practice by focusing on the educational contexts in which research is situated. The rows represent the theoretical context by highlighting issues relevant to learning theory, including theories of human potential and pedagogy. These dimensions of the framework are discussed in more detail next.

Educational Contexts in Which Research Is Situated

The columns of the LTC Framework focus on the educational contexts in which various programs are situated and studied—contexts that range from isolated laboratory settings to classrooms to connected sets of schools. The framework includes three categories along the contexts of usage dimension:

1. *In vitro* laboratory settings;
2. *In vivo* settings involving individual classrooms or sometimes schools; and
3. *Connected* settings involving sets of connected classrooms and schools.

When one works in these different settings, different theoretical and practical issues become relevant.

In vitro laboratory settings (Column 1) include experiments conducted in university-based research laboratories as well as experiments in schools where researchers do the teaching and assessment in order to test particular ideas.

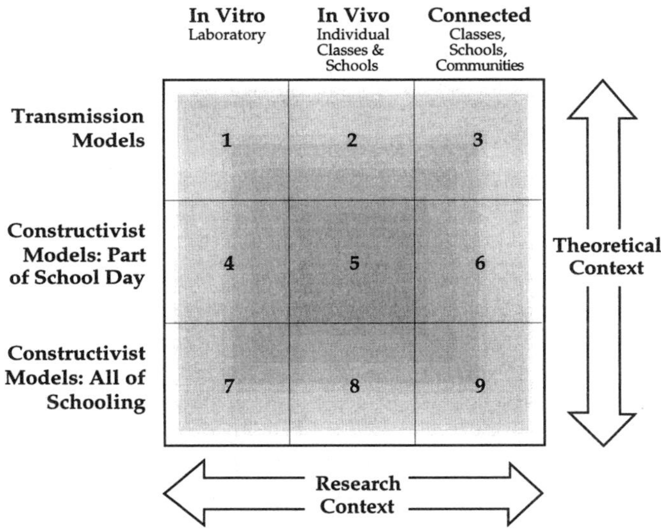

Cell 1: Studies of drill and practice programs in math, spelling, or particular content areas that are administered by research staff.
Cell 2: Studies of drill and practice programs in math, spelling, or particular content areas that are administered by classroom teachers.
Cell 3: Studies of distance learning connecting various classrooms that involve lectures and traditional tests.
Cell 4: Studies of constructivist-oriented programs (e.g., Logo, Voyage of the Mimi, *Jasper*) where the teaching and assessment is conducted by research staff.
Cell 5: Studies of constructivist-oriented programs (e.g., Logo, Voyage of the Mimi, *Jasper*) where the teaching and assessment is conducted by regular classroom teachers.
Cell 6: Studies of constructivist-oriented programs (e.g., Logo, Voyage of the Mimi, *Jasper*) where the teaching and assessment is conducted by regular classroom teachers and the classrooms are linked through telecommunications and interact on the project involved.
Cell 7: Studies of constructivist-oriented programs that fill the entire school day and take place in an experimental school with specially trained staff.
Cell 8: Studies of constructivist-oriented programs that fill the entire school day and take place in normal classrooms; however, the classrooms tend to operate independently of one another.
Cell 9: Studies of constructivist-oriented programs that fill the entire school day and take place in linked classrooms that interact on common problems and projects.

FIG. 7.1. The LTC Framework.

Advantages of this context include greater experimental precision and fidelity of implementation. By the same token, many issues that are important for educational success never need be addressed (see next).

In vivo classroom settings (Column 2) include studies conducted in individual classrooms by the classroom teachers. A research team may collect the data, but the intervention is managed by the teachers rather than the researchers from the lab. This type of arrangement brings one into contact with a host of important new issues. For example, researchers who have moved from laboratory to classroom settings have discovered that their programs may require more extensive professional development for administrators and classroom teachers than was anticipated, or may require a restructuring of typical school schedules from 50-minute class periods to larger blocks of time (e.g., see Hawkins & Collins, in press; Lamon et al., 1996; McGilly, 1994).

Connected settings (Column 3) are composed of connected classrooms and schools, and involve studies that explicitly attempt to break the isolation of classrooms and schools and connect them to form broad-based learning communities. An important reason for creating learning communities is to attempt to deal with issues of equity (e.g., Hawkins, 1991; Hawkins & Sheingold, 1986). Many schools do not have access to teachers of specialized subject matters nor to a broad range of reference materials. By connecting classrooms together, scarce resources can be shared. A second reason for connecting classrooms is that they provide authentic audiences that allow students to share ideas, data, and opinions (e.g., Bruce, Peyton, & Batson, 1993; CTGV, 1994; Levin, Kim, & Riel, 1990; Levin, Riel, Boruta, & Rowe, 1985; Levin, Riel, Miyake, & Cohen, 1987; Newman, 1992; Riel, 1990a, 1990b; Riel & Levin, 1990). A third reason for connecting classrooms is to facilitate the professional development needed to begin and sustain educational reform. This includes issues of scaling up and moving beyond laboratory or hothouse schools (e.g., CTGV, 1996a; Hawkins & Collins, in press; Mandinach & Cline, 1994).

Theoretical Context

The rows of the LTC framework refer to the theoretical context for one's technology-based applications. The theoretical context affects assumptions about curriculum, instruction, and assessment, and these assumptions have important implications for implementation and research efforts.

Especially important is the congruence between the theoretical context of a particular program and the educational context or setting (laboratory, classroom, connected classrooms) in which the program is placed. When the theoretical context and the setting are congruent, it is easy to assimilate one's application into the context of existing practice. When the assumptions of the program and the setting are incongruent, one faces greater challenges because of the need to transform traditional classroom practices.

Many classrooms involve instructional practices that are consistent with transmission models of instruction rather than constructivist-oriented models. As Greeno (1991) noted; students mostly listen, watch, and mimic things that the teacher and textbook tell and show them. When technology programs are congruent with transmission models, they can be assimilated quite easily into traditional classroom settings. The first row of the LTC framework reflects implementations of technology that can be assimilated without fundamental change in theoretical perspective on learning, instruction, and assessment.

Technology implementations that are based on constructivist theories cannot simply be assimilated to traditional classroom practices. Instead, the classrooms must be transformed (e.g., Bereiter, 1994; Bransford, Goldman & Vye, 1991; Cobb, 1994; Cobb, Yackel, & Wood, 1992; Collins, 1991; Pea, 1992; Resnick & Klopfer, 1989; Savery & Duffy, 1995). The LTC framework emphasizes that there are multiple levels at which transformation can be attempted. Challenges increase as one moves from attempts to transform only part of the school day (Row 2) to attempts to transform the entire nature of schooling (Row 3). These efforts include attempts to transform linkages between schools and the home and community, as well as transform what happens in classrooms.

Combining the Two Dimensions of Context

The matrix created by the two dimensions of context, that is, the educational and the theoretical, yields nine cells in the LTC framework. These can be used to characterize a vast array of possible studies. Examples of the kinds of studies that fit in each cell are provided in Fig. 7.1. One cannot do this with 100% certainty, but one can do it approximately. By situating a study in a particular cell, what emerges is a better picture of what has been learned and how that information can be generalized. We strongly believe that research in all cells of the LTC framework is valuable. The value of the framework is to help researchers know where they are in the general space of things.

JASPER AND THE LTC FRAMEWORK

Our work with *Jasper*, and with the projects that gave rise to *Jasper*, has involved us in many of the cells of the LTC framework. In the following discussion, we consider the advantages and disadvantages of working in various cells.

Pre-*Jasper* Work on Well-Defined Word Problems

As discussed in Chapter 2, initial work that led to the development of *Jasper* involved efforts to help students learn to solve traditional, well-defined word problems. The middle school students with whom we worked were having a difficult time understanding the problems they were being asked to solve and, instead, were simply looking for numbers in problems, plus key words that suggested whether they should use these numbers to add, subtract, multiply, or divide. We used videodisc technology to provide visual support for problem comprehension. When we taught in this context, students who previously had experienced considerable difficulty learned and transferred their knowledge quite well.

This initial work fell into Cell 1 of the LTC framework (see Fig. 7.1). Word problems were already a part of the existing curriculum, and all the research was carried out in laboratory contexts with researchers functioning as the teachers. These arrangements allowed a considerable degree of experimental control. By the same token, we never had to face issues such as working with classroom teachers to help them learn to teach this way. And we never had to think about the issue of restructuring the curriculum in order to find a place to introduce new experiences and ideas.

A Move to More Complex Problems and an Emphasis on Self-Generation

As our research progressed, we began to realize that successful everyday problem solving requires people to generate their own problems and goals rather than to always solve well-defined problems that others gave them. Therefore, we designed environments, such as *The River Adventure*, that asked students to generate all the subgoals they would need to consider in order to achieve an overall goal, plus identify data relevant to each subgoal (see Chapter 2).

This change in emphasis marked a transition from Cell 1 in the LTC framework to Cell 4 (see Fig. 7.1). The problems we were proposing to introduce into the curriculum were becoming quite different from typical well-defined word problems. In addition, we began to view them as contexts for teaching basic concepts of mathematical thinking rather than only as applications problems to be used after the mathematical ideas were learned in the first place. As a result, the instruction we began to envision deviated more and more from the traditional instruction found in typical classrooms. Nevertheless, we conducted our studies in laboratory contexts where researchers did all the instruction and assessment. This helped experimental control, but it also deprived us of lessons involved in working with teachers who were beginning to change their teaching and assessment practices.

We eventually talked with teachers about using *The River Adventure* in their own classrooms, which involves a move to Cell 5 in the LTC framework (see Fig. 7.1). When we did, we ran into objections that we had not anticipated. The teachers helped us see that we were a special event when we operated in Cell 4, which was outside the context of normal instruction. As a special event, even the opportunity to work with the poorly produced *The River Adventure* was motivating to students because they got out of class. Teachers argued that the requirements to operate in Cell 5 were much different. Thanks to their support, Vanderbilt helped us fund the production of two professional-quality *Jasper* adventures.

Research on *Jasper*: Cells 4, 5, and 6

Our research on *Jasper* has occurred in Cells 4, 5, and 6 in the LTC framework (see Fig. 7.1). Work in each cell had advantages and disadvantages.

An example of work in Cell 4 involves studies to compare the effects on transfer of having students work with *Jasper* versus work for the same amount of time with the same sub-problems that are found in *Jaspers*, but without the integrated problem context (see the discussion in Chapter 4). By using people from our own research team in the context of laboratory studies, we were able to ensure a high degree of fidelity of implementation for both our experimental and control conditions. By focusing on a relatively small number of students, we were able to conduct in-depth assessments that asked students to think aloud as they attempted to solve new transfer problems (Goldman, Vye, et al., 1991; Van Haneghan et al., 1992). These studies allowed us to document that opportunities to work in integrated problem contexts such as *Jasper* were very important (e.g., CTGV, 1993b; Van Haneghan et al., 1992).

In contrast to laboratory research, studies of *Jasper* that have involved classrooms (Cell 5) have revealed a different set of problems and opportunities. Some of our work in Cell 5 involved our efforts to study the effects of *Jasper* as it was taught by a variety of classroom teachers in nine different states (CTGV, 1992c; Pellegrino et al., 1991).

Our attempts to study *Jasper* as it was used in actual classrooms posed problems from a research perspective. One was that we were unable to study the fidelity with which *Jasper* was implemented in each classroom. Another problem was that the best we could do for comparison groups was to find students with similar levels of achievement and economic status who received regular classroom instruction in mathematics rather than *Jasper*. A third problem was that we had to settle for paper-and-pencil assessment rather than in-depth performance assessments. Overall, it was impossible to be as precise about the *Jasper* instruction, and the instruction received by comparison classes, as it was when we conducted our studies in laboratory contexts. Nevertheless, the opportunity to study *Jasper* across a large number of different sites was extremely beneficial (CTGV, 1992c; Pellegrino et al., 1991).

We have also studied *Jasper* in the context of connected sets of classrooms (Cell 6). The *Jasper* SMART Challenge series was designed to connect groups of classrooms and teachers so that they could learn from one another (CTGV, 1994). Data indicate that this increased the achievement of students relative to *Jasper*-only instruction, and it also helped change teachers' teaching styles (e.g., Barron, Vye, et al., 1995; CTGV, 1994). Note, however, that attempts to study connected sets of classrooms means that they are no longer independent of one another. If something affects one classroom positively or negatively it is also likely to also affect all the others. This raises issues of statistical interpretation that are not as problematic when classes are truly independent of one another (e.g., Bryk & Raudenbush, 1992).

Jasper in Cells 7, 8, and 9

We noted in Chapter 6 that *Jasper* is also part of the Schools for Thought program that attempts to restructure students' entire day. This places *Jasper* in Cells 7, 8, and 9. Opportunities to work in these cells has been extremely informative; they have allowed us to create environments that have the potential to truly transform students' thinking and learning because important opportunities for learning are supported throughout the day rather than supported only for part of a day. It is beyond the scope of this book to report more on the Schools for Thought project here. A preliminary report on Schools For Thought can be found in Lamon et al. (1996). Additional information is available on our Web site (http://peabody.vanderbilt.edu/projects/funded/sft/general/ sftbut1.map).

Adding a Dimension to the LTC Framework

In our discussion so far, the scope of research within each cell in the LTC framework has been left undefined. For example, when we discussed constructivist approaches that attempt to transform all of schooling in connected classrooms (Cell 9), we did not specify whether the scope of analysis was a single grade, middle school, preK–12 or preK–college. The scope of most research projects involves only a single grade level or, at most, two or three consecutive grade levels. There are important differences between thinking about changes within a single grade or small set of grades, and thinking about changes throughout the progression of preK–12 or preK–college. These differences are illustrated in Fig. 7.2.

Brown and Campione's (1994) Community of Learners project is a good example of a project with a broad-scope focus. They emphasized the importance of deep principles in areas such as biology (deep principles might be interdependence, biological diversity and so forth). Most important for the present discussion, Brown and Campione also explicitly attempted to create curricula and instructional opportunities that enabled students to understand deep principles at early ages, and to then have the opportunity to expand their understandings as they progressed throughout the grades. One advantage is that students can develop a level of

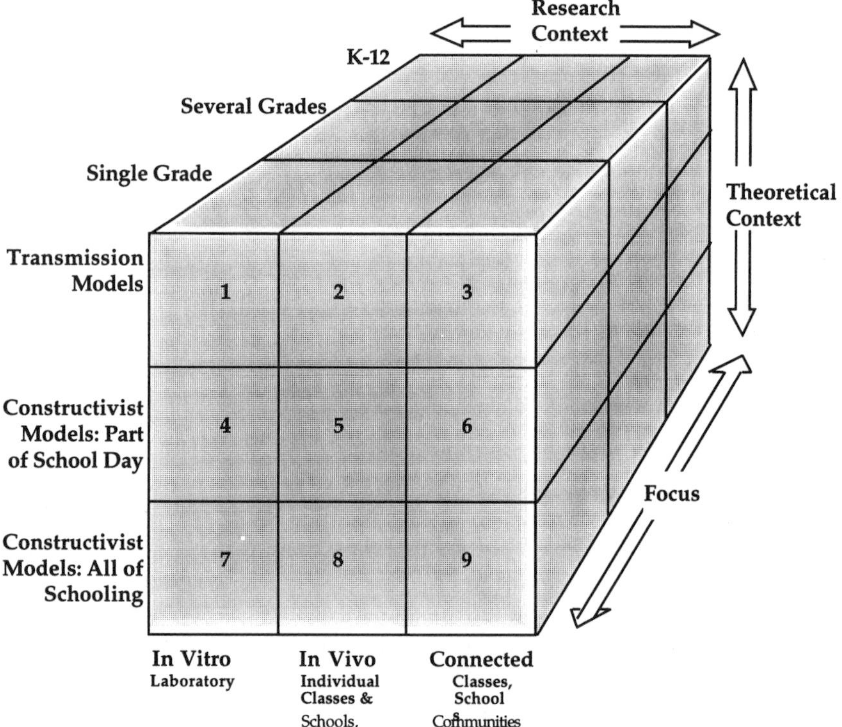

FIG. 7.2. Three-dimensional LTC Framework.

expertise in particular domains that is extraordinary by current standards. Another advantage is that students can engage in cross-age tutoring sessions that include highly sophisticated discussions. In order to take this approach, one must be willing to rethink existing curricula, instruction, and assessment across multiple grades.

Kaput and Lesh (1994) have discussed the importance of a broad-scope focus in the area of mathematics. Why, they ask, should students suddenly be confronted with the course in algebra or geometry or calculus? Similar to Brown and Campione, they argued that there are big ideas in mathematics that can be introduced early and gradually refined over the years.

We agree that a broad scope focus may be necessary for truly profound changes in academic achievement. In addition to helping students acquire more in-depth knowledge, it can provide new avenues to expertise that are denied to many students who are expected to learn an entire subject matter all at once when they receive the course in algebra, genetics, and so forth. Ideally, broad-scope approaches to education will attempt to integrate curricula from preK to college so that mathematics, science, literature, and other subject matters may be learned synergistically (Bransford, Sherwood, et al., 1988). To achieve these ideals, technology-based applications must be designed with broad-scope goals in mind.

We have begun to explore how *Jasper* adventures can be used across multiple years in order to develop an understanding of deep principles that underlie subject matters such as geometry, algebra, and statistics. For example, some teachers have used the first adventure in trip planning, statistics, geometry, and pre-algebra in fifth grade, the next *Jasper* adventure in these areas in the sixth grade, and so forth. (See Fig. 1.1 in Chapter 1.) Other teachers have used different combinations of *Jasper* adventures to create a *Jasper* corridor in mathematics.

Summary of the LTC Framework

We close this discussion of the LTC framework by re-emphasizing that work in every cell of the framework is important. Each cell has unique advantages and disadvantages that are important to keep in mind.

The primary advantages of working in laboratory contexts (Cells 1, 4, and 7) are that one can control important sets of variables and ensure high degrees of fidelity of program implementation. Disadvantages of working in these cells are that many issues relevant to real classrooms and real schools are not dealt with, thereby limiting the applicability of the findings to real classroom settings. Work in Cells 5–6 and 8–9 has helped us begin to understand a number of issues that were invisible to us when we worked exclusively in Cells 1 and 4.

For us, the most important use of the LTC framework is to help us know where we are in the space of research possibilities. When we began working in education, many of us worked exclusively in Cells 1, and to some extent, 4. However, we had absolutely no qualms about telling people who worked in Cells 8 and 9 how to make things better. We had no idea of the distance between Cells 1–4 and 8–9. Now we do.

IMPORTANT LESSONS

Opportunities to move among the cells in the LTC framework have taught us a number of lessons about learning and education. Our goal in this section is to summarize several that seem most important. Probably the most far-reaching lesson involves a much clearer appreciation of the importance of understanding learning from a sociocultural as well as an individual perspective. As noted elsewhere (Barron et al., 1995; Bransford, 1981), sociocultural contexts are often as invisible to researchers (especially researchers whose primary focus has been on individual cognition) as water is to a fish.

After working in numerous settings, it has become clear to us that culture is not an option. Classrooms, schools, and communities develop sets of cultural norms about learning and knowing that are more important than any particular product such as *Jasper*. For example, we have seen *Jasper* used in classrooms that were organized around teacher-directed lessons complete with drill-and-practice worksheets, and where the primary norms of the classroom seemed to be "find the right answer" and never being caught not knowing. When *Jasper* was introduced into these settings, it was often assimilated into the existing classroom culture and used in ways that were vastly different from the purposes for which it was designed.

The cultural norms of classrooms, schools, and communities also affect the degree to which teachers keep their teaching practices private versus actively attempt to learn from one another as well as from other community members. In settings where there are strong learning communities of teachers, programs such as *Jasper* can flourish because people keep finding ways to improve how they are used.

Clearly, the importance of the cultural norms that affect classrooms, schools, and communities is not a new idea; it has been elegantly discussed by many different researchers (e.g., Brown & Campione, 1994; Cobb, 1994; Cobb, Yackel, & Wood, 1992; Cohen, McLaughlin, & Talbert, 1993; Talbert & McLaughlin, 1993). We needed to experience the importance of culture for ourselves in order to truly understand its importance.

Ideally, educational resources such as *Jasper* can help transform existing classroom, school, and community cultures rather than simply be at the mercy of the cultural norms that are currently in operation. Our teacher-collaborators have helped us discover some uses of *Jasper* that facilitate the development of classroom, school, and community cultures—cultures that encourage and support ongoing learning by adults as well as students. In short, the teachers have helped us see how resources such as *Jasper* can be used to help build learning communities. Several issues relevant to community building are discussed later.

A major lesson we learned from our experiences with *Jasper* revolved around the importance of community building. As noted in Chapter 6, opportunities to work in Cells 5–6 and 8–9 of the LTC framework helped us appreciate the importance of helping teachers transform typical classroom structures into ones that functioned as learning communities. In addition, teachers needed to form their own learning communities so that they could continue to learn. We learned that there are important differences between an appreciation of the importance of learning communities and knowledge of how to build them. A number of lessons relevant to building community are discussed in the following.

Common Grounds for Community Building

The teachers helped us realize that a major strength of video-based problems such as *Jasper* was one that we had not originally anticipated. Teachers used them to build community. They did so by inviting parents, administrators, business leaders, and other interested parties to watch a *Jasper* adventure and then attempt to solve it. Students acted as guides to keep the adults out of trouble when they got too far off-track. These experiences helped the adults appreciate the amount of thinking necessary to solve *Jasper* adventures. In addition, the adults appreciated the expertise of the students. The fact that *Jasper* adventures include potential connections to a host of areas (e.g., principles of flight, endangered species, elections, recycling, business planning, etc.) had additional advantages. Adults watching the adventures often identified areas of expertise that they could share with the students. This resulted in numerous visits to classrooms by adult experts, field trips by students to relevant sites, electronic communications among students and adults, and other opportunities to share expertise.

The Importance of Outside Challenges

A second lesson we learned involves the role of outside challenges in community building. The *Jasper* SMART Challenge series evolved over time from a purely summative event to one that also provided multiple opportunities for feedback, reflection, and revision (see Chapters 4 and 5). Nevertheless, a constant feature of every SMART Challenge was the presence of an outside challenge that required teachers and students to work together in order to prepare.

Outside challenges can fulfill the role of a common enemy that unites people in order to defeat it. Our *Jasper* Challenges seemed to fulfill this role. They helped students and teachers realize that they were all on the same side because the challenges were being posed by someone outside the classroom. Because the challenges were voluntary, teachers and students chose to respond to them. In addition, the goal of the challenges was made quite clear at the beginning of the process. These features make the feelings associated with participation in the *Jasper* Challenge series very different from the negative feelings that both students and teachers often experience when they face the prospect of taking achievement tests to assess how much has been learned.

The Importance of Combining Instruction With Assessment

A third major lesson we learned involved the importance of formative assessment and feedback for successful learning. It is noteworthy that we knew about the importance of feedback for learning (see Chapter 5) well before the first *Jasper* adventure ever entered our collective consciousness. Nevertheless, there are extremely important differences between knowing about a particular factor and using it to guide one's practice. In our early work in classrooms, much of our knowledge about the importance of ongoing feedback remained inert (see Whitehead, 1929).

Our discussion in Chapters 4 and, especially, 5 illustrates the changes in our thinking as we became increasingly aware of the importance of providing frequent opportunities for feedback, reflection, and revision. Feedback cycles were explicitly built into our later SMART Challenges (see Chapter 5). In addition, even when SMART Challenges were not available, we began to recommend the use of the I DARE cycles discussed in Chapter 5.

Providing Support for Learning and Reflection

The more we worked in classrooms, the more we realized the need to provide support for learning and reflection. Much of the support was to help students understand problem situations, see possible models for the solution, and view other students attempting to solve similar problems. Other support was designed to help teachers make difficult concepts easier to teach and make it easier to manage the task of providing students with feedback so that they could improve their work and their thinking.

Overall, our attempts to provide support for learning and reflection represent attempts to adapt case-based and problem-based instruction for middle school and high school students. Most uses of case- and problem-based instruction have occurred in professional schools such as medicine, law, business, and educational leadership (e.g., Barrows, 1985; Bridges, 1992; Bridges & Hallinger, 1995; Williams, 1992). Our experiences with *Jasper* indicate that it is important to provide younger learners with scaffolds (e.g., Vygotsky, 1978, 1986) that enhance understanding and learning. Examples of different types of support (scaffolds) are discussed next.

Advantages of the Visual Medium

One feature of the *Jasper* series that scaffolds learning is the fact that *Jasper* problems are visual in nature. When *Jasper* adventures are read as scripts rather than viewed as movies, the difficulty of conveying a large amount of complex information in writing becomes clear. It is often difficult to imagine all the details of the problem situation. In addition, people who have access only to *Jasper* as a script have a difficult time knowing where to search for relevant data that were embedded in the story.

The visual nature of *Jasper* adventures also provides opportunities for noticing subtle clues that are required to solve the *Jasper* Challenge. For example, in many of the adventures data critical for the solution is shown visually but not explicitly mentioned. As discussed in Chapter 4, teachers have told us how these opportunities for noticing provide occasions for insight by students who traditionally do not do well in mathematics class and reading class. In many cases, the students' status in the group changes as they become able to contribute and participate.

The visual nature of *Jasper* also makes it possible to embed a wealth of data relevant to extensions into other areas such as science, history, and social studies. In addition, it helps us portray positive role models and community values that appear to be very important for children.

Despite the many advantages of using a visual format, we do not want to imply that all problems for K–12 must be visual rather than written. Written cases work especially well if they elaborate on situations that were first portrayed through video (e.g., see Sharp et al., 1995). We are also experimenting with the use of radio plays as anchors for problems. These preserve some of the advantages of movies (e.g., each actor speaks in a different voice), but are much easier to produce. In addition, under conditions where listeners have all the background knowledge necessary to understand the radio plays, we suspect that it is better to get listeners to generate their own images rather than rely on images that are supplied by us (for a discussion of the generative learning literature, see Slamecka & Graf, 1978; Soraci et al., 1994).

Embedded Data

Our work with *Jasper* has also prompted us to add features to our problems that facilitate students' discussions and understanding. One feature is the use of embedded data that must be consulted in order to arrive at a solution to the *Jasper* challenge. We believe that the use of embedded data in *Jasper* adventures allows students to engage in reasoned decision making rather than simply engage in opinion swapping because of a lack of data to back up one's claims. Embedding data serves to constrain the problem solving and give all students common information to consider. By including both relevant and irrelevant data, students must decide what is important to use in solving each part of the problem.

Elsewhere, we discuss some examples of problem-solving simulations that do not provide information that supports reasoned decision making (Bransford, Stein, et al., 1986). In these situations, students eventually learn how to successfully navigate through the simulations. However, they seem to do so through trial and error (e.g., "let's see what happens if we choose this path") and memorization of the consequences of particular choices. We wanted to encourage students to learn to use available knowledge resources in order to make informed decisions rather than guess. However, we also wanted to make sure that students were not simply given a list of resources (e.g., data) that they could consult when solving *Jasper* challenges. As noted earlier, students who receive data sheets tend to use them to guide their thinking. This strategy is not very useful in everyday settings: Most of life's problems do not come with a complete data sheet.

Embedded Teaching

The more we observed *Jaspers* being used in classrooms, the more we saw the need to include embedded teaching in the adventures. *Embedded teaching scenes* provide models or worked-out examples (e.g., Chi et al., 1989) that illustrate how to solve certain classes of problems. For example, in our geometry adventures, embedded teaching scenes show how to read topographic maps or how to use graph paper to determine answers to problems that otherwise would require trigonometry. In our algebra adventures, embedded teaching scenes show examples of Smart Tools that can be used to solve a variety of problems.

Our embedded teaching scenes never directly provide answers to *Jasper* challenges; instead, they provide models that have to be adapted in order to solve the challenge. Students return to embedded teaching scenes as they discover.

Our experiences indicate that embedded teaching scenes contribute to classroom discussion and student understanding. Students access these scenes on a need-to-know basis. Once they do, a great deal of thinking is required in order to adapt embedded teaching scenes to the challenges that students face. Our observations suggest that, without the embedded teaching scenes, students would often be lost and would need to rely too much on outside help. Teachers report that embedded teaching scenes also deepen their understanding of motivations and its applications.

Teaching Tools

Despite their advantages, too many embedded teaching scenes get in the way of the story line. As a result, we have also included teaching tools on the videodisc of the *Jasper* adventures. These have been important for helping students understand key concepts and ideas. Examples of teaching tools include dynamic scenes for helping students learn to use a compass and to triangulate (these are relevant to the *Jasper* geometry adventures); scenes that show real geological structures and their representations on topographic maps; dynamic scenes that help students translate from minutes to hours. These can be accessed and viewed in a just-in-time, as-needed basis.

As noted earlier, the advantage of including these scenes as teaching tools on the videodisc rather than as examples of embedded teaching is that too many instances of the latter interfere with the story line of the adventure. A disadvantage of teaching tools is that there is no simple way for students to know that they exist. As a consequence, the use of teaching tools is usually under teacher control.

In our SMART Challenge series (see the discussion in Chapter 5), we have added classroom-based CD-ROMs that include extra video, audio, and text resources for enhancing learning. Students learn about the availability of these resources by watching the Challenge shows. They have the opportunity to return to various aspects of these shows on a just-in-time basis. As discussed in Chapter 5, data indicate that students make excellent use of CD-ROM resources as they work on problems and projects in class.

We have also seen the value of providing teachers and students with software tools that can facilitate feedback and reflection. Examples included the software that teachers could use to give students feedback about their blueprints for a playground, and visual tools that provide information about concepts that are difficult to explain in words (e.g., what a swing set looks like when viewed from straight above it). Examples are provided in Chapter 5.

In Chapter 5, we also discussed software such as the *Jasper Adventure Player* software that provides multiple opportunities for feedback and reflection. Data indicate that the coaching and feedback components of this software have strong effects on students' abilities to learn (e.g., Crews et al., in press).

Support for What-if Thinking

Our work with *Jasper* has also helped us appreciate some features of problem- and project-based instruction that are important for increasing the flexibility with which students can use their knowledge to transfer to new problems. As discussed in Chapter 4, our early research with *Jasper* suggested that students learned a great deal and increased their positive attitudes toward mathematics and problem solving. Nevertheless, more in-depth assessments suggested that students' understanding was not as flexible as we wanted it to be. As a result, we added *Jasper* analog and extension problems that encouraged students to revisit each adventure and ask what-if questions such as, "How would a change in the speed of the ultralight from 30 to 40 miles per hour affect my rescue plans?" Data discussed in Chapter 4 indicate that the use of analog and extension problems increases the flexibility with which students can transfer to new problems.

Problem-Based Learning As Scaffolds or Project-Based Learning

As noted in Chapters 1 and 5, problem-based curricula such as *Jasper* can also be viewed as scaffolds for subsequent project-based learning. There are a number of reasons for encouraging curricula that are project-based.

First, projects that involve connections with students' local communities are extremely motivating (e.g., Collins et al., 1991). As discussed in Chapter 5, interviews conducted with students a year after they have been involved in *Jasper*-related projects indicate that these represented particularly significant accomplishments for a large number of the students. They enjoyed solving the *Jaspers*, but they especially enjoyed the chance to do something meaningful for their community such as design a playhouse that was actually built and used in the community, or plan and successfully manage a fun fair for their entire school.

Second, projects provide additional challenges that help students deepen their understanding of concepts and issues and develop more flexible knowledge. For example, when conducting surveys to create their own business plans, students have to deal with issues of optimal sample size for their population, as well as random sampling. When attempting to create dream houses, students must develop a general ability to estimate, measure, and draw to scale.

For present purposes, the important point involves data indicating that projects are of a higher quality when they are preceded by problem-based activities that help students prepare for the projects (see Chapter 5). Experiences with relevant problem-based curricula help students establish a common vocabulary of content and procedures, learn to collaborate, and acquire relevant concepts (e.g., representative sampling, drawing to scale) necessary to carry off their projects with a high level of confidence and skill (e.g., Moore et al., 1996).

Although problem-based learning can enhance project-based learning, it is noteworthy that the reverse is also true. Project-based activities that build on the *Jasper* experiences enhance students' learning beyond what they gain by solving only an adventure, plus its analogs and extensions. For example, pursuing a project that requires taking a random sample within one's school provides a challenge that builds on and extends the sampling issues involved in the *Jasper* statistics adventures (e.g., Barron et al., 1995). When designed properly, projects provide multiple opportunities for what-if thinking because they involve issues and situations that are similar to the ones encountered in the *Jasper* adventures, yet different as well.

NEW PROJECTS BASED ON *JASPER*

Our experiences with *Jasper* have had a strong influence on other research and development projects being conducted by our center. Some of these projects focus on different subject matters, such as science and literacy, and on a variety of ages ranging from kindergarten to adults. One of the projects, Schools for Thought, integrates all subject matters as it attempts to restructure students' entire school day.

The idea of anchoring learners' experiences in meaningful contexts plays a prominent role in all our current work. A major benefit of anchors is the support they provide for building communities of learners that connect classrooms, schools, and communities. We are also experimenting with additional ways to scaffold teacher and student learning so that it becomes easier for teachers to change their teaching practices. In addition, we are exploring ways to continue to increase student and teacher learning by explicitly integrating programs such as *Jasper* with the rest of the curriculum and providing more opportunities to make students' thinking visible and to engage in frequent, formative assessments by using the Internet. Examples of LTC projects, plus next steps for our research, are discussed later in this chapter.

During the past several years, we have had the opportunity to collaborate with teachers to develop several additional projects that build on our experiences with *Jasper*. We briefly describe several of these and then explain how they are involved in our plans for future work.

Scientists in Action

The *Scientists in Action (SIA)* series is similar in design to *Jasper*, but its major focus is on science (Goldman, Petrosino, Sherwood, et al., 1996; Sherwood, Petrosino, Lin, Lamon, & CTGV, 1995). Because there is so much specific knowledge required to understand most science problems, we do not attempt to embed all the data in the stories as we do in *Jasper*. Instead, information required to solve the challenges is made available through access to research materials that exist outside the video—either as printed materials or materials that reside on a CD-ROM or on the Internet. SMART Challenges are also being designed for the *SIA* series. (An example is discussed later in this chapter.)

The first *SIA* adventure, *The Stones River Mystery*, allows students to explore issues of assessing water quality. In that context, they become familiar with ecosystems and the complex set of interacting factors that create healthy streams and rivers. Prior to working with this adventure, many middle school students believe that a healthy river is one that is free of bacteria and bugs, and has water that is safe for humans to drink.

The second *SIA* adventure, *Return to Rochester*, recreates events in Rochester, New York in the 1960s. Emergency room physicians began to notice that a rising number of young children were being admitted who shared some very severe symptoms. Thanks to a community effort organized by a chemist, it was eventually realized that the problem was lead poisoning that resulted from young children eating paint chips. Students who work with this adventure have opportunities to explore a number of issues including the effects of heavy metals such as lead on the human system, experimental detective techniques for isolating the causes of various disorders, and the importance of community efforts to solve problems that people face.

The third *SIA* adventure, *The Lost Letters of Laslo Clark*, involves the discovery of a time capsule that contains information about some ancient petroglyphs. During an initial trip to find the petroglyphs, students have to turn back because of problems involving contaminated water, poisonous plants, poor preparation for nutritious food, and inadequate protection from the weather. Students watching the video are then challenged to conduct the research needed to plan a second trip. They have to understand important phenomena (e.g., hypothermia, threats to water contamination and how to handle them, essentials of nutrition) in order to properly plan.

The fourth *SIA* adventure is entitled *Border Blues*. Its purpose is to help students deepen their understanding of ecosystems—this time, with a focus on plants.

The story begins with a student's experiences with customs as he and his family return to the United States from a trip abroad. He has a plant that a shopkeeper promised would repel mosquitoes if he planted it. He cannot wait to try it out. But the customs officials refuse to let the plant into the country. The rest of the story focuses on two issues: Is it really possible that some plants repel insects—and if so, how and why do they do so? Why might the customs agents have confiscated the plant?

Accompanying each *SIA* adventure are a variety of materials, including simulations related to each anchor that let students test their mettle. The *SIA* adventures are also being integrated with Internet-based challenges that allow students to compare their answers to those that others provide.

Young Children's Literacy Series

A second project that is based on our experiences with *Jasper* is The Young Children's Literacy series—a multimedia language and literacy program for beginning readers. Designed in collaboration with Little Planet Publishing, its no-floor, no-ceiling design is learner-centered and is based on 4 years of research with a wide range of students, including students at risk of school failure and students well on the road to learning to read.

The Young Childrens' Literacy Project is structured around video stories that anchor a series of activities targeting deep comprehension, composition, and oral language along with traditional print-based skills. New extensions to the program include instructional activities involving science and mathematics.

The Video Anchor Stories

There are currently two anchor stories in the series. Each video sets the stage for a semester's worth of activities, and each begins the semester's work by challenging the children to write a book. In the first story, the characters on the little planet are visited by a stranger named Wongo. Wongo convinces the animals that they need to buy his magic hats if they want to use their imaginations and tell good stories. All of the animals are taken in by his pitch except for Ribbit. As the story progresses, Ribbit learns to use components of the scientific method to test whether the hats really are magic. With these tests, all the animals soon discover they have been duped. They get their money back from Wongo, but they learn that he plans to take his hats to other parts of the planet. This leaves the animals with a challenge: How can they prevent other animals from being tricked by Wongo? The answer, of course, is to write a book, and the animals enlist the aid of children in the classroom to do so.

In the second anchor story, Glowbird disappears after the other animals unthinkingly destroy her habitat. As she searches for a new home, she travels to a desert, an arctic region, a wetlands "area," and a tropical swamp. In each place she finds animals that have adapted well to life there, but she discovers that she is not adapted to live there. Meanwhile, Glowbird's friends work diligently to learn from books how to restore the environment, just in time for Glowbird's weary return. The story ends as Glowbird challenges the children to make books that tell her story and the stories of animals with similar problems. This sets the stage for early research activities about real, endangered animals that lead into bookmaking activities.

Each anchor video is accompanied by a book that tells these stories in print form. However, as with *Jasper,* the video is integral to the program in several respects:

1. *Community Building*: Children who may differ greatly in the background knowledge they possess can use the visual support in the videos to quickly develop shared understandings and vocabulary that make it possible for them to participate in collaborative activities. In addition, teachers can easily share the curriculum with children's families from all literacy backgrounds by distributing the anchor stories on videotape.

2. *Conceptual Richness*: Each anchor story is more narratively complex and dense with information than print-based stories targeted to this age. The key to the success of the stories is that they can be explored and re-explored so that children develop

deep understandings over time. By placing the video stories on laserdisc, CD-ROM, and computer, we allow nonreaders and early readers to control the exploration—something they cannot do with the print medium alone.

3. *Extended Knowledge Building.* A curriculum that fosters deep expertise is heavily dependent on a context that maintains interest over long periods of time. Well-designed video stories are inherently motivating to young children, providing a critical springboard for long-term student engagement.

Activities That Accompany the Anchors

The activities in the program make use of computer and laserdisc tools that provide support for rich discussions and enable children to share their readings and written work with authentic audiences. Examples of technology-supported activities are illustrated in Figs. 7.3, 7.4, and 7.5.

A Web page published by Little Planet Publishing features *The Little Planet Times.* The *Times* includes literacy-based challenges that end with a dilemma. Students are

Story Sequencing

- Children order pictures from the story that represent important story events.
- Software allows the children to:
  - move the pictures into any order that they wish;
  - receive dynamic visual help as needed (e.g., if they can't remember the events that a picture represents, clicking on the picture makes it dynamic and that portion of the story is replayed).
- During sequencing, teachers encourage discussion about the order to events.

Reciprocal Teaching (Palincsar and Brown, 1984)

- Children take turns playing the role of teacher and leading the other children through the steps of Questioning, Summarizing, and Clarifying each scene in the story.
- Playing the role of teacher is consistently motivating and deepens comprehension.

FIG. 7.3. Story sequencing and reciprocal teaching for deep comprehension.

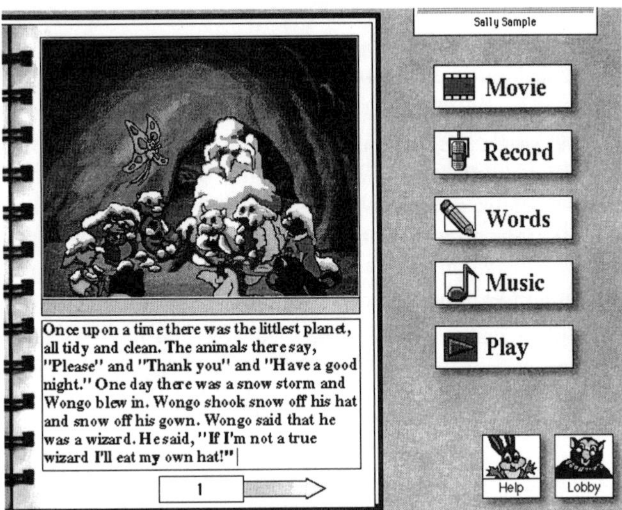

Multimedia Storybook Maker Features:

- Pictures from the sequencing activity are used to construct a book in childrens' own words.
- The "Picture" button turns the still picture into a dynamic but silent clip from the story. (This provides dynamic retrieval prompts.)
- The "Record" button is used to orally record what the students want to write for this page. (The recording phase is collaborative; all children from the group add at least one sentence per page.)
- The "Write" button helps students sound out words and select candidates from a list. Alternatively, children or teachers can use the keyboard to write.
- The "Music" button allows children to select from a variety of musical clips ranging from "fast-happy" music to "slow-sad" music. (As children select clips, teachers guide discussions regarding which musical clips are best suited for the emotional tone of the page.)
- The "Play" button lets children see the dynamic visual clip, hear their voices, see the text, and listen to the music they have chosen.
- When all of the pages are completed, the book is printed out in a traditional format, and the children read along in their books as they listen to the integrated-media version on the computer. The children also take the books home to share with their families.

FIG. 7.4. Multimedia Storybook Maker.

encouraged to write their responses, which are then published. The address for the site is http.//www.LittlePlanet.com.

We are currently extending the Young Children's series to include mathematics and science activities (CTGV, 1996b). Eventually, it will provide the foundation for a Young Children's Schools for Thought.

Schools for Thought

A third project that builds on our experiences with *Jasper* is the Schools for Thought project. As discussed in Chapter 6, the Schools For Thought project is designed to restructure the entire school day in Grades 6, 7, and 8. It involves the integration of three different projects: *Jasper*; the Fostering Communities of Learners (FCL) project developed by Brown and Campione (e.g. Brown & Campione, 1994); and Scardamalia and Bereiter's Computer Supported Intentional Learning Environments (CSILE) project (Scardamalia & Bereiter, 1994).

The ability to restructure the entire school day in the Schools For Thought project provides an important opportunity to see the potential benefits of creating learning communities organized around problem- and project-based curricula. We believe that the effects of programs such as *Jasper* can be even greater in environments such as Schools for Thought because other aspects of the students' day facilitate their work in *Jasper* and vice versa (CTGV, 1996a).

NEXT STEPS

We envision several next steps that continue to build on our experiences with *Jasper*. One involves a new idea for making problem-based learning curricula such as *Jasper* easier to teach by combining them with a set of contrasting cases that scaffold students' discussions and provide increased opportunities for assessment because they help make students' thinking more visible. A second next step involves making *Jasper* integral to mathematics courses rather than being simply a supplement. A third next step involves uses of Internet technologies to help teachers create communities of learning that foster high achievement for all students. Examples are discussed next.

The Composition Software provides multiple types of help for composition.

- Story starters use familiar characters and themes from the anchor to begin a story that children complete; children can also write stories from scratch.
- A clip-art library and drawing tools allow children to create their own pictures.

Problem-Solving Extensions include related stories that students are asked to compare to the anchor story. Examples include "The Emperors New Clothes" and "The Lion and The Mouse."

- Extensions also revisit anchor and other stories by taking a specific mathematical or scientific focus.

FIG. 7.5. Communication through composition and problem-solving extensions.

Additional Scaffolds for Teaching With *Jasper*

A concept that has the potential to make it easier to teach with problem-based curricula such as *Jasper* involves the idea of providing students with contrasting cases that can scaffold their thinking, communication, and assessment. The best way to introduce the idea of contrasting cases is to discuss uses of *Jasper* with and without these cases. Toward this end, we consider the *Jasper* adventure *Working Smart.*

Working Smart Without Contrasting Cases

The adventure *Working Smart* involves a flashback to the 1960s where a young Jasper and his friends Larry and Emily have to compete in a game show that involves answering questions related to trip planning (see Appendix B). They have to answer as quickly and accurately as possible. The challenge for the students in the classroom is to create Smart Tools that help Jasper, Larry, and Emily win the game show. Several different types of problems occur on the show. One category of questions is Are We There Yet?

Consider preparing Smart Tools to answer questions about this category. The problems are all related to a map (see Fig. 7.6) that is given to students; it shows

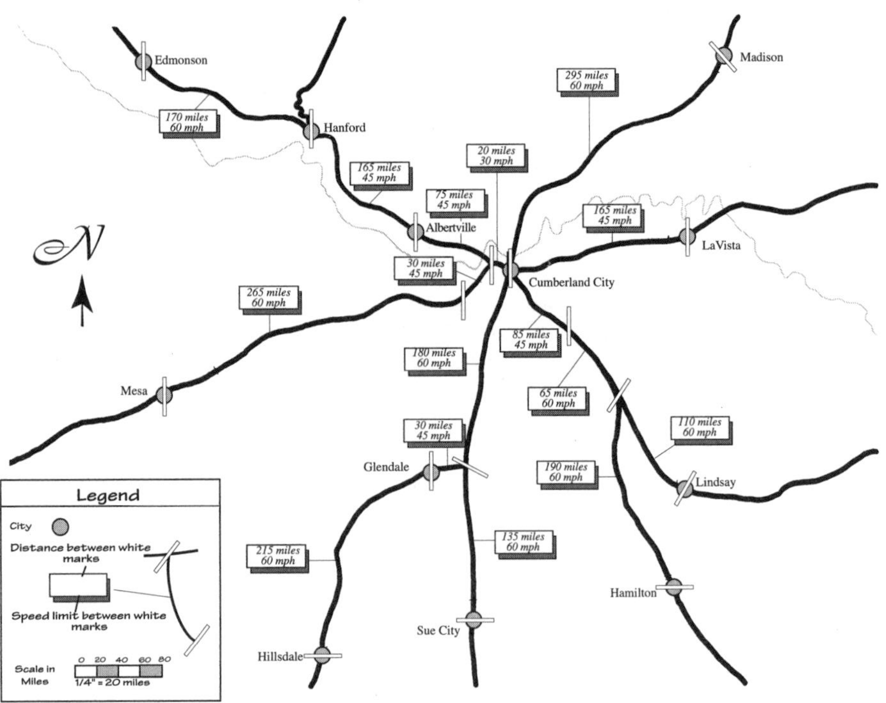

FIG. 7.6. Working Smart map.

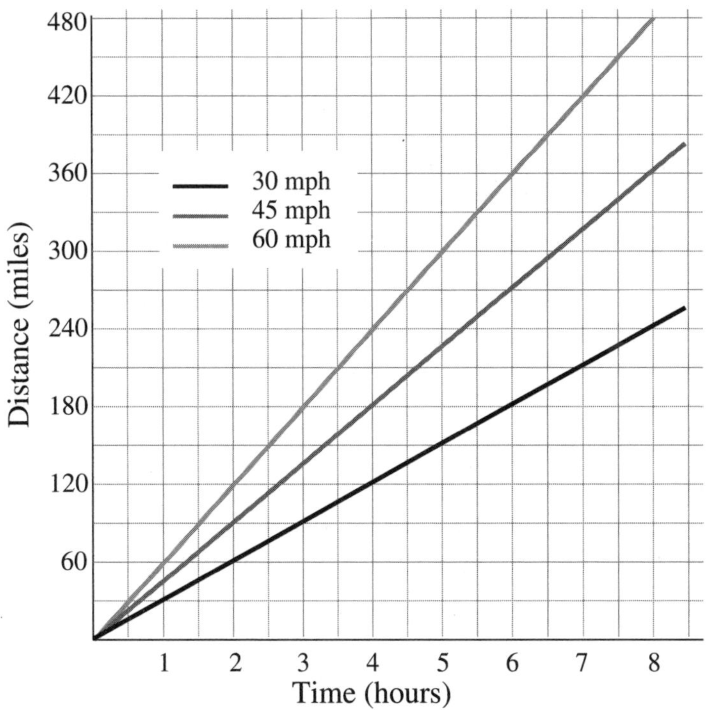

FIG. 7.7. Smart Tool for category Are We There Yet?

relevant distances and speed limits. Given the map and their Smart Tools, students are asked to solve problems such as the following:

1. How long should it take me to get to Sue City by car?
2. I've been driving for 2 hours at 60 mph and I'm in the country. Can you tell me the nearest town?
3. If I drive 45 mph rather than 60 mph, how much longer will it take me to get to Hanford (which is 260 miles away)?

A graph like the one illustrated in Fig. 7.7 provides an excellent Smart Tool for helping students answer a variety of questions about the category Are We There Yet? Students usually do not create an appropriate graph on their first try; we give them several trials in order to create and revise their Smart Tool. Students then proceed to work on different categories of problems (e.g., Catch 'em If You Can, Beat This Deal). Each type of problem requires the construction of different types of Smart Tools.

It is not easy to implement *Working Smart* and similar problem-based activities (e.g., Bransford, Zech, Schwartz, et al., 1996). Students initially have little idea about how to approach complex problems. This is especially true in classrooms where students have had little experience working in groups and little experience in attempting to solve complex problems. Unfortunately, there are many classrooms such as this.

Problem Solving With Contrasting Cases

Appropriate uses of contrasting cases make it much easier for both teachers and students to begin working in problem-solving contexts such as *Working Smart*. In our studies, we have presented students with catalogs of potential tools and asked them to choose one or two for solving a particular class of problems. For example, the catalog illustrated in Fig. 7.8 shows tools that are potentially relevant to the Are We There Yet? category of problems noted earlier. Students work in groups to choose two tools to purchase. Each group then explains its choices to the rest of the class. Eventually students receive examples of their tools and get to test their mettle in actual problem-solving situations. They get to revise their choices of tools and try them with new problems before moving on to new categories of problems to solve.

Observations from our pilot studies suggest that the use of catalogs containing contrasting cases makes it much easier to get the class thinking about *Working Smart*. First, students in our pilot studies were highly motivated to look through the catalog. Second, students' conversations were focused because they organized their discussions around the design features that differentiated the contrasting tools. Third, students received more chances for feedback because the catalog contrasts helped structure their thinking and make it more visible. In addition, when different groups explained their choices of tools to the other groups, their presentations were clear and they received useful feedback from the rest of the class.

For the next several categories of problems in *Working Smart*, students in the contrasting cases group again received catalogs of contrasting items. However, this time the items required student-generated elaboration before students were able to use them as tools (e.g., students had to actually draw in various functions rather than receive them predrawn in various tools). For the last category of problems, students in the catalog group generated their own Smart Tools, just as students in the noncatalog group had done all along. We used the catalog to scaffold (e.g., Vygotsky, 1978, 1986) students' abilities to generate their own tools. Our pilot data suggest that students who receive the catalogs of appropriately contrasting cases end up generating better sets of tools than the students who have consistently been asked to generate tools without catalogs of contrasting cases.

One of the teachers with whom we work recently provided an interesting perspective on the advantages of using contrasting cases. She had first taught *Working Smart* without a catalog and found that all her students tended to generate the same Smart Tool each time. When she later used a Smart Tool catalog, there was much more variability in the students' initial choices and, hence, much more meaningful discussion. After thinking about her teaching, the teacher realized that the first time she had taught *Working Smart*, she had led her students to create a

SMART TOOLS CATALOG

Item A:

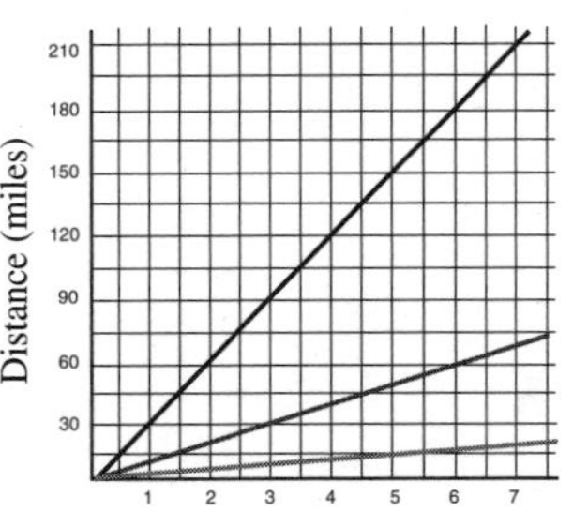

Item B:

Distance (miles)	Time (min) Rate 1	Time (min) Rate 2	Time (min) Rate 3	Time (min) Rate 4	Time (min) Rate 5	Time (min) Rate 6	Time (min) Rate 7
10	20	17	15	13	12	11	10
20	40	34	30	27	24	22	20
30	60	51	45	40	36	33	30
40	80	69	60	53	48	44	40
50	100	86	75	67	60	55	50
60	120	103	90	80	72	65	60
70	140	120	105	93	84	76	70
80	160	137	120	107	96	87	80
90	180	154	135	120	108	98	90
100	200	171	150	133	120	109	100
110	220	189	165	147	132	120	110
120	240	206	180	160	144	131	120
130	260	223	195	173	156	142	130
140	280	240	210	197	168	153	140
150	300	257	225	210	180	164	150

Item C:

From Cumberland City to:	Distance (miles)
Albertville	95
Edmonson	430
Glendale	210
Hamilton	340
Hanford	260
Hillsdale	425
LaVista	165
Lindsay	260
Madison	295
Mesa	285
Sue City	315

Item D:

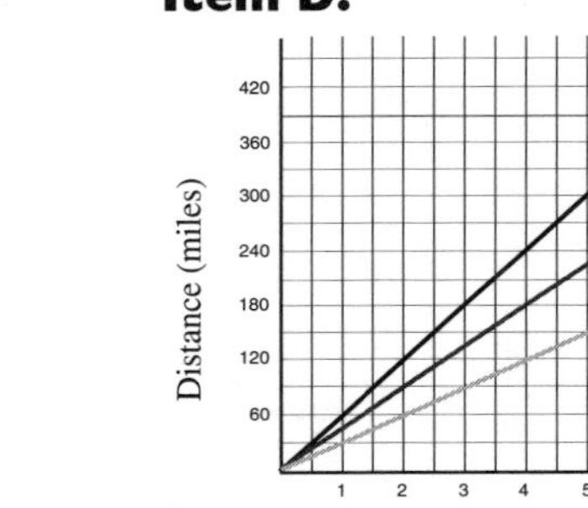

FIG. 7.8. Sample catalog items.

particular type of Smart Tool without realizing that she had done so. The use of the catalog made it much easier to keep from being too directive. This motivated exciting discussions among students who then became eager to test the value of their particular tools.

Overall, our pilot data suggest the fruitfulness of using contrasting cases as a way to naturally scaffold teaching and learning in a *Jasper* context. We are also exploring the idea that the use of contrasting cases in a context of anchored inquiry can enhance instruction in all subject matters. We are currently experimenting with the idea in science and literature.

Making *Jasper* Integral to Mathematics Courses

At the present time, *Jasper* is still only a supplement to schools' mathematics instruction. As discussed throughout this book, data indicate that *Jasper* can be a very useful supplement. Nevertheless, our experiences strongly suggest that *Jasper* would be much more powerful if it were closely linked to students' entire mathematics curriculum. We are eager to work toward this goal.

Our current thoughts about creating curricula organized around *Jasper* involve the Smart Tools concept that emerged in our efforts to create the *Jasper* algebra adventures (e.g., see Bransford, Zech, Schwartz, et al., 1996). An emphasis on encouraging students to create Smart Tools, and to test the mettle of their tools, seems to have a number of advantages. First, it helps students focus on the idea that modeling the world by mathematizing it enables them to solve entire classes of problems rather than only a single problem. Second, it helps students focus on the concept of distributed cognition—on the idea that people are smart, in part, because of the tools they invent (e.g., Bransford, Zech, Schwartz, et al., 1996; Norman, 1993; Pea, 1993; Salomon, 1993). Third, an emphasis on creating multipurpose tools helps students appreciate the power of understanding abstract mathematical concepts such as rate, functions, and proportionality. Fourth, the creation of Smart Tools that can be used to solve a variety of problems provides an excellent context for the SMART Challenge series discussed in Chapter 5.

One of our plans is to redo typical approaches to teaching geometry and algebra in the seventh and eighth grades. Many programs are encouraging more students to take these courses. In our community, however, the students are still focusing primarily on computational procedures; they have very little understanding of the concepts they are learning. Our initial work with Smart Tools suggests that they hold promise for transforming students' understanding of geometry and algebra into forms that make them exciting and understandable. We will begin with visual tools and then help students transform them into symbolic tools (Bransford, Goldman, & Hasselbring, 1995; Bransford, Zech, Schwartz, et al., 1996).

Using the Internet to Support Community Building

A third next step in our research efforts is to use the Internet in ways that help teachers build learning communities that focus on the acquisition of important information relevant to mathematics, science, social studies, and literacy. For example, an Internet site for Schools for Thought will allow new teachers to feel part of an international community, and gain access to information about theory, SFT sites, and most importantly, advice from other teachers who have tried SFT in their classrooms. We also plan to build on our work with SMART Challenges (see Chapter 5) by extending it to the Internet and allowing teachers and students chances to test their mettle, receive feedback, reflect, and revise.

An experiment being completed as this book goes to press involves an Internet-based SMART Challenge organized around the *SIA* adventure *The Stones River Mystery*. Students first watch the initial part of the *SIA* adventure on CD-ROM; it takes them to the point of seeing that a river might be polluted and needing to collect and analyze data. At this point students work in groups to make decisions about how to collect data on the river, how to analyze it, and how to interpret their results.

As a scaffold for enhancing inquiry, discussion, and self-assessment, students receive a catalog of possible devices that can be used to take samples from the river (see Fig. 7.9). Students know that they are to choose only one item and must explain why.

FIG. 7.9. A sample of items in a catalog for ordering tools for Macroinvertebrate Testing.

The catalogs are specially designed to include contrasting cases that help students discover the need to know certain kinds of information. For example, the Hochmeister kick net comes in several different sizes of mesh. By looking at these items, students realize they need to understand the size of macroinvertebrates. Similarly, by comparing catalog items for eliminating macroinvertebrates (students often have the misconception they cause pollution) versus items for capturing macroinvertebrates and using them to estimate the health of the river, students begin to explore issues that are relevant to frequently held misconceptions.

Once groups of students make their choice of a catalog item, they access SMART WEB on the Internet (see Fig. 7.10). The catalog items are displayed on the Web, and students make their choices and explain why they either did or did not choose each item. Their responses go to a database that organizes all the data from their classroom, plus data from other classrooms as well. Students also receive feedback on their choices.

Students can also access a Kids Online section that includes audio of other students explaining their choices from the catalog.

The visit to the Internet provides students with general feedback about their choices. As they work to revise, students have opportunities to look up text-based resources that provide more in-depth information about science content relevant to various choices. For example, the text resources explain the need to break macroinvertebrates into categories that are pollution-tolerant, semi-pollution-intolerant, and pollution-intolerant. Students can use this information to understand why the Tetra Ben Laser counter, which counts all macroinvertebrates but does not sort them, does not provide the kinds of data they would need.

After revising their thinking, students again visit the SMART WEB Internet site and make new choices of catalog items and new justifications. They can then see summarized data from their class and other classes and see how the data have changed. Following the correct choice of an appropriate object (in this case, the .5 mm Hochmeister kick net), students work with a CD-ROM simulation that allows them to see a sample of macroinvertebrates, calculate a water quality index, and compare their results with baseline data from previous years (see Fig. 7.11). Although each student gets a different sample of macroinvertebrates, each set of data shows that there is a serious absence of pollution sensitive macroinvertebrates—hence something is wrong.

The SMART Challenge continues by next having students choose items for doing an oxygen test. Again, they make their choices via the Web and see data that summarizes the choices of other classes. Also, students gain access to text-based resources (which sometimes reside in other Internet sites) that help them understand the science underlying various choices. And they eventually get to do some experiments on their own. For example, students are encouraged to test the amount of dissolved oxygen in a tank of water prior to putting fish in it and after the fish have lived in it for at least 1 day. With appropriate testing instruments, data show that there is less dissolved oxygen in the water after the fish have been there. For classrooms that cannot do actual tests, simulated, computer-based tests are available.

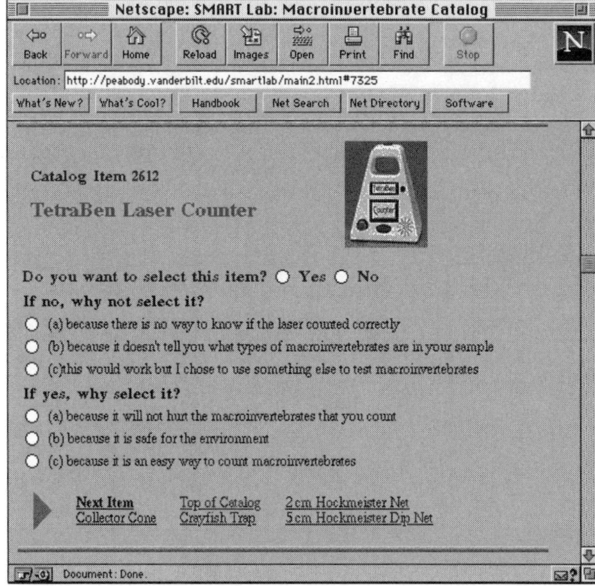

FIG. 7.10. Smart Web and an example of a catalog item.

FIG. 7.11. Software for sampling and classifying Macroinvertebrates.

As noted earlier, our work with SMART WEB challenges is just beginning: *The Stones River Mystery* challenge is the first we have attempted. Our plans are to create additional Web-based challenges around the choice and creation of SMART Tools relevant to *Jasper* adventures and, eventually, around the Young Children's Literacy series. By providing students and teachers with frequent opportunities for formative assessment and revision, we believe that we can better help them reach the goals of the National Standards in areas such as mathematics and science (e.g., NCTM, 1989; National Research Council, 1996). We are also developing Web Challenges that focus on big ideas in areas such as social studies and literature. This will allow us to use SMART Challenges for programs such as Schools for Thought.

An exciting opportunity for implementing Web-based challenges is provided by the American Schools Directory (ASD). Designed to become the Internet home for all K–12 schools in America, the ASD will provide free Web pages for each of the country's 106,000 schools, as well as for each teacher and, ultimately, each student. A major goal of the ASD is to create school-centered communities with access to the world.

Members of our center are involved in the development of The Education Connection, a component of ASD that includes links to a number of important Web sites and Web-based tools for students, educators, and parents. The Education Connection also includes the Challenge Zone, where students test their mettle, publish their responses to various challenges, and compare them to others' from around the country. Each challenge is accompanied by offline and online resources that are relevant for solving the challenges. The research reported in this book suggests that Web-based challenges can help break the isolation of classrooms and increase student achievement as well as teacher learning. The ASD provides an ideal mechanism for implementing challenges and assessing their effects.

SUMMARY AND CONCLUSIONS

Our goal in this chapter was to summarize the intellectual journey made possible by *Jasper* and discuss some of the important lessons and next steps.

We described our intellectual journey from the perspective of the LTC framework. Work with *Jasper* involved us in many of the cells in the framework. We noted that each research cell was important; different things could be learned by working in different cells. The most important advantage of the LTC framework is that it helps us know where we are in the general space of possibilities.

We noted that one of the major lessons learned from our journeys through the LTC framework involves a much deeper appreciation of the importance of sociocultural contexts and their effects on learning. Teachers helped us see how features of programs such as *Jasper* could be used to build learning communities within classrooms and schools, across classrooms and schools, and between schools, classrooms, and the broader community.

New research and development projects being undertaken in our LTC have been strongly influenced by our experiences with *Jasper.* We continue to organize our instructional environments around anchors that provide shared contexts for inquiry, and we continue to look for ways to provide frequent opportunities for formative assessment. Our current work has also been influenced by the development of CD-ROM and Internet technologies that were not widely available when we began our work with *Jasper.* They offer opportunities that are promising and exciting.

We are extremely grateful to the teachers and students who worked with us and taught us so much, and to the granting agencies who gave us the opportunity to develop and study *Jasper.* We hope that this book helps repay some of their investment by providing information that is valuable to others. We also look forward to the next 10 years of research—it is going to be quite an adventure!

APPENDIX A. Story Summary of *Rescue at Boone's Meadow*

Larry Peterson, a friend of Jasper Woodbury, flies an ultralight plane over Cumberland City. Soon, Larry begins to teach Emily Johnson to fly the ultralight. He gives her some information about the plane: Its total weight is 250 pounds. It can carry a payload of up to 220 pounds. Larry explains that payload is the weight; payload includes the weight of the pilot, the fuel, and cargo. Larry then show Emily a box used for carrying extra cargo. The box weighs 10 pounds when it is empty. The cargo box holds a 1-gallon gas can.

Emily comes closer to the ultralight so she can see as Larry is teaching her. He explains that the propeller does the pushing, just like it does with a boat; the wing does the lifting. He then demonstrates how the unique shape of the wing helps lift the plane.

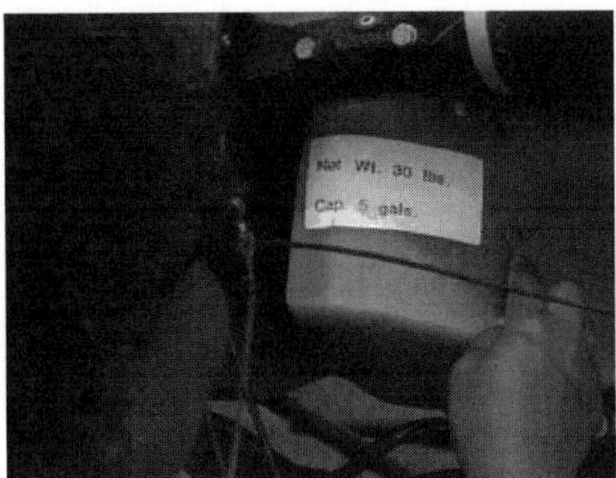

A few days later, Larry teaches Emily about the engine of the ultralight. He tells her that his ultralight's engine was originally used for a snowmobile, so it uses regular fuel and not aviation fuel. The net weight of the 5-gallon fuel tank is 30 pounds. Emily points out that 1½ gallons of fuel are left in each of the 2 sides of the fuel tank. She asks Larry how far he flew on the two gallons missing from the tank. He tells her that he had filled up the fuel tank in the morning and had flown over to Headlyville and back, which was about 30 miles. She asked him how long that took. Larry replied, "My rule of thumb is 1 mile every two minutes—on a calm day, that is." Larry tells Emily that he only needs a field 100 yards long to take off.

A few weeks later, Emily takes her first flight. Emily, Larry, and Jasper go out to supper to celebrate. At the restaurant, Jasper talks about his plans for a fishing trip. He says that he plans to drive the 60 miles from Cumberland City to Hilda's Service Station and then hike to his favorite fishing spot, which is about 18 miles on foot. Larry mentions that he flew his ultralight to see Hilda the previous week and that he landed in the field next to her service station.

For dessert, Emily orders a dish of strawberry ice cream and Larry orders lemon jello in a sugar cone. Their bill comes to $17.50. Emily suggests they include a 20% tip, and they agree to split the check equally. They each put money down on the table: Jasper puts $11.00 down, Emily puts $12.00, and Larry puts $9.00 down. Larry calculates the total bill and makes change for each of them.

Before leaving the restaurant, Emily and Larry weigh themselves. The scale shows that Emily weighs 120 pounds and Larry weighs 180 pounds.

While fishing, Jasper hears a gunshot. He discovers that an eagle has been shot. After giving first-aid to the eagle, he makes an emergency call to Hilda on his two-way radio.

A customer in a convertible drives up to Hilda's. The speed limit on the road is 60 miles per hour. Hilda is pumping gas for her customer as Jasper radios for help. When Hilda is finished, the gas pump shows that the customer got a total of 13.9 gallons and that gas costs $1.259 per gallon. Her customer records his mileage and tells Hilda that he got 312 miles on his last tank of gas. His bill for the gas comes to $17.50, and he pays for it with a $20.00 bill.

When Hilda answers Jasper's emergency call, Jasper tells her about the wounded eagle and explains that he needs to get it to Dr. Ramirez, a veterinarian in Cumberland City, ASAP. Jasper tells Hilda that he is at Boone's Meadow, which is about a 5-hour walk from her service station. He asks Hilda to call Emily Johnson and explain the situation.

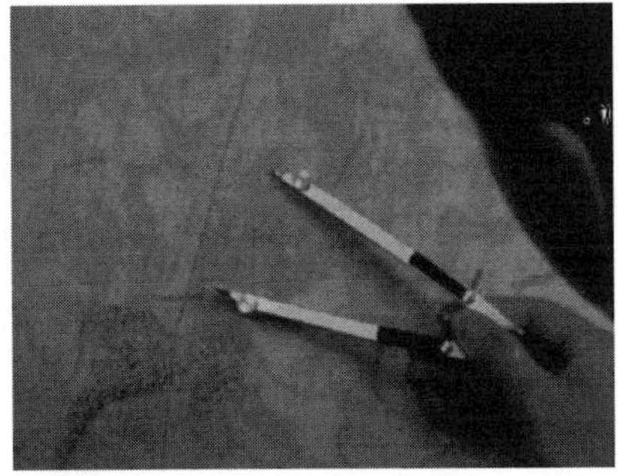

Emily drives to Dr. Ramirez's office. They go into his office, where he has a map of the area on his wall. He marks the locations of his office in Cumberland City, Boone's Meadow, and Hilda's. Dr. Ramirez points out that Hilda's is right off the highway and that there are no roads leading into Boone's Meadow. Emily asks how much a bald eagle weighs. Dr. Ramirez estimates that it would weigh about 15 pounds.

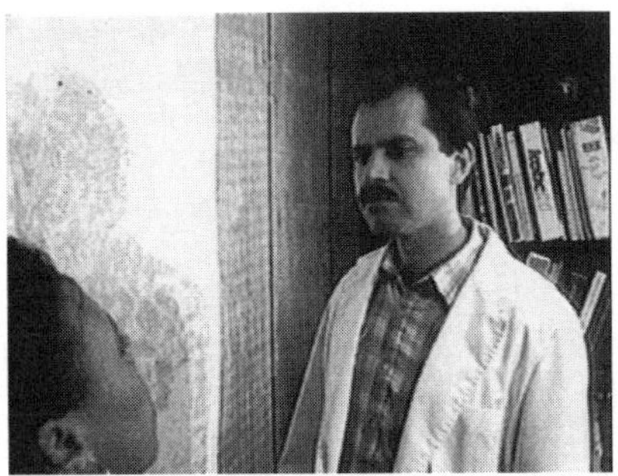

On the map, Dr. Ramirez determines that the distance by air between Boone's Meadow and Cumberland City is about 65 miles. He tells Emily that most planes need about 2,000 feet of runway and Boone's Meadow is just half that long. Before he leaves, Dr. Ramirez tells Emily that the sooner he can treat the eagle, the better chance he has of saving it.

Emily plans for the eagle's rescue. She uses the map to determine that the distance by air between Boone's Meadow and Hilda's is approximately 15 miles. Next, she calls Larry, who is just down the road. She learns that Larry is available to fly, that the ultralight is fueled up and ready, and that the winds are calm.

Emily thinks about the information she has gathered. She estimates that if the ultralight is used in the rescue, she had better add 5 minutes for each stop.

Challenge
Emily wants to know two things:

- The quickest way to move the eagle to Cumberland City;
- And how long will that take?

APPENDIX B. Synopses of the *Jasper* Adventures

1. DISTANCE / RATE / TIME

Trip Planning: "Journey to Cedar Creek"

Students meet Jasper Woodbury one morning as he is reading the newspaper. His interest is piqued by an advertisement for an old boat for sale. Jasper decides to go see the boat, and the viewers follow him up the Cumberland River to Cedar Creek Marina. There, he meets the boat owner, test drives the boat, and learns that its running lights are not working and that it has a temporary fuel tank. He decides to buy the boat. Students are challenged to help Jasper determine if he can make it home before sunset without running out of fuel.

Trip Planning: "Rescue at Boone's Meadow"

The story opens with Jasper's friend Larry teaching another friend, Emily, to fly an ultralight airplane. Jasper and his friends discuss an upcoming fishing/camping trip that he is taking to Boone's Meadow. On his trip, Jasper finds a badly wounded eagle that needs emergency treatment to survive. The overall problem deals with alternatives that Emily must consider in helping Jasper get the eagle to the veterinarian.

Trip Planning: "Get Out the Vote"

When metropolitan Trenton threatens to dump its excess garbage in Cumberland City, Jasper visits Trenton to investigate the story for his newspaper. There he meets Lenore Clayton, a candidate for mayor. A key to Ms. Clayton's winning will be making sure voters who are most likely to vote for her are able to get to the polls. Tracy and Marcus, Ms. Clayton's teenage children, are helping their mother with her campaign. Two days before the election, Ms. Clayton's campaign manager gets sick and is unable to finish the driver itineraries for transporting voters. Students are challenged to help Tracy and Marcus prepare plans to drive as many voters as possible to the polls on election day.

2. STATISTICS AND PROBABILITY

Business Planning: "The Big Splash"

Jasper's young friend Chris wants to help his school raise money to buy a new camera for the school TV station. His idea is to have a dunking booth in which teachers would be dunked when students hit a target. He must develop a business plan for the school principal in order to obtain a loan for his project. The overall problem centers on developing this business plan, including the use of a statistical survey to help him decide if this idea would be profitable.

Business Planning: "Bridging the Gap"

A group of eight students from high schools around Trenton and two executives from a local wildlife preserve are challenged to develop a grant proposal for projects that will protect threatened or endangered species and benefit the surrounding community. The proposal will be judged in a national competition. The winning group will be given a $5,000 grant to carry out its proposal. The students must be able to include 60% of all their schools' population as volunteers in the projects. Students learn about statistical concepts and their environment as they look for worthy projects.

Business Planning: "A Capital Idea"

A group of high school students, along with Jasper's friend Larry, become involved in a project to recycle aluminum beverage cans. They need to raise money to continue the Mayor's fund for an annual high school trip to Washington, D. C. The students conduct a survey to predict how many families would recycle aluminum cans. The challenge is to prepare a business plan to gain the Mayor's support for their aluminum can recycling project.

3. GEOMETRY

Architectural Design: "Blueprint for Success"

Christina and Marcus, two students from Trenton, visit an architectural firm on Career Day. While learning about the work of architects, Christina and Marcus hear about a vacant lot being donated in their neighborhood for a playground. This is exciting news because there is no place in their downtown neighborhood for children to play. Recently, several students have been hurt playing in the street. The challenge is for students to help Christina and Marcus design a playground and ballfield for the lot.

Way-Finding: "The Right Angle"

Paige Littlefield, a young Native American, has been left a challenge by her grandfather to find a cave with a family heirloom. Paige wants to find the heirloom in time for the powwow, which is coming up soon. As the story unfolds, the viewer learns from Larry and others about topographic maps, as well as about important concepts of geometry (e.g., isosceles right triangles) and their usefulness for measurement. At the end of the story, the students need to use the information about maps and geometry to locate the cave by following Paige's grandfather's directions. They then need to determine the fastest way to get to the cave.

Way-Finding: "The Great Circle Race"

Jasper's newspaper sponsors a Great Circle Race in which contestants can start anywhere outside a circle that is centered at a specific finish point and has a radius of 5 miles. Only nonmotorized vehicles are allowed in the race. Students have to predict who will win the race and in what time. In order to do so, they need to interpret a topographic map, correctly draw the legal race area on the map, interpret data about the speed of various nonmotorized vehicles, and use compass clues to determine racers' starting locations and routes.

4. ALGEBRA

Smart Tool Building: "Working Smart"

Larry tells William and Annie a story that occurred in 1968 when he was a teenager. In the story, Jasper, Emily, and Larry compete in a problem-solving contest sponsored by a local travel agency. If the three teenagers do well in the contest, they win an all-expenses-paid trip to anywhere in the United States. The trio decides that studying geography is the best way to prepare. To their dismay, they learn at the preliminary round that the contest is not about geography. They set about creating mathematical Smart Tools that will allow them to solve several classes of travel-related problems efficiently and quickly so they can succeed in the final round.

Smart Tool Building: "Kim's Komet"

At the regional soapwood derby competition, Kim's model race car has the second-fastest time trial and qualifies for the Grand Pentathlon. In the Grand Pentathlon race, cars must compete in five different events. Kim must decide where to place her car on the ramp of the race track so that it is going the right speed to successfully complete each event. One of her competitors, Darlene, uses an electrical device and a computer to calculate the speed of her car. With the help of her brother Greg and former soapwood derby winner Larry Peterson, Kim times her car and creates the Smart Tools that will allow her to quickly and accurately determine the best starting points for each event.

Smart Tool Building: "The General Is Missing"

Larry's grandfather is kidnapped by three villains who want him to turn over the design for his latest invention. The kidnappers take Grandpa to a secret hideout where he must stay until they are sure that the design he gives them is authentic. Grandpa convinces the kidnappers that he must send a note to Jasper, Emily, and Larry or they will get suspicious about his disappearance. Using algebra, Grandpa discreetly communicated information about the location of the hideout. Jasper, Emily, and Larry must decipher Grandpa's note, locate the hideout, and help rescue Grandpa.

References

Adams, J. L. (1979). *Conceptual blockbusting: A guide to better ideas*. NY: Norton.

Adams, L., Kasserman, J., Yearwood, A., Perfetto, G., Bransford, J., & Franks, J. (1988). The effects of facts versus problem-oriented acquisition. *Memory & Cognition, 16*, 167–175.

Anderson, J. R. (1983). A spreading activation theory of memory. *Journal of Verbal Learning and Verbal Behavior, 22*, 261–296.

Anderson, J. R. (1987). Skill acquisition: Compilation of weak-method problem solutions. *Psychological Review, 94*, 192–210.

Asch, S. E. (1969). A reformulation of the problem of associations. *American Psychologist, 24*, 92–102.

Baron, J. (1987). Evaluating thinking skills in the classroom. In J. Baron & R. J. Sternberg (Eds.), *Teaching thinking skills: Theory and practice* (pp. 221–248). New York: Freeman.

Barron, B. (1991). *Collaborative problem solving: Is team performance greater than what is expected from the most competent member?* Unpublished doctoral dissertation, Vanderbilt University, Nashville, TN.

Barron, B. J. (1996, April). *Building in opportunities and resources for revision: Social and technological designs for formative assessment.* Paper presented at the meeting of the American Educational Research Association, New York.

Barron, B. J., Bransford, J. D., Kulewicz, S., & Hasselbring, T. S. (1989, April). *Uses of macrocontexts to facilitate mathematical thinking*. Paper presented at the meeting of the American Educational Research Association meeting, San Francisco.

Barron, B. J., Mayfield-Stewart, C., Schwartz, D., & Czarnik, C. (1996, April). *Students' use of tools for formative assessment.* Paper presented at the meeting of the American Educational Research Association, New York.

Barron, B. J. S., Vye, N. J., Zech, L., Schwartz, D., Bransford, J. D., Goldman, S. R., Pellegrino, J., Morris, J., Garrison, S., & Kantor, R. (1995). Creating contexts for community-based problem solving: The Jasper challenge series. In C. N. Hedley, P. Antonacci, & M. Rabinowitz (Eds.), *Thinking and literacy: The mind at work* (pp. 47–71). Hillsdale, NJ: Lawrence Erlbaum Associates.

Barrows, H. S. (1985). *How to design a problem-based curriculum for the preclinical years*. New York: Springer.

Bereiter, C. (1984, Spring). How to keep thinking skills from going the way of all frills. *Educational Leadership, 42*, 75–77.

Bereiter, C. (1994). Implications of postmodernism for science, or, science as progressive discourse. *Educational Technology, 29*, 3–12.

Borasi, R. (1987, November). Exploring mathematics through the analysis of errors. *For the Learning of mathematics, 7*(3), 1–8.

Borasi, R. (in press). *Learning mathematics through inquiry: A study of practice.* Portsmouth, NH: Heinmann.

Bransford, J. D. (1981). Social-cultural prerequisites for cognitive research. In J. H. Harvey (Ed.), *Cognition, social behavior, and the environment* (pp. 557–569). Hillsdale, NJ: Lawrence Erlbaum Associates.

Bransford, J. D. (1993). Who ya gonna call? Thoughts about teaching problem-solving. In P. Hallinger, K. Leithwood, & J. Murphy (Eds.), *Cognitive perspectives on educational leadership* (pp. 171–191). New York: Teachers College Press.

Bransford, J. D., Delclos, V., Vye, N., Burns, S., & Hasselbring, T. (1987). Approaches to dynamic assessment: Issues, data and future directions. In C. Lidz (Ed.), *Dynamic assessment: An interactional approach to evaluating learning potentials* (pp. 479–495). New York: Guilford.

Bransford, J. D., Franks, J. J., Morris, C. D., & Stein, B. S. (1979). Some general constraints on learning and memory research. In L. S. Cermak & F. I. M. Craik (Eds.), *Levels of processing in human memory* (pp. 331–354). Hillsdale, NJ: Lawrence Erlbaum Associates.

Bransford, J. D., Franks, J. J., Vye, N. J., & Sherwood, R. D. (1989). New approaches to instruction: Because wisdom can't be told. In S. Vosniadou & A. Ortony (Eds.), *Similarity and analogical reasoning* (pp. 470–497). New York: Cambridge University Press.

Bransford, J. D., Goin, L. I., Hasselbring, T. S., Kinzer, C. K., Sherwood, R. D., & Williams, S. M. (1988). Learning with technology: Theoretical and empirical perspectives. *Peabody Journal of Education, 64*(1), 5–26.

Bransford, J. D., Goldman, S. R., & Hasselbring, T. S. (1995, April). *Marrying constructivist and skills-based approaches: Could we, should we, and can technology help?* Symposium presented at the annual meeting of the American Educational Research Association, San Francisco. (Audiotape available from AERA.)

Bransford, J. D., Goldman, S. R., & Vye, N. J. (1991). Making a difference in peoples' abilities to think: Reflections on a decade of work and some hopes for the future. In L. Okagaki & R. J. Sternberg (Eds.), *Directors of development: Influences on children* (pp. 147–180). Hillsdale, NJ: Lawrence Erlbaum Associates.

Bransford, J. D., Hasselbring, T., Barron, B., Kulewicz, S., Littlefield, J., & Goin, L. (1988). Uses of macro-contexts to facilitate mathematical thinking. In R. I. Charles & E. A. Silver (Eds.), *The teaching and assessing of mathematical problem solving* (pp. 125–147). Hillsdale, NJ: Lawrence Erlbaum Associates and National Council of Teachers of Mathematics.

Bransford, J. D., & Heldmeyer, K. (1983). Learning from children learning. In J. Bisanz, G. Bisanz, & R. Kail (Eds.), *Learning in children: Progress in cognitive development research* (pp. 171–190). New York: Springer.

Bransford, J. D., & Johnson, M. K. (1972). Contextual prerequisites for understanding: Some investigations of comprehension and recall. *Journal of Verbal Learning and Verbal Behavior, 11*, 717–726.

Bransford, J. D. & Johnson, M. K. (1973). Considerations of some problems comprehension. In W. Chase (Ed.), *Visual information processing* (pp. 383–438. New York: Academic Press.

Bransford, J., Kinzer C., Risko, V., Rowe, D., & Vye, N. (1989). Designing invitations to thinking: Some initial thoughts. Cognitive and social perspectives for literacy research and instruction. In S. McCormick, J. Zutrell, P. Scharer, & P. O'Keefe (Eds.), *Cognitive and social perspectives for literacy research and instruction: 38th Yearbook-National Reading Conference* (pp. 35–54). Chicago: National Reading Conference.

Bransford, J. D., & McCarrell, N. S. (1974). A sketch of cognitive approach to comprehension. In W. Weimer & D. Palermo (Eds.), *Cognition and the symbolic processes* (pp. 189–229). Hillsdale, NJ: Lawrence Erlbaum Associates.

Bransford, J. D., & Schwartz, D. (1996, April). *Implications for the future: Design principles for useful assessment.* Paper presented at the meeting of the American Educational Research Association, New York.

Bransford, J. D., Sherwood, R., & Hasselbring, T. (1988). The video revolution and its effects on development: Some initial thoughts. In G. Foreman & P. Pufall (Eds.), *Constructivism in the computer age* (pp. 173–201). Hillsdale, NJ: Lawrence Erlbaum Associates.

Bransford, J. D., Sherwood, R. D., Hasselbring, T. S., Kinzer, C. K., & Williams, S. M. (1990). Anchored instruction: Why we need it and how technology can help. In D. Nix & R. Spiro (Eds.), *Cognition, education, and multi-media: Exploring ideas in high technology* (pp. 115–141). Hillsdale, NJ: Lawrence Erlbaum Associates.

Bransford, J. D., Sherwood, R. D., Vye, N. J., & Rieser, J. (1986). Teaching thinking and problem solving: Research foundations. *American Psychologist, 41*, 1078–1089.

Bransford, J. D., & Stein, B. S. (1993). *The IDEAL problem solver* (2nd ed.). New York: Freeman.

Bransford, J. D., & Stein, B. S. (1984). *The IDEAL problem solver*. New York: Freeman.

Bransford, J. D., Stein, B. S., Delclos, V. R., & Littlefield, J. (1986). Computers and problem solving. In C. K. Kinzer, R. Sherwood, & J. D. Bransford (Eds.), *Computer strategies for education* (pp. 147–180). Columbus, OH: Merrill.

Bransford, J. D., Vye, N., Kinzer, C., & Risko, V. (1990). Teaching thinking and content knowledge: Toward an integrated approach. In B. Jones & L. Idol (Eds.), *Dimensions of thinking and cognitive instruction* (pp. 381–413). Hillsdale, NJ: Lawrence Erlbaum Associates.

Bransford, J. D., Zech, L., Schwartz, D., Barron, B., Vye, N., and the Cognition and Technology Group at Vanderbilt [CTGV]. (1996). Fostering mathematical thinking in middle school students: Lessons from research. In R. J. Sternberg & T. Ben-Zeev (Eds.),*The nature of mathematical thinking* (pp. 203–250). Mahwah, NJ: Lawrence Erlbaum Associates.

Bridges, E. M. (1992). *Problem based learning for administrators with the assistance of Philip Hallinger.* Eugene, OR: Eric Publishing.

Bridges, E. M., & Hallinger, P. (1995). *Implementing problem based learning in leadership development.* Eugene, OR: Eric Publishing.

Brown, A. L., Ash, D., Rutherford, M., Nakagawa, K., Gordon, A., & Campione, J. C. (1993). Distributed expertise in the classroom. In G. Salomon (Ed.), *Distributed cognitions: Psychological and educational considerations* (pp. 188–228). New York: Cambridge University Press.

Brown, A. L., Bransford, J. D., Ferrara, R., & Campione, J. (1983). Learning, remembering and understanding. In J. H. Flavell & E. M. Markman (Eds.), *Handbook of child psychology, Vol. 3: Cognitive development* (4th ed., pp. 77–166). New York: Wiley.

Brown, A. L. & Campione, J. C. (1994). Guided discovery in a community of learners. In K. McGilly (Ed.), *Classroom lessons: Integrating cognitive theory and classroom practice* (pp. 229–272). Cambridge, MA: MIT Press.

Brown, A. L., & Campione, J. C. (1996). Psychological theory and the design of innovative learning environments: On procedures, principles, and systems. In L. Schauble & R. Glaser (Eds.), *Innovations in learning: New environments for education* (pp. 289–325). Mahwah, NJ: Lawrence Erlbaum Associates.

Brown, J. S., Collins, A., & Duguid, P. (1989). Situated cognition and the culture of learning. *Educational Researcher, 18*, 32–41.

Brown, S. I., & Walter, M. I. (1990). *The art of problem posing* (2nd ed.). Hillsdale, NJ: Lawrence Erlbaum Associates.

Bruce, B. C., Peyton, J. K., & Batson, T. (1993). *Network-based classrooms: Promises and realities.* Cambridge, MA: Cambridge University Press.

Bruer, J. T. (1993). *Schools for thought.* New York: MIT Press.

Bryk, A. S., & Raudenbush, S. W. (1992). *Hierarchical linear models: Applications and data analysis methods.* Newbury Park, CA: Sage.

Burton, R. R., Brown, J. S., & Fischer, G. (1984). Skiing as a model of instruction. In B. Rogoff & J. Lave (Eds.), *Everday cognition* (pp. 139–150). Cambridge, MA: Harvard University Press.

Campione, J. C., & Brown, A. L. (1987). Linking dynamic assessment with school achievement. In C. S. Lidz (Ed.), *Dynamic assessment: An interactional approach to evaluating learning potential* (pp. 82–114). New York: Guilford.

Charles, R., & Silver, E. A., (Eds.). (1988). *The teaching and assessing of mathematical problem solving.* Hillsdale, NJ: Larence Erlbaum Associates& National Council for Teachers of Mathematics.

Chi, M. T., Bassok, M., Lewis, P. J., & Glaser, R. (1989). Self-explanations: How students study and use examples in learning to solve problems. *Cognitive Science, 13*, 145–182.

Chi, M. T. H., Glaser, R., & Farr, M. (1991). *The nature of expertise.* Hillsdale, NJ: Lawrence Erlbaum Associates.

Clement, J. (1982). Algebra word problem solutions: Thought processes underlying a common misconception. *Journal of Research in Mathematics Education, 13*, 16–30.

Cobb, P. (1994). Where is the mind? Constructivist and sociocultural perspectives on mathematical development. *Educational Researcher, 23*(7), 13–20.

Cobb, P., Yackel, E., & Wood, T. (1992). A constructivist alternative to the representational view of mind in mathematics education. *Journal for Research in Mathematics Education, 19*, 99–114.

Cognition and Technology Group at Vanderbilt. (1990). Anchored instruction and its relationship to situated cognition. *Educational Researcher, 19*(6), 2–10.

Cognition and Technology Group at Vanderbilt. (1991). Technology and the design of generative learning environments. *Educational Technology, 31*, 34–40.

Cognition and Technology Group at Vanderbilt. (1992a). The Jasper series: A generative approach to mathematical thinking. In K. Sheingold, L. G. Roberts, & S. M. Malcolm (Eds.), *This year in science series, 1991: Technology for teaching and learning* (pp. 108–140). Washington, DC: American Association for the Advancement of Science.

Cognition and Technology Group at Vanderbilt. (1992b). The Jasper experiment: An exploration of issues in learning and instructional design. *Educational Technology Research and Development, 40*, 65–80.

Cognition and Technology Group at Vanderbilt. (1992c). The Jasper series as an example of anchored instruction: Theory, program description, and assessment data. *Educational Psychologist, 27*, 291–315.

Cognition and Technology Group at Vanderbilt. (1993a). The Jasper series: Theoretical foundations and data on problem solving and transfer. In L. A. Penner, G. M. Batsche, H. M. Knoff, & D. L. Nelson (Eds.), *The challenges in mathematics and science education: Psychology's response* (pp. 113–152). Washington, DC: American Psychological Association.

Cognition and Technology Group at Vanderbilt. (1993b, March). Anchored instruction and situated cognition revisited. *Educational Technology, 33*, 52–70.

Cognition and Technology Group at Vanderbilt. (1994). From visual word problems to learning communities: Changing conceptions of cognitive research. To appear in K. McGilly (Ed.), *Classroom lessons: Integrating cognitive theory and classroom practice* (pp. 157–200). Cambridge, MA: MIT Press.

Cognition and Technology Group at Vanderbilt. (1996a). Looking at technology in context: A framework for understanding technology and education research. In D. C. Berliner & R. C. Calfee (Eds.), *The handbook of educational psychology* (pp. 807–840). NY: MacMillan Publishing.

Cognition and Technology Group at Vanderbilt. (1996b). A multimedia literacy series that celebrates authorship and books. *Communications of the Association for Computing Machinery* (ACM), *39*(8), 106–109.

Cognition and Technology Group at Vanderbilt. (in press). The Jasper series: A design experiment in complex, mathematical problem-solving. In J. Hawkins & A. Collins (Eds.), *Design experiments: Integrating technologies into schools*. New York: Cambridge University Press.

Cohen, D. K., McLaughlin, M. W., & Talbert, J. E. (Eds.). (1993). *Teaching for understanding: Challenges for policy and practice*. San Francisco, CA: Jossey-Bass.

Collins, A. (1991). The role of computer technology in restructuring schools. *Phi Delta Kappan, 73*, 28–36.

Collins, A., Hawkins, J., & Carver, S. M. (1991). A cognitive apprenticeship for disadvantaged students. In B. Means, C. Chelemer, & M. S. Knapp (Eds.), *Teaching advanced skills to at-risk students* (pp. 216–243). San Francisco: Jossey-Bass.

Corey, S. M. (1944). Poor scholar's soliloquy. *Childhood Education, 33*, 219–220.

Cosden, M. A., Goldman, S. R., & Hine, M. S. (1990). Learning handicapped students' interactions during a microcomputer-based writing activity. *Journal of Special Education Technology, 10*, 220–232.

Crews, T. R., Biswas, G., Goldman, S. R., & Bransford, J. D. (in press). Macrocontexts plus microworlds: An anchored instruction approach to intelligent learning environments. *Journal of AI in Education*.

deBono, E. (Ed.). (1974). *Eureka, an illustrated history of inventions from the wheel to the computer; A London Sunday Times Encyclopedia*. New York: Holt, Rinehart & Winston.

Dewey, J. (1933). *How we think, a restatement of the relation of reflective thinking to the educative process*. Boston: Heath.

Duffy, G. G. (1992, April). *Learning from the study of practice: Where we must go with strategy instruction*. Paper presented at the AERA annual meeting, San Francisco.

Duffy, T. M., Lowyck, J., & Jonassen, D. (Eds.). (1993). *Designing environments for constructivist learning*. Heidelberg: Springer.

Dunker, K. (1945). Experiments demonstrating functional fixedness were conducted on problem solving. *Psychological Monographs, 58*(5).

Eiser, L. (1993, March). Math for a reason. *Technology & Learning Magazine*, pp. 52–58.

Fennema, E., & Sherman, J. (1977). The study of mathematics by high school boys and girls: Related variables. *American Educational Research Journal, 14*, 159–168.

Feuerstein, R. (1979). *The dynamic assessment of retarded performers: The learning potential assessment device, theory, instruments, and techniques*. Baltimore: University Park Press.

Feuerstein, R., Rand, Y., & Hoffman, M. B. (1979). *The dynamic assessment of retarded performers: The learning potential assessment device, theory, instruments, and techniques*. Baltimore: University Park Press.

Feuerstein, R., Rand, Y., Hoffman, M. B., & Miller, R. (1980). *Instrumental enrichment*. Baltimore: University Park Press.

Franks, J., Bransford, J., Brailey, K., & Purdon, S. (1991). Understanding memory access. In R. Hoffman & D. Palermo (Eds.), *Cognition and the symbolic processes: Applied and ecological perspectives* (pp. 281–299). Hillsdale, NJ: Lawrence Erlbaum Associates.

Frederiksen, J. R., & Collins, A. (1989). A systems approach to educational testing. *Educational Researcher, 18*(9), 27–32.

Furman, L., Barron, B., Montavon, E., Vye, N. J., Bransford, J. D., & Shah, P. (1989, April). *The effects of problem formulation training and type of feedback on math handicapped students' problem solving abilities.* Paper presented at the meeting of the American Educational Research Association meeting, San Francisco.

Gibson, J. J. (1977). The theory of affordance. In R. Shaw & J. Bransford, (Eds.), *Perceiving, acting, and knowing* (pp. 67–82). Hillsdale, NJ: Lawrence Erlbaum Associates.

Gick, M. L., & Holyoak, K. J. (1980). Analogical problem solving. *Cognitive Psychology, 12*, 306–365.

Gick, M. L., & Holyoak, K. J. (1983). Schema induction and analogical transfer. *Cognitive Psychology, 15*, 1–38.

Goldman, S. R., & the CTGV (1991, August). *Meaningful learning environments for mathematical problem solving: The Jasper problem solving series.* Paper presented at the Fourth European Conference for Research on Learning and Instruction, Turku, Finland.

Goldman, S. R., Cosden, M. A., Hine, M. S. (1992). Working alone and working together: Individual differences in the effects of collaboration on learning handicapped students' writing. *Learning and Individual Differences, 4*, 369–393.

Goldman, S. R., Mertz, D. L., & Pellegrino, J. W. (1989). Individual differences in extended practice functions and solution strategies for basic addition facts. *Journal of Educational Psychology, 81*, 481–496.

Goldman, S. R., Pellegrino, J. W., & Bransford, J. D. (1994). Assessing programs that invite thinking. In E. Baker & H. F. O'Neil, Jr. (Eds.), *Technology assessment in education and training* (pp. 199–230). Hillsdale, NJ: Lawrence Erlbaum Associates.

Goldman, S. R., Pellegrino, J. W., & Mertz, D. L. (1988). Extended practice of basic addition facts: Strategy changes in learning disabled students. *Cognition & Instruction, 5*, 223–265.

Goldman, S. R., Petrosino, A., Sherwood, R. D., Garrison, S., Hickey, D., Bransford, J. D., & Pellegrino, J. (1996). Anchoring science instruction in multimedia learning environments. In S. Vosniadou, E. De Corte, R. Glaser, & H. Mandl (Eds.), *International perspectives on the design of technology-supported learning environments* (pp. 257–284). Hillsdale, NJ: Lawrence Erlbaum Associates.

Goldman, S. R., Vye, N. J., Williams, S., Rewey, K. L., & Hmelo, C. (1992, April). *Planning net representations and analyses of complex problem solving.* Paper presented at the annual meeting of the American Educational Research Association, San Francisco.

Goldman, S. R., Vye, N. J., Williams, S., Rewey, K. L., Pellegrino, J. W., & the CTGV (1991, April). *Problem space analyses of the Jasper problems and students' attempts to solve them.* Paper presented at the American Educational Research Association, Chicago.

Goldman, S. R., Williams, S., Vye, N. J., Bransford, J. D., & Pellegrino, J. W. (1993, March). *Flexible knowing in complex problem solving situations.* Paper presented at the meeting of the Society for Research in Child Development, New Orleans, LA.

Gragg, C. I. (1940, October 19). Because wisdom can't be told. *Harvard Alumni Bulletin*, 78–84.

Greeno, J. G. (1991, November). *Situations for productive learning.* Preprint of paper presented at the University of South Florida Conference on Contributions of Psychology to Science and Math Education. Tampa.

Hallinger, P., Leithwood, K., & Murphy, J. (Eds.), (1993). *Cognitive perspectives on educational leadership.* New York: Teachers College Press.

Hanson, N. R. (1970). A picture theory of theory meaning. In R. G. Colodny (Ed.), *The nature and function of scientific theories* (pp. 233–274). Pittsburgh, PA: University of Pittsburgh Press.

Hasselbring, T., Goin, L., & Bransford, J. D. (1988). Developing math automaticity in learning handicapped children: The role of computerized drill and practice. *Focus on Exceptional Children, 20*(6), 1–7.

Hasselbring, T. S., Sherwood, R. D., Bransford, J. D., Fleenor, K., Griffith, D., & Goin, L. (1988). An evaluation of a level-one instructional videodisc program. *Journal of Educational Technology Systems, 16*(2), 151–169.

Hawkins, J. (1991). Technology-mediated communities for learning: Designs and consequences. *Annals, AAPSS, 514,* 159–174.

Hawkins, J., & Collins, A. (Eds.). (in press). *Design experiments: Integrating technologies into schools.* New York: Cambridge University Press.

Hawkins, J., & Sheingold, K. (1986). The beginning of a story: Computers and the organization of learning in classrooms. In A. Culbertson & L. L. Cunningham (Eds.). In A. Culbertson & L. L. Cunningham (Eds.), *Microcomputers and education* (85th Yearbook of the National Society for the Study of Education). Chicago, IL: NSSE distributed by University of Chicago.

Hayes, J. R. (1990). Individuals and environments in writing instruction. In B. F. Jones & L. Idol (Eds.), *Dimensions of thinking and cognitive instruction* (pp. 241–263). Hillsdale, NJ: Lawrence Erlbaum Associates.

Hayes, J. R., & Simon, H. A. (1977). Psychological differences among problem isomorphs. In N. J. Castelan, D. B. Pisoni, & C. R. Potts (Eds.), *Cognitive theory* (Vol. 2, pp. 21–42). Hillsdale, NJ: Lawrence Erlbaum Associates.

Hine, M. S., Goldman, S. R., & Cosden, M. A. (1990). Error monitoring by learning handicapped students engaged in collaborative microcomputer-based writing. *Journal of Special Education, 23,* 407–422.

Hmelo, C. E. (1994). *Development of independent learning and thinking: A study of medical problem solving and problem-based learning.* Unpublished doctoral dissertation, Vanderbilt University, Nashville, TN.

Holt, J. (1964). *How children fail.* New York: Dell.

Jenkins, J. J. (1979). Four points to remember: A tetrahedral model and memory experiments. In L. S. Cermak & F. I .M. Craik (Eds.), *Levels of processing in human memory*_(pp. 429–446). Hillsdale, NJ: Lawrence Erlbaum Associates.

Johnson, R. (1987). *The ability to retell a story: Effects of adult mediation in a videodisc context on children's story recall and comprehension.* Unpublished doctoral dissertation, Vanderbilt University, Nashville, TN.

Johnson-Laird, P. N. (1985). Deductive reasoning ability. In R. J. Sternberg (Ed.), *Human abilities: An information-processing approach.* New York: Freeman.

Kaput, J., & Lesh, R. (1994, May). *Rethinking mathematics education.* Presentation at a National Science Foundation Conference on "Research using a cognitive science perspective to facilitate school-based innovation in teaching science and mathematics," Sugarloaf Conference Center, Chestnut Hill, PA.

Kolodner, J. L. (1991, summer). Improving human decision making through case-based decision aiding. *Artificial Intelligence Magazine,* pp. 52–68.

Lamon, M., Secules, T. J., Petrosino, T., Hackett, R., Bransford, J. D., & Goldman, S. R. (1996). Schools for thought: Overview of the international project and lessons learned from one of the sites. In L. Schauble & R. Glaser (Eds.), *Innovations in learning: New environments for education* (pp. 243–288). Hillsdale, NJ: Lawrence Erlbaum Associates.

Lave, J. (1988). *Cognition in practice: Mind, mathematics, and culture in everyday life.* Cambridge, England: Cambridge University Press.

Lefrancois, G. R. (1982). *Psychology for teaching.* Belmont, CA: Wadsworth.

Lehrer, R., Lee, M., & Jeong, A. (1994). *Reflective teaching of Logo.* Unpublished manuscript.

Lesgold, A. (1988). Problem solving. In R. J. Sternberg & E. E. Smith (Eds.), *The psychology of human thought* (pp. 188–213). New York: Cambridge University Press.

Levin, J. A., Kim, H., & Riel, M. M. (1990). Analyzing instructional interactions on electronic message networks. In L. M. Harasim (Ed.), *Online education: Perspectives on a new environment* (pp. 185–213). New York: Prager.

Levin, J. A., Riel, M. M., Boruta, M., & Rowe, R. (1985). Muktuk meets jacuzzi: Computer networks and elementary school writers. In S. W. Freedman (Ed.), *The acquisition of written language: Response and revision,* (pp. 160–171). Norwood, NJ: Ablex.

Levin, J. A., Riel, M. M., Miyake, N., & Cohen, M. (1987). Education on the electronic frontier: Teleapprentices in globally distributed educational contexts. *Contemporary Educational Psychology, 12,* 254–260.

Lidz, C. S. (1987). *Dynamic assessment: An interactional approach to evaluating learning potential.* New York: Guilford.

Lin, X. D., Bransford, J. D., Kantor, R., Hmelo, C., Hickey, D., Secules, T., Goldman, S. R., Petrosino, T., & the CTGV (1995). Instructional design and the development of learning communities: An invitation to a dialogue. *Educational Technology, 35*(5), 53–63.

Linn, M. C. (1986). *Establishing a research base for science education: Challenges, trends, and recommendations.* Report of a National Science Foundation national conference. Berkeley: University of California.

Lipman, M. (1985). Thinking skills fostered by philosophy for children. In J. Segal, S. Chipman, & R. Glaser (Eds.), *Thinking and learning skills: Relating instruction to basic research* (Vol. 1, pp. 83–108). Hillsdale, NJ: Lawrence Erlbaum Associates.

Littlefield, J., Delclos, V. R., Bransford, J. D., Clayton, K. N., & Franks, J. J. (1989). Some prerequisites for teaching thinking: Methodological issues in the study of LOGO programming. *Cognition and Instruction,* 6(4), 331–366.

Littlefield, J., Delclos, V., Lever, S., Clayton, K., Bransford, J., & Franks, J. (1988). Learning Logo: Method of teaching, transfer of general skills, and attitudes toward school and computers. In R. E. Mayer (Ed.), *Teaching and learning computer programming* (pp. 111–135). Hillsdale, NJ: Lawrence Erlbaum Associates.

Lockhart, R. S., Lamon, M., & Gick, M. L. (1988). Conceptual transfer in simple insight problems. *Memory & Cognition,* 16, 36–44.

Mandinach, E. B., & Cline, H. F. (1994). *Classroom dynamics: Implementing a technology-based learning environment.* Hillsdale, NJ: Lawrence Erlbaum Associates.

Mann, L. (1979). On the trail of process: A *historical perspective on cognitive processes and their training.* New York: Grune & Stratton.

Mayer, R. E. (Ed.). (1988). *Teaching and learning computer programming: Multiple research perspectives.* Hillsdale, NJ: Lawrence Erlbaum Associates.

McGilly, K. (Ed.). (1994). *Classroom lessons: Integrating cognitive theory and classroom practice.* Cambridge, MA: MIT Press/Bradford Books.

McLarty, K., Goodman, J., Risko, V. J., Kinzer, C. K., Vye, N., Rowe, D. W., & Carlson, J. (1990). Implementing anchored instruction: Guiding principles for curriculum development. In J. Zutell & S. McCormick (Eds.), *Literacy theory and research: Analysis for multiple perspectives* (39th NRC Yearbook, pp. 109–120). Chicago: National Reading Conference.

McLennan, B. (1991, August). Prevent problems by considering the dog's viewpoint. *Dogfancy Magazine,* p. 68.

McNamara, T. P., Miller, D. L., & Bransford, J. D. (1991). Mental models and reading comprehension. In R. Barr, M. Kamil, P. Mosenthal, & T. D. Pearson (Eds.), *Handbook of Reading Research.* (Vol 2. pp. 490–511). New York: Longman.

McNeese, M. (1992). *Analogical transfer in situated cooperative learning.* Unpublished doctoral dissertation, Vanderbilt University, Nashville, TN.

Meece, J. L., Wigfield, A., & Eccles, J. S. (1990). Predictors of math anxiety and its influence on young adolescents' course enrollment intentions and performance in mathematics. *Journal of Educational Psychology,* 82, 60–70.

Michael, A. L., Klee, T., Bransford, J. D., & Warren, S. (1993). The transition from theory to therapy: Test of two instructional methods. *Applied Cognitive Psychology,* 7, 139–154.

Minstrell, J. A. (1989). Teaching science for understanding. In L. B. Resnick & L. E. Klopfer (Eds.), *Toward the thinking curriculum: Current cognitive research* (pp. 129–149). Alexandria, VA: ASCD.

Montavon, E., Furman, L., Barron, B., Bransford, J.D., & Hasselbring, T. S. (1989, April). *The effects of varied context training and irrelevant information training on the transfer of math problem solving skills.* Paper presented at the meeting of the American Educational Research Association meeting, San Francisco.

Moore, A., Sherwood, R., Bateman, H., Bransford, J. D., & Goldman, S. R. (1996). Using problem-based learning to prepare for project-based learning. In J. D. Bransford (Chair), *Enhancing project-based learning: Lessons from research and development.* Symposium conducted at the 1996 Annual meeting of the American Educational Research Association, New York.

Morris, C. D., Bransford, J. D., & Franks, J. J. (1979). Levels of processing versus transfer appropriate processing. *Journal of Verbal Learning and Verbal Behavior, 16,* 519–533.

National Council of Teachers of Mathematics. (1989). *Curriculum and evaluation standards for school mathematics.* Reston, VA: Author.

National Council of Teachers of Mathematics. (1991). *Professional Standards for Teaching Mathematics.* Reston, VA: Author.

National Research Council (1996). *National science education standards.* Washington, DC: National Academy Press.

Newell, A., & Simon, H. A. (1972). *Human problem solving.* Englewood Cliffs, NJ: Prentice-Hall.

Newman, D. (1992). Technology as support for school structure and school restructuring. *Phi Delta Kappan, 74,* 308–315.

Nickerson, R. S. (1988). On improving thinking through instruction. *Review of Research in Education, 15,* 3–57.

Norman, D. A. (1993). Things that make us smart: Defending human attributes in the age of the machine. New York: Addison-Wesley.

Novick, L. R. (1988). Analogical transfer, problem similarity, and expertise. *Journal of Experimental Psychology: Learning, Memory, & Cognition, 14,* 510–520.

Palincsar, A. S., & Brown, A. L. (1984). Reciprocal teaching of comprehension-fostering and comprehension monitoring activities. *Cognition and Instruction, 1,* 117–175.

Palincsar, A. S., & Brown, A. L. (1989). Instruction for self-regulated reading. In L. B. Resnick & L. E. Klopfer (Eds.), *Toward the thinking curriculum: Current cognitive research* (pp. 19–39). Alexandria, VA: ASCD.

Papert, S. (1980). *Mindstorms: Children, computers, and powerful ideas.* New York: Basic Books.

Pea, R. D. (1992) Augmenting the discourse of learning with computer-based learning environments. In E. De Corte, M. C. Linn, H. Mandl, & L. Verschaffel (Eds.), *Computer-based learning environments and problem solving* (pp. 313–344). New York: Springer-Verlag.

Pea, R. D. (1993). Practices of distributed intelligence and designs for education. In G. Salomon (Ed.), *Distributed cognitions: Psychological and educational considerations* (pp. 47–87). New York: Cambridge University Press.

Pellegrino, J. W., Hickey, D., Heath, A., Rewey, K., Vye, N. J., & the CTGV (1991). *Assessing the outcomes of an innovative instructional program: The 1990–1991 implementation of the "Adventures of Jasper Woodbury"* (Tech. Rep. No. 91–1). Vanderbilt University: Learning Technology Center, Nashville, TN.

Perfetto, G. A., Bransford, J. D., & Franks, J. J. (1983). Constraints on access in a problem solving context. *Memory and Cognition, 11,* 24–31.

Peterson, P. L., Fennema, E., & Carpenter, T. (1991). Using children's mathematical knowledge. In B. Means, C. Chelemer, & M. S. Knapp (Eds.), *Teaching advanced skills to at-risk students* (pp. 68–111). San Francisco: Jossey-Bass.

Porter, A. (1989). A curriculum out of balance: The case of elementary school mathematics. *Educational Researcher, 18,* 9–15.

Reed, S. K., Ernst, G. W., & Banerji, R. (1974). The role of analogy in transfer between similar problem states. *Cognitive Psychology, 6,* 436–450.

Resnick, L. (1987). *Education and learning to think.* Washington, DC: National Academy Press.

Resnick, L. B. & Klopfer, L. E. (Eds.). (1989). *Toward the thinking curriculum: Current cognitive research.* Alexandria, VA: ASCD.

Resnick, L. B., & Resnick, D. P. (1991). Assessing the thinking curriculum: New tools for educational reform. In B. R. Gifford & M. O'Connor (Eds.), *New approaches to testing: Rethinking aptitude, achievement and assessment* (pp. 37–76). New York: National Committee on Testing and Public Policy.

Reusser, K. (1988). Problem solving beyond the logic of things: Contextual effects on understanding and solving word problems. *Instructional Science, 17*, 309–338.

Rewey, K. L., Barron, B. J., Rieser, J., Bransford, J. D, & Goldman, S. R. (1992, April). *Small group problem solving in the "Adventures of Jasper Woodbury" environment.* Paper presented at the annual meeting of the American Educational Research Association, San Francisco.

Riel, M. (1990a). A model for integrating computer networking with classroom learning. In A. McDougall & C. Dowling (Eds.), *Computers in Education,* (pp. 1021–1026). North-Holland, Holland: Elsevier.

Riel, M. (1990b). Cooperative learning across classrooms in electronic learning circles. *Instructional Science,* 9, 445–466.

Riel, M. M., & Levin, J. A. (1990). Building electronic communities: Success and failure in computer networking. *Instructional Science,* 19(2), 145–169.

Riesbeck, C. K., & Schank, R. C. (1989). *Inside case-based reasoning.* Hillsdale, NJ: Lawrence Erlbaum Associates.

Risko, V. J., Kinzer, C. K., Goodman, J., McLarty K., Dupree, A., & Martin, H. (1989, April). *Effects of macrocontext on reading comprehension, composition of stories, and vocabulary development.* Paper presented at the annual meeting of the American Research Association in San Francisco.

Salomon, G. (1992, April). *Computer's first decade: Where were we and where are we going next?* Paper presented at the annual meeting of the American Educational Research Association, San Francisco

Salomon, G. (1993). On the nature of pedagogic computer tools: The case of the writing partner. In S. P. Lajoie & S. J. Derry (Eds.), *Computers as cognitive tools* (pp. 179–196). Hillsdale, NJ: Lawrence Erlbaum Associates.

Salomon, G., & Globerson, T. (1989). When teams do not function the way they ought to. *International Journal of Educational Research, 13*, 89–99.

Salomon, G., Perkins, D. N., & Globerson, T. (1991). Partners in cognition: Extending human intelligence with intelligent technologies. *Educational Researcher, 20*(3), 2–9.

Savery, J. R., & Duffy, T. M. (1995). Problem based learning: An instructional model and its constructivist framework. *Educational Technology, 35*, 31–38.

Scardamalia, M., & Bereiter, C. (1991). Higher levels of agency for children in knowledge building: A challenge for the design of new knowledge media. *Journal of the Learning Sciences, 1*, 37–68.

Scardamalia, M., & Bereiter, C. (1994). Computer support for knowledge-building communities. *The Journal of the Learning Sciences*, 265–285.

Scardamalia, M., Bereiter, C., & Lamon, M. (1994). The CSILE Project: Trying to bring the classroom into world 3. In K. McGilly (Ed.), *Classroom lessons: Integrating cognitive theory and classroom practice* (pp. 201–228). Cambridge, MA: MIT Press/Bradford Books.

Schank, R. C. (1990). Case-based teaching: Four experiences in educational software design. *Interactive Learning Environments, 1*, 231–253.

Schank, R. C., & Jona, M. Y. (1991). Empowering the student: New perspectives on the design of teaching systems. *Journal of the Learning Sciences, 1*, 7–36.

Schoenfeld, A. H. (1985). *Mathematical problem solving.* Orlando, FL: Academic Press.

Schoenfeld, A. H. (1988). Problem solving in context(s). In R. Charles & E. A. Silver (Eds.), *The teaching and assessing of mathematical problem solving* (pp. 82–92). Hillsdale, NJ: Lawrence Erlbaum Associates & National Council of Teachers of Mathematics.

Schoenfeld, A. H. (1989). Teaching mathematical thinking and problem solving. In L. B. Resnick & L. E. Klopfer (Eds.), *Toward the thinking curriculum: Current cognitive research* (pp. 83–103). Alexandria, VA: ASCD.

Schwartz, D. L., Goldman, S. R., Vye, N. J., Barron, B. J., & the CTGV (in press). Using anchored instruction to align everyday and mathematical reasoning: The case of sampling assumptions. In S. Lajoie (Ed.), *Reflections on statistics: Agendas for learning, teaching and assessment in K–12.* Hillsdale, NJ: Lawrence Erlbaum Associates.

Schwartz, D. L. (Organizer), & the CTGV (1996, April). *Enhancing project-based learning: Lessons from research and development.* Symposium conducted at the 1996 Annual meeting of the American Educational Research Association, New York.

Segal, J. W., Chipman, S. F., & Glaser, R. (Eds.). (1985). *Thinking and learning skills: Relating instruction to research* (Vol. 1). Hillsdale, NJ: Lawrence Erlbaum Associates.

Senge, P. M. (1990). *The fifth discipline: The art and practice of the learning organization.* New York: Doubleday.

Sharp, D. L. M., Bransford, J. D., Goldman, S. R., Risko, V. J., Kinzer, C. K., & Vye, N. J. (1995). Dynamic visual support for story comprehension and mental model building by young, at-risk children. *Educational Technology Research and Development, 43* (4), 25–42.

Sherwood, R. D., Kinzer, C. K., Bransford, J. D., & Franks, J. J. (1987). Some benefits of creating macro-contexts for science instruction: Initial findings. *Journal of Research in Science Teaching, 24*(5), 417–435.

Sherwood, R., Kinzer, C., Hasselbring, T., & Bransford, J. (1987). Macro-contexts for learning: Initial findings and issues. *Applied Cognitive Psychology, 1*, 93–108.

Sherwood, R. D., Petrosino, A. J., Lin, X., Lamon, M., & the CTGV (1995). Problem-based macro contexts in science instruction: Theoretical basis, design issues, and the development of applications. In D. Lavoie (Ed.), *Towards a cognitive-science perspective for scientific problem solving* (pp. 191–214). Manhattan, KS: National Association for Research in Science Teaching.

Silver, E. A. (1986). Using conceptual and procedural knowledge: A focus on relationships. In J. Hiebert (Ed.), *Conceptual and procedural knowledge: The case of mathematics* (pp. 181–189). Hillsdale, NJ: Lawrence Erlbaum Associates.

Simon, H. A. (1980). Problem solving and education. In D. T. Tuma & R. Reif (Eds.), *Problem solving and education: Issues in teaching and research* (pp. 81–96). Hillsdale, NJ: Lawrence Erlbaum Associates.

Slamecka, N. J., & Graf, P. (1978). The generation effect: Delineation of a phenomenon. *Journal of Experimental Psychology: Human Learning and Memory, 4*, 592–604.

Soraci, S. A., Jr., Franks, J. J., Bransford, J. D., Chechile, R. A., Belli, R. F., Carr, M., & Carlin, M. T. (1994). Incongruous item generation effects: A multiple-cue perspective. *Journal of Experimental Psychology: Learning, Memory, and Cognition, 20*, 1–12.

Sternberg, R. J. (1986). *Intelligence applied.* Orlando, FL: Harcourt Brace Jovanovich.

Talbert, J. E., & McLaughlin, M. W. (1993). Understanding teaching in context. In D. K. Cohen, M. W. McLaughlin, & J. E. Talbert (Eds.), *Teaching for Understanding: Challenges for policy and practice* (pp. 167–206). San Francisco: Jossey-Bass.

Thorndike, E. L. (1913). *Educational psychology* (Vols. 1 and 2). NY: Columbia University Press.

Turnbull, H. W. (1993). *The great mathematicians.* NY: Barnes and Noble.

Van Haneghan, J. P., Barron, L., Young, M. F., Williams, S. M., Vye, N. J., & Bransford, J. D. (1992). The Jasper series: An experiment with new ways to enhance mathematical thinking. In D. F. Halpern (Ed.), *Enhancing thinking skills in the sciences and mathematics* (pp. 15–38). Hillsdale, NJ: Lawrence Erlbaum Associates.

Van Lehn, K. (1990). *Mind bugs: The origins of procedural misconceptions.* Cambridge, MA: The MIT Press.

Vye, N. J., Barron, B., Belynne, K., & Till, L. (1996, April). *Technology-based resources for assessment and revision: Discussion of SMART assessment tools.* Paper presented at the meeting of the American Educational Research Association. New York.

Vye, N. J., Burns, M. S., Delclos,V. R., & Bransford, J. D. (1987). Dynamic assessment of intellectually handicapped children. In C. S. Lidz (Ed.), *Dynamic assessment: An interactional approach to evaluating learning potential* (pp. 327–359). New York: Guilford.

Vye, N. J., Goldman, S. R., Voss, J. F., Hmelo, C., Williams, S., & the CTGV (in press). An analysis of complex mathematical problem solving by individuals and dyads. *Cognition and Instruction.*

Vygotsky, L. S. (1978). *Mind in society: The development of higher psychological processes.* Cambridge, MA: Harvard University Press.

Vygotsky, L. (1986). *Thought and language* (A. Kozulin, Trans.). Cambridge, MA: MIT Press. (original English translation published 1962)

Weisberg, R., DiCamillo, M., & Phillips, D. (1978). Transferring old associations to new situations: A nonautomatic process. *Journal of Verbal Learning and Verbal Behavior, 17*, 219–228.

Whimbey, A. & Lochhead, J. (1985). *Problem solving and comprehension* (3rd ed.). Hillsdale, NJ: Lawrence Erlbaum Associates.

Whitehead, A. N. (1929). *The aims of education*. New York: MacMillan.

Williams, S. M. (1992). Putting case-based instruction into context: Examples from legal and medical education. *The Journal of the Learning Sciences, 2*(4), 367–427.

Williams, S. M. (1994). *Anchored simulations: Merging the strengths of formal and informal reasoning in a computer-based learning environment.* Unpublished doctoral dissertation, Vanderbilt University, Nashville, TN.

Williams, S. M., Bransford, J. D., Vye, N. J., Goldman, S. R., & Carlson, K. (1992, April). *Positive and negative effects of specific knowledge on mathematical problem solving*. Paper presented at the American Educational Research Association, San Francisco.

Williams, S. M., Bransford, J. D.,Vye, N. J., Goldman, S. R., & Hmelo, C. E. (1993, April). *Using an anchored computer simulation to facilitate qualitative reasoning in mathematics*. Paper presented at the American Educational Research Association, San Francisco.

Williams, S. M., Nathan, M., Moore, J. M., Goldman, S. R., & the CTGV (1994, November). *The Adventures of Jasper Woodbury and The AdventureMaker: Technologies that support mathematical problem solving and problem posing for realistically complex problems.* A technology focus group presented at the meeting of the North American Chapter of the International Group for the Psychology of Mathematics Education, Baton Rouge, LA.

Wood, D., Wood, H., & Middleton, D. (1978). An experimental evaluation of four face-to-face teaching strategies. *International Journal of Behavioural Development, 1*, 131–147.

Zech, L., Vye, N. J., Bransford, J. D., Goldman, S. R., Barron, B. J., Schwartz, D. L., Kisst-Hackett, R., Mayfield-Stewart, C., & the CTGV (in press). An introduction to geometry through anchored instruction. In R. Lehrer & D. Chazan (Eds.), *New directions for teaching and learning geometry.* Hillsdale, NJ: Lawrence Erlbaum Associates.

Zech, L., Vye, N. J., Bransford, J. D., Swink, J., Mayfield-Stewart, C., Goldman, S. R., & the CTGV (1994). Bringing the world of geometry into the classroom with videodisc technology. *Mathematics Teaching in the Middle School, 1*(3), 228–233.

Author Index

Subject Index

PC HARDWARE AND SOFTWARE REQUIREMENTS

PC 486 with 66 Mhz or higher (Pentium Processor recommended)
Double-speed CD-ROM drive or faster (Quad-speed recommended)
7 MB of UNUSED memory (RAM) in its largest block (8MB or more preferred)
13" color monitor or larger with 8 bit color (256 colors) or better
Windows 3.x or Windows 95
QuickTime 2.1 or later (QuickTime 2.1 may be loaded from this CD-ROM)

MACINTOSH HARDWARE AND SOFTWARE REQUIREMENTS

Macintosh 68040 or higher
Double-speed CD-ROM drive or faster
7 MB of UNUSED memory (RAM) in its largest block (8MB or more preferred)
13" color monitor or larger with 8 bit color (256 colors) or better
System Software 7.x or later
QuickTime 2.1 or later (QuickTime 2.1 may be loaded from this CD-ROM)
QuickTime PowerPlug (for Power Macs only), Apple Multimedia Tuner, and Apple CD- ROM driver version 4.0.2 or 5.0.1

As you view the *Rescue at Boone's Meadow* video, please take note that safety is an important part of camping and hiking. We encourage you and your class to contact fire and park officials in your area and learn how to properly extinguish a campfire. The bald eagle that appears to be wounded in this episode is actually a rehabilitated raptor that is not able to fly and no longer lives in the wild. Raptors are birds adapted for seizing prey and are protected by federal law. Bald eagles are listed by the U.S. Fish and Wildlife Service as an endangered species. These and other raptors should only be handled by people who are licensed to do so. Federal or state wildlife authorities should be contacted if a raptor is found injured in the wild. No warranty, guarantee or representation either expressed or implied is made by the authors or publisher as to the correctness or sufficiency of any information herein. Neither the authors nor the publisher assumes any responsibility or liability for the use of the information herein, nor can it be assumed that all necessary warnings and precautionary measures are contained in this publication.